Black Music Matters

Black Music Matters

Jazz and the Transformation of Music Studies

Ed Sarath

ROWMAN & LITTLEFIELD
Lanham • Boulder • New York • London

Published by Rowman & Littlefield
An imprint of The Rowman & Littlefield Publishing Group, Inc.
4501 Forbes Boulevard, Suite 200, Lanham, Maryland 20706
www.rowman.com

Unit A, Whitacre Mews, 26-34 Stannary Street, London SE11 4AB

Copyright © 2018 by The Rowman & Littlefield Publishing Group, Inc.

All rights reserved. No part of this book may be reproduced in any form or by any electronic or mechanical means, including information storage and retrieval systems, without written permission from the publisher, except by a reviewer who may quote passages in a review.

British Library Cataloguing in Publication Information Available

Library of Congress Cataloging-in-Publication Data

Names: Sarath, Ed, author.
Title: Black music matters : jazz and the transformation of music studies / Ed Sarath.
Description: Lanham : Rowman & Littlefield, 2018. | Includes bibliographical references and index.
Identifiers: LCCN 2018015357 (print) | LCCN 2018016767 (ebook) | ISBN 9781538111710 (electronic) | ISBN 9781538111703 (cloth) | ISBN 9781538158258 (pbk) Subjects: LCSH: Music—Instruction and study. | Jazz—Instruction and study. | Curriculum change. | Musicology.
Classification: LCC MT1 (ebook) | LCC MT1 .S268 2018 (print) | DDC 780.71—dc23
LC record available at https://lccn.loc.gov/2018015357

In memoriam Geri Allen

Contents

Introduction	ix
I: Jazz and the Creativity Turn	**1**
1 Creativity as New Organizing Principle	3
2 Multiculturalism, Transculturalism, and Race	25
3 Music School for a Transcultural Age	53
4 New Conversations with Conservatives	79
II: Jazz and the Consciousness Turn	**101**
5 A Jazz-Based Integral Perspective on Consciousness	103
6 A Consciousness-Based Integral Perspective on Improvisation	131
7 Jazz and the Integral Revolution	161
Epilogue	187
Notes	191
References	211
Index	219
About the Author	225

Introduction

> Your creating—it comes from the heart, the spirit, the soul. You're not manufacturing somebody else's plan, somebody else's blueprint, somebody else's idea that's not yours. . . . It comes from within you.[1] —Alice Coltrane

If, as held by cultures from time immemorial, music is a direct expression of the soul, then the question looms large for a country as diverse as twenty-first-century America: What constitutes the nation's musical soul? What music, in other words, most directly emanates from the deepest recesses of our country's individual and collective consciousness, and in so doing reflects the totality of forces that shape national identity, and represents our most distinct contribution to the cultural mosaic of humanity?

This book is predicated on the view that black music, with a particular focus on jazz, is this distinctly American musical expression, and on the importance of this music–culture relationship not only in musical practice and studies but also for education and society at large. A society disconnected from its musical roots is disconnected from its soul, and thus prone to all manner of internal and external divisions, conflicts, and pathologies. A society with its musical/spiritual roots intact is capable of sustaining vitality and wholeness in all facets of life, and also serving as a transformative catalyst for all humankind. When the U.S. House of Representatives in 1997 declared that jazz is a "national treasure" that needs to be "preserved, understood, and promulgated,"[2] ramifications could be inferred on both accounts: not only is it imperative that this African American musical idiom, which has unfortunately been marginalized in our country's educational systems and national identity, be recognized as central to our own cultural integrity, but it is also imperative to recognize jazz as a quintessentially American contribution to world culture with important ramifications for arts-driven planetary healing.

Extending on prior work, an emergent, consciousness-based worldview called Integral Theory informs my inquiry. Integral Theory unites the analytical rigors of science, the deep interiors of spirituality, and the robust creativity of the arts in a remarkably expansive vision of human nature and evolutionary potential that I believe is particularly timely at the present juncture in human history. A jazz-driven, integral paradigm of music studies—one that harnesses the unmatched capacities inherent in the genre to support wide-ranging musical navigation—has the capacity to not only revolutionize how musicians, music teachers, and music scholars are trained, but also re-enliven the inextricable connection between music and soul that is key to a new vision for our world.[3] Moreover, rather than merely joining the ever-growing chorus of appeals for music studies reform, I take a further step—that of critically interrogating limiting patterns in the change conversation itself. The time has come for a shift from what I call "lower order" reform discourse to "higher order" visioning if the broader transformation is to ensue. This will require change agents to fundamentally rethink the underlying assumptions that guide the conversation and the prevailing language and terminology—including the very term *jazz*—that reify these assumptions, and also recognize how these and a host of related patterns have been inherited from the very framework the reform of which is sought.

DEFINING BLACK MUSIC

What do I mean by "black music"? Where does jazz fall within this broad category? What about the multitude of other genres within black music when it comes to defining American musical identity, let alone the place of European and other musical traditions in this identity? What are the transformative features of black music that justify the above claims regarding its significance in American culture, global culture, and broader transformative impact?

To begin: black music comprises a long legacy of African-based and African American–based forms and practices that have evolved through contact with a wider range of cultural influences, and in turn have significantly impacted musical practice across wide-ranging cultural boundaries. Defined in terms of its manifestations on America's shores alone, the black music spectrum is indeed vast, encompassing the field hollers, ring shouts, work songs, and spirituals that first surfaced on southern plantations, the powerful musical practices that evolved from those times to this day in the African American church, and the larger continuum including blues, funk, rock, bebop, techno pop, hip hop, and more that extends from these roots and pervades the broader society. When—moving beyond American borders—one delves into the African roots of this expanse, as well as its many global extensions, the enormity of the black music wave on a planetary scale is all the more striking.[4] Jeff Pressing's account alone of the ubiquitous impact of "Black Atlantic Rhythm" across the global musical landscape, while clearly underscoring the sheer range of this particular kind of black music fruit, may also reveal much about the depth of its roots, as he suggests connections between these practices and the innermost dimensions of human consciousness.[5] LeRoi Jones's powerful case for key "Africanisms" not only surviving the holocaust of slavery and its transcontinental uprooting of people and traditions, but also further evolving and exhibiting broader impact, points in the same direction.[6]

Unfortunately, awareness of black music as this powerful cultural, artistic, and spiritual resource has been minimal in our overall educational systems, and particularly in our music schools. Providing perhaps the most sobering evidence of this point: An American music education major is still likely to graduate from an American music school with certification to teach music in American public schools with little or no hands-on engagement, let alone substantive skills, in this core aspect of American musical culture.[7] If, moreover, as Michelle Obama has asserted, this important facet of our cultural identity must occupy a central place "in every single school in America," then this must first take hold at the higher education level—where not only music teachers but also the broader spectrum of classroom instructors and administrators receive their training.[8] Until this happens, American society will remain disconnected from its musical soul, key to its cultural and spiritual identity, rendering the nation oblivious to its most distinctive contribution to global culture, at a time when connection with this transcendent and robustly creative source has never been more urgently needed. A closer look at jazz supports this perspective.

Jazz as Embodiment of Key Black Music Features

While any one of the constituent black music styles is so vast that it could be (and has been) the focus of entire volumes, jazz is where key elements of black music have blossomed on unprecedented scales. Key features include African-based rhythmic foundations, prevalence of improvisation in individual and collective formats, blues roots, highly personalized expression amidst rich collective interaction, self-transcending connections, and spirituality. Considered independently, these features reveal jazz to be what I call a uniquely robust process-structure region—which is how I prefer to characterize genres—in the overarching musical world. But when considered collectively, thereby taking into account the synergistic, coevolutionary relationships between the various elements, the richness of jazz becomes exponentially evident. I view jazz as not only the crest of the black music wave in the twenty-first-century musical ocean, but also the crest of the Western music wave in that same ocean. Jazz provides the most compelling basis for Christopher Small's provocative, yet self-evident assertion:

> By any reasonable reckoning of the function of music in human life, the Afro-American tradition is the major music of the west in the 20th century, of far greater human significance than those remnants of the great European classical tradition that are to be heard today in the concert halls and opera houses of the industrial world, east and west.[9]

Also inspired by Small, I argue for the nexus of jazz and European classical music as key to the further evolution of both lineages as well as a range of global connections. I will have more to say on that below and throughout the book.

Turning at the moment to key jazz features that promote this aim: It is difficult to imagine any such inventory that does not begin with rhythm, and particularly jazz's foundations in swing. This propulsive rhythmic core, continually evolving yet also grounded in essential characteristic properties, anchors much of jazz to this day. Along with an important even-eighth note rhythmic stream informed by Afro-Carribean, mid-Eastern, Indian, European classical, and other rhythmic influences, a jazz rhythmic universe of unmatched breadth and power has engulfed our country and world. Indeed, as I elaborate, whereas the topic of rhythm in music studies is typically confined to rhythmic *accuracy*, jazz situates this focus within the broader context of rhythmic *languages*.

Coevolving with jazz's rhythmic roots is an exquisitely rich creative process scope, anchored by a jazz improvisatory line that features multiple constituent languages of its own, including tonal/harmonic, modal, globally influenced improvising, and a range of more open frameworks such as "free jazz" and what has come to be simply called "improvised music"[10] given the highly syncretic musical terrain it typically broaches. Alongside this improvisatory spectrum, a robust and co-evolutionary compositional component has become increasingly prominent in the idiom. Although jazz musicians from early on have typically been composers as well as improvisers, recent decades have seen increasing exploration of multimovement forms, involving large ensembles of various kinds, that are informed by European classical music while adding important African American and other influences to the jazz compositional mix. Developing in close conjunction to the idiom's rhythmic and creative facets is a jazz pitch spectrum that extends from foundations in the blues—which can be thought of as much a rhythmic dimension as a harmonic/melodic one—to encompass a rich modal-tonal-transtonal continuum that broaches the outer edges of Western harmony.[11]

Jazz also exemplifies the interplay of individual and ensemble that runs deep in black music. "Pursuit of individualism within an egalitarian frame," writes George Lewis, "has been central to not only the jazz moment, but to African American music before and after that moment."[12] In the evolution of the jazz solo, provision for personal freedom of expression reached its zenith, while the succession of soloists—so everyone gets space to shine—and interaction between soloist and collective equally highlight the democratic dimensions of musical performance. Even in instances, increasingly evident, where clear-cut boundaries between soloist and ensemble would dissolve in more expansive approaches to jazz-inspired improvised music, the two realms—personal freedom and leadership against collective responsibilities for listening and background roles—still maintain their integrity. As I emphasize, the evolution of the individual creative voice—what I call, inspired by the work of C. G. Jung, "musical individuation"—is unsurpassed as it unfolds in jazz.[13] I examine this deep blossoming of the personal voice as the basis for self-organizing, student-driven pedagogy. I also extrapolate from this premise far broader ramifications: the very need for our nation to recognize jazz as central to its collective cultural voice also finds its localized manifestation in the quest, which jazz holds at a premium, for each musician to find his/her personal artistic voice.

It is also important to emphasize the principle of musical embodiment in defining jazz and black music. In other words, where there is rhythm and creativity, particularly of the collective improvisatory type, there are human bodies in motion. In most African traditions, music is typically accompanied by dance (or one could rephrase it as dance is typically accompanied by music).[14] Although jazz in recent decades is typically not performed in direct conjunction with dance, the music exhibits a physicality that nonetheless reflects these roots. Even when jazz broaches highly subtle textures, soft dynamic levels, or realms of abstraction that are devoid of underlying pulse, its physical nature—even if the bodily response elicited is one of utmost, meditative stillness—is palpable. Jazz-based embodiment, paralleling the principle of Black Atlantic Rhythm, is another essential aspect of the broader navigation called for in our time, even if this aspect eludes attention in change conversations predicated on this very navigational goal.

As noted above, the ultimate power of these and other elements of jazz and black music resides in their integrative nature—their synergistic interaction within a dynamic musical wholeness. This is key to the spiritual or transformative capacities often associated with jazz. Rhythmic, groove-oriented, collective creativity catalyzes transformations in consciousness among all participants—players and listeners alike—that exemplify the highest ideals of an arts-driven spirituality, one that transcends cultural and denominational boundaries yet at the same time invites connections with those boundaries as individuals are inclined. As I put it, jazz delivers an expansive spiritual vision that accommodates both the "church and the changes"—meaning formal spiritual/religious engagement of many kinds as well as the improvisation-driven transcendent experience that is increasingly acknowledged for its transformative ramifications across fields. If these aspects are to be harnessed, an entirely new understanding of the word *jazz* needs to guide future visioning in music studies.

Jazz as Self-Transcending Musical Gateway

The point is not to place jazz on a pedestal that overshadows the rest of the black music continuum, let alone the broader musical landscape. Rather, my intention is the opposite—to underscore a particularly rich and powerful process-structure region in the twenty-first-century musical landscape that, unsurpassed in its capacities to open up connections to a wide range of musical and extramusical terrain, happens to be called "jazz." Jazz excels in its "self-transcending"[15] capabilities, by which practitioners penetrate beyond the localized horizons of a given domain and embark on wide-ranging excursions of inquiry, interconnectedness, transformation, and growth. On launching upon such excursions, jazz is not discarded in the process, nor is grounding in the idiom diluted. Rather, the idiom is at once reintegrated within the newfound expanse and conducive to even deeper engagement within its horizons. Integral approaches to knowledge systems "transcend and include,"[16] rather than jettison, their points of departure, yielding more expansive and differentiated approaches to all points along the self-transcending continuum.

Key is the principle of diverse epistemologies, or diverse ways of knowing, being, and creative expression. Jazz is epistemically rich, as seen above in its creative spectrum, and thus a powerful self-transcending gateway that opens up to wide-ranging destinations. Musicians with "jazz" grounding, particularly when the idiom is defined as *writ large*—to encompass its outer edges that often elude categorization—are therefore able to arrive at whatever destinations they choose from a significantly broader and integrative skill set than other kinds of grounding. What, if anything, is being privileged, then, is not a particular genre, or kind of music, but rather a creative process scope that enhances, rather than precludes, engagement with wide-ranging genres and knowledge categories. This is not to imply that tradition-specific immersion in any given destination is therefore unnecessary upon developing jazz foundations, but that these foundations are unmatched in the tools they offer immersion in a given area. There is no replacement for the rigors of North Indian raga/tala improvisation, European classical performance or composition, or Turkish *maqam* to attain mastery in those traditions. However, there is a fundamental skill set inherent in the African American core of American musical culture that is unmatched in how it prepares musicians for these kinds of pursuits.

Nor do I wish to suggest that the primary purpose of rebuilding music studies around jazz foundations is to gain skills that lead elsewhere than jazz per se. In a single stroke, jazz foundations link musical identity with the black roots of American musical culture and also provide musicians with a creative infrastructure that opens up to an infinitude of horizons.

Unfortunately, conventional jazz education—inheriting aspects of compromised creativity from music studies (and education) at large—has not been securely grounded in these intrinsic aspects of the jazz heritage. Important light is shed on this topic by a look at the contrasting vision that underlies the Association for Advancement of Creative Musicians (AACM), an important movement that originated in the community of black musicians in Chicago in the 1960s, and that—despite its impact on jazz and contemporary music—has sadly been only peripherally recognized, its fruits barely harvested, in the continually burgeoning realm of jazz studies. The AACM, as George Lewis recounts in his landmark book on the initiative, was driven by exploration of "new and expanded ideas about timbre, sound, collectivity, extended technique, relationship between improvisation and composition, intermedia, invented instruments, and installations."[17] Disconnected from this self-transcending creative thrust that is inherent in the jazz tradition, conventional jazz education would instead remain constrained by self-confining approaches "that cordon off musicians from interpenetration with other musical art worlds, and cannot account for breakdown of genre definitions or the mobility of practices that informs the present-day musical landscape."[18] If the jazz-driven transformation of music studies is to transpire, jazz study itself needs to reconnect with the creative and spiritual roots of the music as embodied in the AACM and other initiatives that have minimally informed academic jazz study.[19]

From Multicultural to Transcultural Diversity Platforms

Central to understanding the emergent, integral conception of jazz, as well as harnessing its transformative capacities, is a shift from prevailing multicultural approaches to contemporary musical navigation to a transcultural framework. The multicultural platform tends to be ambivalent about epistemology and views the musical world in terms of an infinite series of separate cultural compartments to be taken up one by one in aspirations for a culturally diverse awareness. By contrast, the transcultural vision is one of robust interconnectedness, creative dynamism, and self-transcending engagement. The central pulse of the musical landscape from a transcultural perspective lies not in the language-bound categories that dominate academic and commercial awareness, but in the creative processes that gave rise to genre categories in the first place. The transcultural, however, does not reject genre-specific engagement. Rather, it regards genres as tributaries that flow into the central syncretic current. Important to the transcultural vision, moreover, is creative grounding in the music of one's own culture as gateway to the broader musical world. In chapter 2, I identify close to twenty distinguishing features between multicultural and transcultural frameworks.

I characterize conventional jazz education as multicultural in nature, as I do other areas of music studies—such as ethnomusicology, music education, and more recently, popular music studies—that are ostensibly predicated on expanding the cultural horizons of music studies ethnomusicology. In other words, in response (or more aptly, reaction) to the monocultural orientation of the conventional music studies paradigm, with its focus on interpretive performance and analytical studies of European classical repertory, the diversity quest in music schools has become locked into a paradigm, typically unexamined, of its own that in important ways undermines this quest. Because change is often sought through additions to the prevailing model rather than foundational redesign, I call this "lower order" change discourse. To the contrary, an integral conception of jazz, construed as *writ large*, exemplifies transcultural principles and underpins a "higher order" level of change visioning that is driven by the quest for foundational overhaul.[20]

My point is not to categorically discredit musical multiculturalism, but rather to situate its contributions within the more expansive transcultural perspective. As I state, "Anything multiculturalism can do, transculturalism can do better." However, this is not just a matter of simple expansion of the horizons of the first in order to accommodate those of the second. Multiculturalism inheres foundational roadblocks that need to be identified and removed.

Language as Paradigmatic Indicator

Among the important steps in this process is the recognition of how language and terminology—what we call things—reify prevailing paradigms in a given field. As I discuss in chapter 2, the word *jazz*, from a multicultural and thus epistemically ambivalent standpoint, indicates a self-confining musical destination—a cultural compartment that exists among an infinite spectrum of other compartments—that comes early on under the *J*s in the musical alphabet. Moreover, and I encounter this regularly in ethnomusicological and other circles, arguments for jazz to play a foundational role in contemporary musical navigation may indeed be rejected by multiculturalists as a form of privileging. However, the same word—*jazz*—from a transcultural perspective, characteristic of higher order visioning, designates a creativity-rich, self-transcending region with unmatched capacities for culturally diverse interaction and infusion. Again, the transcultural apprehension of musical reality lies not in overarching categories but in underlying processes.

Important ramifications extend to the intersection of jazz and European classical music, with contrasting readings inferred in prevailing terminology, often uttered uncritically by multiculturalists and monoculturalists alike, that further reflects radically different paradigmatic vantage points that need to be identified if substantive change is to transpire. The heading "classical music" (or "art music," which I consider distinctly problematic) from a multicultural standpoint (as well as conventional monocultural standpoint) typically refers to a tradition in which the majority of musicians focus on interpretive performance, with composition undertaken by a distinct minority, and improvisation is virtually absent. The same heading—"classical"—from a transcultural perspective points to a tradition of Contemporary Improvisers Composers Performers (CICP), from which the Interpretive Performance Specialist (IPS) model—which I thus call neo-Eurocentric—is a stark deviation. In other words, Bach, Beethoven, Clara Schumann, Franz Liszt, and the majority of their peers improvised, composed, and performed in the languages of their times—as do today's jazz musicians. Whereas multicultural conceptions of the words *jazz* and *classical*, confined by epistemically weak conditioning inherited from the conventional music studies paradigm, perpetuate divisions between these two great lineages, transcultural understanding highlights the common creative thread uniting these lineages, thus unveiling powerful strategies for harnessing their intersection. As I commonly assert in my speaking and writing on the topic, the problem with music studies—from a transcultural vantage point—is *not* that it is too Eurocentric, but that *it is not Eurocentric enough*. Meaning, of course, that a truly Eurocentric paradigm would restore the contemporary creative foundations of European classical music to music studies, at which point the African American foundations of twenty-first-century creativity—and musical inquiry and understanding—would loom large in any music degree program in America.

Therefore, when it comes to the question posed above, and likely harbored by many readers, regarding the place of European classical music in American musical identity, new perspectives also come into view on this topic from an integral, transcultural vantage point. Indeed, there is no denying the importance of the European tradition in this identity. However, the following questions must first be addressed: What European classical paradigm is one talking about? Is it the prevailing neo-Eurocentric, interpretive performance framework? Or the epistemically broad and creativity-rich CICP model? The paradigmatic lens through which these questions are posed, and from which responses are proffered, must be identified if the inertia of lower order reform discourse is to be overcome.

Higher order, transcultural responses to these questions lay conceptual groundwork for entirely new approaches that overcome this inertia. While the neo-Eurocentric paradigm has long been predominant in American musical life, this is a distinctly European contribution to world musical culture, not an American one. If one cites the CICP paradigm as the central European model in question, then a different consideration comes to the fore—that this process scope has been ushered into American musical life through African American, not European, culture. Restoring the process or epistemic foundations of musical inquiry, understanding, and navigation, the transcultural perspective underscores the centrality of jazz in American musical culture and, in so doing, redirects entanglement in kinds of music as competing to a celebration of their creativity-based coevolution. To invoke further wisdom from Christopher Small: "The meeting between African and European music has been one of the most fruitful exchanges in the entire history of music."[21] While one need not look far within both jazz and classical lineages to see the fruits of this merging, I take a further step in viewing it as still in its embryonic stages, with extraordinary vistas of creativity and syncretism waiting to blossom in the years ahead providing the higher order transformation of music studies is realized.

In sum, this book seeks to distance itself from prevailing arguments for the need to change the conventional music studies paradigm through multicultural modifications. However well intended, these approaches fall short of the creativity/epistemic revolution at the heart of my vision. Inspired by, yet in fact extending, Small's notion of "musicking," jazz impels us to flip the ontological switch from structure to process, from a view of musical reality dominated by objective features and discrete genre categories, to the creative processes by which those criteria came into being in the first place, and which occupy the central pulse of musical reality. The emergent perspective is not oblivious to structural concerns, but reconceives them atop process-rich creative foundations, resulting in synergistic process-structure interactions that underpin new levels of achievement, understanding, and transformative impact. At which point, the higher order, integral vision that takes hold in music studies can then extend to broader arts-driven educational and societal practice.

An emergent worldview called Integral Theory sheds light on what the improvised musical art form called jazz has to offer this transformation.

JAZZ AS INTEGRAL TEMPLATE

Little elaboration is needed on the scope of the challenges confronting today's world, and the questions they raise about the very future of civilization as we know it. The assertion by Anthony Braxton that "the West is in its 11th hour"[22] could just as readily apply on a planetary scale. My vision for an arts-driven revolution in creativity and consciousness is inspired by both this kind of sobering assessment and also an unwavering optimism about the capacity for humanity to dig deep into its wellsprings of evolutionary potential and triumph in this moment. Following Buckminster Fuller, I have argued that the kind of transformation that the present challenges call for will not only suffice to ensure our survival but also catapult humankind to an entirely new developmental plateau.[23] For this to occur, a new worldview, or account of human creative and spiritual potential, needs to guide and inform every facet of life. I view Integral Theory as uniquely equipped to serve as this guiding narrative. In the words of the preeminent American philosopher Ken Wilber, largely regarded as the primary exponent of integral thought, Integral Theory synthesizes and makes available the "knowledge, experience, wisdom, and reflection of all major human civilizations," from the timeless insights of "the ancient shamans and sages" to the latest "breakthroughs in cognitive neuroscience."[24] In so doing, Integral Theory at once expands the vision of future possibilities for the world and also offers powerful diagnostic tools that help identify and understand, from their roots on up, important obstacles to be encountered and addressed along the way.

A look at three primary integral maps—structure, process, and diagnostic—supports the case for jazz as an unmatched embodiment of integral principles in and beyond music.

Integral Structural Maps

Integral structural maps involve the inner-outer dimensions of human experience and reality, and the core evolutionary purpose of human existence, which is interior-exterior wholeness, or union. Here the terms *yoga* and *religion*, both indicating this inner-outer integration, can be understood as synonymous. Following Wilber, integralists fathom greater nuance within the interior-exterior expanse by viewing it in terms of three interpenetrating dimensions—first-person, second-person, and third-person, or subjective, interactive/process, and objective.[25] First-, second-, and third-person dimensions correlate with and are perhaps more readily grasped as "I," "we," and "it," or the familiar domains of spirituality, art, and science. Here, however, it is important to understand the domains both as conventionally construed and as manifestations of primordial subject-process-object impulses that permeate every instant of time, space, and human experience.[26] In other words, science from an integral vantage point not only comprises such fields as physics, biology, and chemistry but also represents a third-person, objective dimension of reality and experience that manifests itself in all human endeavor. Similarly, art comprises not only disciplines such as music, dance, and painting, but also a second-person, creative/interactive impulse that can be enlivened to pervade engagement in all aspects of life; spirituality in the same way encompasses not only interior transformative practices and ideas but also a first-person subjective impulse that pervades all of existence.[27] As creativity and consciousness evolve, engagement in any given moment in any endeavor becomes more integral through the interweaving of spiritual, artistic, and scientific (first-, second-, and third-person) dimensions, which renders the activity and overall development optimally self-transcending.

Much as seen previously with music, familiar labels take on new meaning. The word *science* approached integrally designates a self-transcending gateway that opens up to art and spirituality, *art* designates a gateway that integrates spirituality and science, and *spirituality* similarly unites science and art. Just as musical engagement that fails to open up to the broader landscape is self-confining, approaches to spirituality, art, and science that fail to open up to the totality are correspondingly self-confining. At which point, a second type of integral map, having to do with the processes by which this self-transcending integration happens, comes into view. If integral structural maps indicate the "what" of Integral Theory and its vision of human development, integral process maps indicate the "how."

Integral Process Maps

Here is where another principle already encountered, that of epistemological diversity—diverse ways of knowing, being, and creative expression—comes into play. The Contemporary Improviser Composer Performer process scope is epistemically rich; the Interpretive Performance Specialist scope that underpins conventional music studies is epistemically limited. The greater the epistemic breadth, the greater the self-transcending capacities (as in the CICP profile), from which the reverse follows (as in the neo-Eurocentric), where epistemological dearth breeds self-confinement. When we shift the ontological lens as noted earlier from structure to process, now applied more broadly, we realize that spirituality, art, and science correlate with respective epistemologies that need to be represented in balance for any endeavor to be realized in a fully integral manner. Regardless of the nature of the gateway discipline, as designated by the terms *spiritual*, *artistic*, or *scientific* or some subset, self-transcending engagement is optimal when first-person/interior (spiritual), second-person/creative (artistic), and third-person/objective (scientific) ways of knowing and expression work in tandem.

Jazz, again construed integrally as self-transcending, and thus writ large, exemplifies a key principle within the notion of diverse epistemologies that powerfully supports this aim. This is the interplay of what I call "parts-to-whole" and "whole-to-parts" (PW/WP) methodologies.[28] Parts-to-whole is creativity-based in that it proceeds from engagement in a given domain of activity and opens up to more unified and integrative experience—what is often called "flow" or "peak experience."[29] Improvisation is therefore a powerful parts-to-whole vehicle because it involves intensive physical/technical, inventive, interactive, mental, and emotional activity en route to the transformed episodes of consciousness that improvisers commonly report. Whole-to-parts is contemplative or consciousness-based, in that it proceeds from the deep, interior silence invoked in meditation and through related contemplative modalities, which over time infuses itself into the realm of action. Features and benefits associated with these practices and experiences include mind-body integration, where ideas flow and are executed effortlessly, transformed sense of time, heightened connections between performers and listeners, inner calm, exceptional well-being, and joy, much of which finds support in a growing body of literature on development of consciousness.[30]

The jazz tradition boasts a long legacy of musical innovators—including John Coltrane and Alice Coltrane, John McLaughlin, Herbie Hancock, Wayne Shorter, Don Cherry, Charles Lloyd, and Mary Lou Williams—who have also significantly engaged with contemplative traditions in order to enrich their work and lives.[31] Muhal Richard Abrahms writes, "The new musicians have a need for mind expansion . . . so (music making) can get way past the intellect, into what I call the spiritual plane. Intuition takes what it needs from the intellect when they meet; emotion is used to develop beauty once it gets to this plane."[32]

The parts-to-whole/whole-to-parts epistemic template offers a powerful model for self-transcending engagement and growth that can be applied across fields to catalyze first-second-third person, or spirituality-art-science synthesis. I view John and Alice Coltrane as particularly strong exemplars of the PW/WP framework, with both being consummate improvisers and devoted meditators, and with Alice—in her immersion in Vedantic practice—as uniquely definitive of the latter.[33] As I emphasize in chapter 5, where I delineate a range of contemplative methodologies, my point is not to prescribe a specific framework that everyone might follow, but to illuminate principles that help individuals arrive at pathways that suit their personal needs and proclivities. Among these principles is the delicate interplay between rigorous immersion and highly personalized expression and exploration that is as essential to spirituality/consciousness evolution as it is to creative development. Just as today's musicians are challenged to find ways of navigating an infinitude of musical possibilities, a parallel challenge is evident in the broad spectrum of practices and pathways available to contemporary spiritual aspirants. I believe an integral conception of jazz, particularly as it takes shape in the PW/WP framework, offers important guidance for both types of navigation, and thus emergence of new paradigms of music studies and overall education.

Integral Diagnostic Maps

Which leads to the third integral map, having to do with the model's diagnostic faculties. It is not enough to delineate an expanded vision of human potential and reality (the what), or ways of navigating the interior-exterior dimensions of that reality (the how); it is also important to dig deep into limiting patterns in individual and collective thinking in order that they may be addressed (hence, the "how not"). The integral diagnostic realm includes several key features. The first and most general is what integralists—following Freud, Jung, and the tradition of depth psychology—call the "shadow," or repository of repressed emotions, anxieties, and unresolved desires that, left unaddressed, give rise to pathological tendencies. Shortly I will deal with racism/ethnocentricism in music as a key example. Integral Theory, however, offers more nuanced analyses that place shadow content and tendencies within a broader context that enhances rectifying strategies.

Among the key principles to this is that knowledge systems evolve from less differentiated toward more differentiated wholeness. Or put another way, from lesser to greater complexity. The self-transcending engagement examined above is richly differentiated.

Second is that the thrust toward differentiation is often punctuated by periods of dissociation, where a given line of engagement (or discipline), as it opens up to increased complexity, becomes severed from its connection to the science-art-spirituality wholeness and takes on a life of its own. Now self-transcending engagement succumbs to self-confining. Wilber vividly illustrates this dissociative, self-confining tendency in terms of the science-religion split, where both domains needed to evolve beyond the crude fusion that prevailed in earlier times. The fact that "Galileo could not look freely through his telescope and report the results because art, morals and science were all fused under the Church, (which) defined what science could—and could not do," was symptomatic of a paradigm in which science and religion could not develop as independent, co-evolutionary lines. The two domains, however, didn't just differentiate as part of a unified, more complex wholeness, but rather took the further step and "flew apart"—hence dissociated—from one another, resulting in the lingering ideological conflict that continues to this day.[34] The more that dissociated science confines the human being and cosmos to a material substrate, the more that dissociative tendencies are fueled in religion, as it retreats behind its equally rigid dogmas.[35] The time has come, as Wilber forcefully asserts, for both domains "to grow up"[36] and escape these cycles of extremism by recognizing that the pathway forward for each, and the whole of human development, lies in transcending their discipline-specific boundaries and opening up to each other. In so doing, celebration of the unique facets of each domain (e.g., correlations between human experience and neurobiological activity revealed by science, and physically transcendent dimensions of consciousness and reality as disclosed by religion) is possible.

Application of these ideas is immediately evident to music. What I call above the neo-Eurocentric paradigm in European classical music can be seen as an example of differentiation—the organic yet interdependent growth of improvisation, composition, and performance along their respective developmental pathways—succumbing to dissociation, where composition was relegated to a minority and improvisation fell by the wayside in the hegemonic ascendance of interpretive performance. Tensions between dissociated models of science and religion thus directly parallel those between dissociated classical music and the broader musical world, all of which are reified by language. As discussed earlier with the word *jazz* being conceived quite differently from multicultural and transcultural perspectives, the words *science* and *religion* are also subject to radically different understandings mediated by respective kinds of ideological baggage that reify tensions between them, or noetic insight that reveals within them deeper, synergistic meaning and interconnectedness. While fundamentalism is commonly ascribed to religion, whereby religious extremists reject not only science but also other forms of religion, a less commonly recognized, but equally pernicious fundamentalism in science—sometimes called scientism—must also be identified. Here, science, in categorically rejecting religious perspectives, functions antithetically to integral models of human nature and development in which science and religion are both essential. The integral framework enables even more nuanced understanding. Recall, as one example, the above correlation between *religion* and *yoga*, whereby both denote union in consciousness, thus providing a basis for tensions (usually harbored in Christian extremist ranks that are averse to Eastern and other spiritual practices) between the two areas to be resolved. The same yoga/religion correlation is also essential to, in turn, countering antireligious sentiments harbored among some who identify as "spiritual but not religious," which when categorically dismissing religion, can be recognized as its own form of extremism (albeit operating under a politically correct guise). The fact that common to extremism, which is sustained by unexamined language and terminology, is limited epistemic engagement underscores the important contributions that the arts in general, and its epistemically unmatched subdomain of jazz in particular, have to offer a world riddled by these kinds of fragmentation and division.

A further integral diagnostic feature involves identification of shadow tendencies as both interior, within a given system, and parts of overarching patterns. Now dissociative scientific materialism and musical materialism can be seen as related, as aspects of what I call an overarching "Matrix of Materialism"[37] that also includes tendencies in education at large to reduce learning to ingestion of information at the expense of a broader epistemic scope. Much of the legacy of educational criticism can be seen as directed at this very deficiency, which the Matrix of Materialism reveals as rooted in the overarching view of the human being as largely physical in nature, thus denying any sort of spiritual dimension (if not essence) that has been inherited from the prevailing ideology of scientism that dominates the academy. Parallels between scientism as a deviation from a prior, broader paradigm of scientific inquiry, and neo-Eurocentrism as a deviation from a prior, broader European classical music paradigm underscore the diagnostic utility of the Matrix of Materialism model, and the integral framework overall. While it may take no great powers of imagination to fathom the correlation between the reduction of human consciousness (invoking materialism in its most extreme form) to the neurophysiology of the brain to the reduction of musical reality to the composed-notated art object (not to be conflated with the act of composition), the integral account takes the further diagnostic leap in revealing multicultural efforts to rectify the problem as constrained by, hence further manifestations of the overarching materialist veil, the very epistemic crisis from which it (multiculturalism) arises. This richly differentiated recognition of localized, domain-specific patterns as aspects of broader tendencies underscores at once their tenacity, and the paradigmatic nature of the reform needed for liberation therefrom.

Here is where integral distinctions between horizontal and vertical change come to the fore. Horizontal change involves modifications of paradigms; vertical change entails foundational overhaul from their conceptual core on up. Applied to what I characterize above as lower order and higher order models of change visioning in music studies, lower order involves ornamental adjustments to the prevailing neo-Eurocentric paradigm, usually through the introduction of cursory experiences in improvisation and composition and engagement with diverse musics atop the existing foundations. I call this the "neo-Eurocentric-plus" approach in order to emphasize how it falls short of the foundational overhaul needed. Higher order change visioning is predicated on wholesale transformation around the CICP paradigm, which when expanded to include a broader spectrum of musical and extramusical inquiry—including consciousness—I term the CICP-plus model.

Integral application of progressive scales from developmental psychology is also helpful in diagnosing obstacles. For example, growth in self-development from egocentric, to ethnocentric, to worldcentric, which integralists extend to cosmocentric, illuminates how individuals and even entire fields can be stuck at a given evolutionary platform.[38] The decidedly ethnocentric status of music studies is underscored in this context, which sheds light on the steps needed for the field to move forward.

In sum: Self-transcending, integral approaches to domains are not only broader in their interior-exterior scope but also more differentiated in every instant of engagement, and conducive to optimal achievement in mainstream areas as well as robust connections across fields. Such approaches also render fields more self-organizing, adaptable to changing circumstances, and self-critical, whereby practitioners are able to step back and critically interrogate lingering patterns and begin to free themselves from dogma. And as I elaborate in part II, self-transcending models are more differentiated, and thus robust, pathways to the soul. Unfortunately, with the disappearance of improvisation and its creative foundations, classical music—and thus the prevailing music studies framework—has distanced itself from these self-transcending capacities and become riddled by dissociation and the hegemonic by-products inherent in compromised epistemic systems. Application of the above principles to music studies sheds light on the key role jazz will play in the integral transformation of the field and beyond.

CHAPTER-BY-CHAPTER OVERVIEW

The book is divided into two parts, which correspond to the two prongs of the parts-to-whole (PW)/whole-to-parts (WP) interplay introduced above. Part I correlates with the PW creativity-driven thrust and is thus called *Jazz and the Creativity Turn*. Part II correlates with the WP consciousness angle, and is called *Jazz and the Consciousness Turn*. The closely intertwined nature of creativity and consciousness, however, is evident throughout; one cannot delve significantly into one without broaching the other.

This is clearly evident in chapter 1, "Creativity as New Organizing Principle." Distinctions between creativity as an add-on and foundational pillar underpin my distinctions between lower order and higher order change visioning. Whereas the lower order platform approaches change by inserting improvisation, composition, and engagement with diverse musical traditions as ornaments atop the existing framework, higher order visioning rebuilds the entire music learning enterprise around the creativity-based CICP identity. The identity shift from music interpreter (who may occasionally improvise and compose) to music creator (who also performs) is key to circumventing what I call the Central Impasse, which is the challenge—facing all fields—of addressing an ever-expanding knowledge base in a nonchanging curricular space (hours-per-week/years-per-degree program). A list of twenty change themes is provided, including diversity, integrative learning, student-centered growth, embodied musicianship, and entrepreneurship, that underscores the need for higher order, foundational rebuilding. A definition of musical creativity and creative development is provided that illuminates how the CICP is uniquely equipped to underpin the broader kind of navigation and that opens up to the interior dimensions of consciousness and thus foreshadows an integral music studies paradigm. Individuation, the blossoming of the distinctly personal artistic voice, is paramount, as it is the basis for rendering musical development self-organizing—shifting the conventional orientation toward institution-based pedagogy to student-driven growth.

Subsequent chapters address the twenty change themes from lower order and jazz-inspired higher order approaches. Chapter 2, "Multiculturalism, Transculturalism, and Race," examines the social justice ramifications of the two change perspectives. The inextricable link between epistemology and ethnology, which has eluded change discourse, assumes front and center stage. From this standpoint, multiculturalism is characterized as a lower order reform perspective, with its fragmented navigational strategies rooted in an underlying ambivalence about epistemology or mode of engagement. The transcultural vision is higher order in that it grounds understanding and contact in creative integration of diverse elements in the individual improvisatory/compositional voice. Whereas the multicultural framework also remains ambivalent about grounding in one's own musical culture, the transcultural paradigm is predicated on creativity-based foundations in the music of one's time and place as key to fathoming deep connections to music of other cultures. In developing its argument that, while conversation about diversity is nothing new in music studies, discourse rarely penetrates to the realm of race, the chapter critically examines the use of language and terminology that reifies ethnocentric/racist tendencies. Headings such as "art music" and "new music" are viewed as examples of exnomination, where terminology that is seemingly neutral and inclusive is typically used in exclusive ways; in other words, while "art music" could theoretically encompass virtually every tradition in the world, the conventional use of the term to solely or largely apply to European classical music creates the effect of marginalization.

Chapter 3, "Music School for a Transcultural Age," presents a higher order account of what a jazz-inspired, creativity-based music studies paradigm might look like. New conceptions are presented of how a music school might be organized, with five new pillars deemed central (and subsuming all existing areas within an expanded framework): music creation, music inquiry and craft, music pedagogy, music and consciousness, and music and society. A radically new core musicianship framework is outlined that unites improvisation, composition, performance, aural skills, theoretical studies, musical embodiment, cultural/aesthetic/cognitive studies, and spirituality/consciousness. A considerably expanded framework is presented for private instruction, even as approaches to mastering an instrument are distributed across the curriculum. A reconceived ensemble program is advanced in which the small creative music ensemble is the central experience, and atop which large ensemble programs—now capable of considerably new horizons (that unite traditional and innovative areas)—are rebuilt. Parallels are considered between the shared challenges of contemporary musical navigation and contemporary spiritual navigation. New perspectives on musical embodiment, technology, and entrepreneurship—among the newest change themes, and perhaps most fashionable buzzwords—are offered.

Chapter 4, "New Conversations with Conservatives," discusses issues that commonly arise in music school reform deliberations in hopes of elevating the dialogue. Whereas much of the critique in the book aims at lower order change thinking, as a result of which critique of the conventional, neo-Eurocentric model may be inferred, this chapter takes the opposite approach in identifying recurring patterns in responses to change by conservatives. I identify a dozen "fallacies" commonly encountered in these conversations that reflect unexamined assumptions. Prominent examples are the notions that creativity- and diversity-driven change necessarily means compromised skills, diluted engagement in a given tradition, or denigration of European classical music. I distinguish between lower order and higher order responses to these misconceptions.

Whereas, as noted, part I presented a parts-to-whole trajectory in which a creativity-driven trajectory opened up to consciousness, part II, *Jazz and the Consciousness Revolution*, complements this with a consciousness-based, whole-to-parts approach that significantly expands future visioning.

Chapter 5, "A Jazz-Based Integral Perspective on Consciousness," grapples with one of the most elusive topics imaginable, yet one that is arguably essential to the navigation of the present juncture in human history, through a jazz-based, integral lens. Contrasting philosophies of mind are considered, including materialism, idealism, dualism, and integralism, with the jazz-based parts-to-whole/whole-to-parts epistemic interplay serving as a basis for an integral perspective. This sheds light on the so-called "hard problem of consciousness," which has to do with how consciousness emerges from a physical substrate; from an integral standpoint, it doesn't—consciousness is ontologically primary in the cosmic scheme. A range of issues related to development of consciousness are considered, including its relationship to improvisatory creativity as well as parallels between challenges inherent in twenty-first-century musical and spiritual navigation. Both involve practitioners having to sort through a morass of options (musical and spiritual pathways), to skillfully balance grounding in tradition with trans-traditional exploration, and to evolve an individual (musical and spiritual) voice. Cutting-edge scientific research into psi or anomalous features of consciousness is examined that supports age-old notions of consciousness as nonlocal, intersubjective, and physically transcendent, consistent with the integral model. The heightened intersubjectivity of peak improvisatory performance is paralleled with the heightened intersubjectivity often reported in group meditation practice.

The more complete grasp of consciousness sets the stage for a fuller understanding of improvisation in chapter 6, aptly titled "A Consciousness-Based Integral Perspective on Improvisation." Dispelling the long-standing notion that improvisation is an accelerated form of composition, the chapter presents a model called Nonlinear Time Dynamics. Multiple tiers of distinctions between the two operations are identified, including contrasting conditions (improvisation [in groups] is collective and happens once; composition is unaccompanied and happens in a discontinuous framework), differing temporal conceptions (improvisation is nonlinear; composition is linear), contrasting cultural origins, distinct pathways to transcendent experience, and contrasting archetypal correlations (improvisation correlates with the feminine archetype; composition the masculine). Further light is shed on the significance of the Contemporary Improviser Performer Composer profile that is central to jazz. I close the chapter with a new paradigm of musical inquiry and understanding called Integral Musicology.

Chapter 7, "Jazz and the Integral Revolution," provides a culminating account of how a transformed paradigm of music studies has the capacity to catalyze broader transformation—what I call a creativity and consciousness revolution in education and society at large. Ramifications for jazz-inspired, integral approaches to educational reform, social justice, creativity and innovation across fields, consciousness/spirituality, and peace are considered.

An epilogue sums up the vision set forth in the book.

A CALL TO LEADERSHIP

I view jazz as not only among the most advanced artistic lineages humanity has ever known, but also among the most advanced "wisdom systems"—by which I mean a robust vehicle for creativity and consciousness evolution—that humanity has ever known. Jazz is the musical soul of America, with important contributions to make in connecting with the world's musical soul. If age-old accounts of the place of music in the broader spectra of consciousness and cosmic wholeness are any guide, this means connecting with the soul of humanity.

Imagine the impact of this vision for the African American child, newly awakening to the harsh realities of racism, and susceptible to its litany of casualties—not the least of which are low self-esteem and self-confidence; lack of role models; constrained vision of possibilities; and for far too many black (and other) youth, day-to-day atrocities (such as hunger and violence) that are endemic to poverty. Imagine the sense of pride and self-worth, and impetus for aspiring toward self-actualization and leadership, that such a child might develop were a seminal African American cultural achievement recognized, in our educational systems and society, as a *seminal human achievement*. Imagine the impact of this vision for the non–African American child—and adolescent or adult—that is also a victim, though perhaps suffering from it differently, of America's racial, and thus cultural and spiritual, confusion and calamities. When, as I argue from an integral, nondual view of human consciousness, we realize that we are all part of an interconnected spiritual web, and that regardless of skin color, we all have black, white, red, yellow, female, and male aspects of our individual and collective soul, it becomes evident that the connection of our society to its black musical/spiritual foundations is of equal importance for individuals of all backgrounds.

Black music matters.

This book is devoted to those individuals who share my belief in the transformative potential of the arts, sense of urgency of harnessing this transformative impact at this moment in human history, and commitment to doing the inner and outer work needed to place a conspicuously overlooked facet of American culture front and center in order for its potential contributions to flow—and enrich and help heal—the precious world we inhabit.

I

Jazz and the Creativity Turn

Chapter One

Creativity as New Organizing Principle

Why, after over fifty years of reform appeals and initiatives, has music studies remained immune to all but the most superficial modifications of a paradigm rooted in interpretive performance and analysis of European classical repertory?[1] How will the expanded set of skills and understanding required of twenty-first-century musicians be integrated into a manageable, coherent, and effective program of study? What is the place of jazz in this broader transformation, and why have the considerable resources this tradition offers been overlooked in reform conversations? Where does European classical music fit into the new vision, and how can connections to this and other genres open up through jazz foundations? How does the jazz paradigm open up to connections beyond music, including spirituality/consciousness, to thus embody the integral vision?[2]

In this chapter, I respond to these and other questions by placing creativity at the center of the change conversation. At first glance, this may seem to be nothing new, with appeals to incorporate improvising and composing in the curriculum long prominent in music studies reform deliberations.[3] However, distinctions between what I call lower order and higher order change visions reveal fundamentally contrasting conceptions for the place of music creation in the music studies framework. Lower order, neo-Eurocentric-plus approaches tend to advocate creativity—as well as other themes associated with change—as add-ons, often as pedagogical aids (e.g., to enhance achievement in music theory and aural skills) within the conventional framework.[4] By contrast, a higher order, early integral account calls for a wholesale shift in artistic identity, and thus curricular foundations, from music interpreter (who may also improvise and compose to moderate extents) to creating artist (who eats, sleeps, dreams, and breathes as improviser-composer).[5]

Recall preliminary correlations between lower and higher order platforms with multicultural and transcultural diversity frameworks, to be explored more fully in chapter 2. As noted, improvisation and composition are core to the emergent transcultural identity and viewed as foundational forms of creativity that, when ceded central status in music learning, promote the growth of creativity in all facets of musical practice and inquiry as well as life as a whole. As the site of the return of the Contemporary Improviser Composer Performer profile that was once prominent in European classical music, jazz has the capacity to catalyze a transformative chain that takes hold in music studies and extends throughout the educational spectrum and far beyond. The creativity aspect of this transformation is the focus of part I of the book; part II deals with consciousness, which is key to a fully integral approach.[6]

I begin with a look at an obstacle confronting all educational disciplines, what I call the "Central Impasse." Indeed, the challenges inherent in addressing an ever-expanding knowledge base without expanding the curricular space—meaning not only credit hours in a given semester but also the number of years that comprise degree programs—is among the most prominent topics in contemporary educational discourse. I identify twenty change themes that commonly appear and underscore the challenge in music studies. I then inquire into the nature of musical creativity to show how development of the personal creative voice, which I view—inspired by C. G. Jung—as "musical individuation," provides an entirely new self-organizing principle for addressing the challenge. The core thrust of music studies and change visioning shifts from horizontal, institution-centered pedagogy, which can be compared to the continual addition of new items to a curricular assembly line, to a vertical, student-driven impetus that is capable of newfound scope and integration within that scope. Now the broad spectrum that is associated with an emergent conception of musical skills and understanding—including improvisation, composition, diversity, integrative learning, critical thinking, theoretical understanding, aural abilities, rhythm/embodiment, history, cultural and cognitive understanding, and transpersonal/spiritual development— may be seen as not only a horizontal inventory, but a vertical unfolding from unified, self-organizing foundations. A systematic approach to improvisation studies, which uniquely integrates the totality, is key to the new model and its self-organizing, student-driven impetus. As I elaborate, student-driven pedagogy does not render institutional resources irrelevant, but in fact enlivens students' receptivity to these resources that make possible entirely new kinds of assimilation and excellence.

The chapter then shifts to a diagnostic focus. I examine the division of labor between creation and performance considered in the introduction as an instance of differentiation, which is considered in the introduction to be an evolutionary norm, taking the extreme step of dissociation, an evolutionary detour. The core, dissociative split in the prevailing neo-Eurocentric worldview, which lower order, neo-Eurocentric-plus discourse fails to heal, continues to permeate the conventional paradigm and efforts to reform it. The jazz-based return of the creativity-rich, CICP paradigm, now in expanded, globally mediated, and powerfully integrative form, restores dissociative tendencies to the richly differentiated template that is key to twenty-first-century musical navigation and transformative impact.

CENTRAL IMPASSE

Today's musicians need a broader spectrum of skills and understanding than their predecessors, which music schools are ill-equipped to provide. The question for music studies change visionaries is not only *what* this spectrum might consist of, which is the relatively easy part of the reform process, but also *how* it can be addressed. This means finding ways not only for its expanded array of components to coexist in already-overcrowded curricular frameworks, but also for these components to coevolve as organically interrelated facets of a unified system of learning and growth. In order to make room for new areas, moreover, some portion of existing requirements must give way, meaning that terrain cherished by some colleagues must be relinquished in favor of that deemed essential by others. Aside from its inherent political tensions, this kind of "curricular horse trading," involving a swapping of, say, a term of music theory for a term of improvisation, is but one example of how horizontal reform strategies fall dramatically short in solving a problem that requires new, vertical organizing principles. The guiding question needs to shift from the lower order "How do we fit everything in?" which in any case is not possible, to the higher order question "How do we enliven robust self-organizing capacities among our students in order that they may embark on careers as lifelong, self-sufficient learners?" As Howard Gardner has succinctly put it, there is simply "too much to know," and education therefore must shift toward "process-rich learning environments" that catalyze student-driven growth.[7]

The following inventory of change themes underscores the nature of the challenge:

Creativity: improvisation and composition occupying a place in the curricular core
Diversity: music studies as reflection of a global society
Integrative learning: connections across the many areas of the curriculum
Critical thinking: critical reflection on music learning, education, artistic and life pathways
Self-sufficiency: capacities for self-driven growth
Aural musicianship: stronger abilities to play by ear, to link visual and aural

Listening skills: to engage deeply in the music sounding at the moment
Embodied musicianship: experiencing music as a whole-body phenomenon
Rigor and understanding: new conceptions of what constitutes musical knowing
Technology: conversance with technological developments
Chamber music: small ensembles that allow for more personalized expression
Contemporary music: engagement with new musical developments
Pedagogical innovation: grounding in traditional and new teaching modalities
Community music: connections to music happening in students' locales
Community service: music as a vehicle for enhancing society
Entrepreneurship: self-promotion and self-marketing skills
Multidisciplinary education: grounding in multiple disciplines
Transdisciplinary understanding: fathoming underlying unifying principles across fields
Neurobiology of human learning: aligning music learning with neurobiological research
Arts advocacy: preparing students as arts ambassadors
Spirituality: grounding in awareness of the interior, sacred dimensions of music

Even a cursory look at the above inventory underscores the point that nothing short of foundational overhaul will suffice to align music studies with the musical world around us. An approach to the problem based in the creativity-consciousness foundations of Integral Theory immediately redirects reform visioning and diagnostics toward the vertical pillars of improvisation and composition. Instead of approaching these processes as curricular add-ons, or pedagogical aids, higher order integral change seeks to rebuild the entire music studies edifice around them. Inquiry into the nature of musical creativity from the standpoint of Integral Theory enables a further step in this vertical realignment, where an unprecedented scope of musical engagement and inquiry can be organized atop an improvisatory core. The case for jazz as paradigmatic change catalyst thus gains strength.

WHAT IS MUSICAL CREATIVITY?

Few questions more fully harness the capacity of Integral Theory to situate conventional thinking in a vastly expanded scope that includes the innermost dimensions of consciousness. Tracing this along the first-second-third person integral continuum encountered in the introduction, musical creativity from a third-person, objective standpoint may be understood largely as an input-output endeavor, where one assimilates skills and concepts and then fashions them, perhaps in novel configurations, in creative expressions of one's own. From a second-person, process-mediated standpoint, musical creativity is measured not only by the objects it produces or melds, but also by a broader spectrum of inventive methodologies and influences. Improvising and composing can thus be seen as primary creative modalities that undergird a much broader creative spectrum that includes interpretive performance, a host of areas in musical inquiry and craft, and extra-musical/artistic domains. Creativity, therefore, is not exclusive to improvising, composing, painting, or sculpting and other artistic media but—as originating in the deepest recesses of consciousness—intrinsic to all human endeavor. Shortly, moreover, I show how improvisation is uniquely equipped to enhance creativity throughout the broader spectrum. Second-person understanding of musical creativity also goes far beyond direct input/output relationships and recognizes a wider scope of cultural, environmental, economic, educational, and other experiences and influences that are, as it were, metabolized into personal expressions.

Where Integral Theory particularly excels, however, is in its situating of third-person and second-person considerations within a yet broader first-person, subjective standpoint—at the core of which is consciousness. Musical creativity may therefore be understood as more than overlying skills and influences from musical and extramusical sources, but most fundamentally a direct manifestation of the innermost regions of the psyche. In other words, while shaped by overlying forces, musical creativity is also a phenomenon with transcendent origins. Now primordial, archetypal influences can be added to the spectrum of influences that shape creative expression, a point to be explored further later.

Furthermore, in light of the integral nonduality thesis, musical creativity from a first-person standpoint can be seen as a direct manifestation of cosmic creativity. It is therefore a relatively small step, as I propose in my "strong nonduality thesis," to view human improvising, at the heart of this creativity-consciousness connection, as a direct manifestation of cosmic improvisation.[8] Meki Nzewi emphasizes that African music, "deriving from a more holistic philosophy of life and the cosmos," demonstrates the "fairly common fundamental creative principle of mediating physical and metaphysical worlds."[9] In part II of the book, I elaborate on this line of thinking by tracing the origins of improvisatory creativity to the realm of *lila*, or eternal play of creation from Indian thought. Insights from Maharishi Mahesh Yogi's commentary on Rig Veda, called Apaurusheya Bhashya, are particularly instructive. Brahman, the divine creative source, reverberating within its own undifferentiated wholeness, generates primordial frequencies that are the most fundamental building blocks of the infinite diversity of the cosmic wholeness. Music is a direct manifestation of this divine play, a notion compatible with age-old worldviews from cultures across the globe. Moreover, while correlations between musical pitch systems and cosmic order—as in the Time Theory of Indian music, or Western notion of Music of the Spheres—have typically been framed from a structural perspective, I take a further step in examining this through the lens of process, viewing improvisation as rooted in the very self-referral, curving back of individual consciousness onto its source that is at the heart of cosmic improvisation. Improvised music may thus be, of all human endeavor, the closest manifestation of divine improvisatory play, from which a principle may be inferred that warrants a place at the forefront of contemporary spirituality—that human beings are co-evolutionary participants in an improvisatory cosmos.[10]

To be sure, not all readers will be disposed to taking first-person, vertical inquiry into musical creativity this far. Nor is my aim to make a case for this admittedly speculative and ambitious proposition. What interests me, however, are principles inferable from this kind of inquiry that may be key to a new paradigm of music studies, as well as harnessing the broader transformative potential of the arts, and particularly an improvised musical art form called jazz. A primary example entails the sequential unfolding of more differentiated domains from less-differentiated primordial roots, and the subsequent synergistic, evolutionary relationship between primordial and emergent domain. When Brahman, an eternal field of consciousness that represents the cosmic core of first-person subjective reality, curves back on its own nature—which is the primordial second-person, process dimension—spirituality (first-person) can be seen as not only primordial to art (second-person) but also co-evolving in a spirituality-art synergistic relationship. Similarly, the generation of primordial frequencies, which correlate with third-person, objective reality, brings science into the mix, yielding a spirituality-art-science synergistic relationship. Inasmuch, as established in the introduction, spirituality-art-science interactions occur not only on macroscales, as between the disciplines per se, but also in their innumerable subdomains, as well as in every instant in time and space; one can readily infer transformative potentialities were these interactions to be enlivened in human knowledge systems. For each synergistic blossoming represents a kind of synapse that promotes the flow of creativity and consciousness from the deepest levels of the soul, or *atma*. Knowledge systems that are entirely structured around the sequential alignment of these synapses are thus endowed with a rich circuitry through which the soul connection informs every component, in every instant of engagement.[11]

I propose a "systematic improvisatory development" framework that operationalizes these principles, integrating the expanded spectrum of skills and understanding required to circumvent the Central Impasse, and yielding a model that exemplifies capacities for arts-based transformation in education and society at large.[12]

SYSTEMATIC IMPROVISATORY DEVELOPMENT FRAMEWORK

The basic concept could neither be simpler nor more powerful: Improvisation contains in overt or seed form the entire scope of music studies, vastly exceeding the horizons of not only the conventional model but also the spectrum of possibilities that are typically envisioned in lower order reform deliberations. Improvisation-based musical development therefore has the capacity to relate an unprecedented range of areas not only to the source in which they originate but also with one another. By grounding the entire endeavor in deeper vertical foundations, music studies may thus access broader overlying horizontal expanse in richly integrative, rigorous, and self-organizing form.

Preliminary grasp of this idea is provided by thinking of the Contemporary Improviser Composer Performer process scope not as a horizontal array, as formidable as that may be, but as a vertical unfolding from an improvisatory source. Improvisation, in other words, directly encompasses aspects of composition and performance and may thus be considered primordial within the musical epistemological spectrum. An improvisation-composition relationship, then, may be identified as a first increment of differentiation within this scheme; engagement in both areas is enhanced by the synergistic interplay of each component. An improvisation-composition-performance relationship may be seen as occupying a next tier of differentiation and synergistic relationship. As the scope expands horizontally, it also increasingly strengthens its vertical, improvisation-based grounding. One can readily envision how the same principle might apply to areas such as music theory and aural skills, let alone a range of conceptual areas. Imagine, then, a music studies program that encompasses multiple approaches to improvisation (stylistically open, style-specific), composition (song form, small and large jazz ensemble, concert music), virtuosic performance skills, rigorous melodic and harmonic studies along a broad modal-tonal-transtonal spectrum, robust grounding in globally resonant rhythmic languages that are united with musical embodiment, strong aural capacities, engagement with wide-ranging musical traditions and influences, cultivation of pedagogical expertise, technology studies, entrepreneurship, and a range of conceptual studies that span historical, cultural, cognitive, aesthetic, and transpersonal dimensions (consciousness/spirituality). While from a lower order standpoint, the expanded scope might appear to be yet another version of the Central Impasse—a vast litany of skill and aptitudes that are easily articulated yet defy curricular implementation—the framework may be understood from a higher order, integral standpoint as an exquisite tapestry of horizontal and vertical relationships by which creativity and consciousness can flow from the primordial, soul level and inform, enliven, and integrate every aspect of the system.

In part II, I further elaborate on key facets of the model that come into focus with a fuller discussion about consciousness. For example, I take issue with conventional tendencies to view improvisation as a subspecies of composition and emphasize the need to understand the two processes on their own terms. A consciousness-based viewpoint reveals that neither is improvisation an accelerated, real-time version of composition, nor composition a slowed down kind of improvisation; rather the two processes represent contrasting—yet complementary—creative, cognitive, and culturally mediated soul pathways to which today's artists have full access. "There is a music that must be composed," wrote Steve Lacy; "there is another that can only be improvised."[13] While I position improvisation as foundational in the above model, it is therefore not to subordinate composition but to ground music studies in an alignment that is ideally suited for both creative faculties to fully blossom in synergistic relationship. The differentiation of the two processes is also key to understanding and harvesting the fruits of the relationship between African American and European musical traditions. The Afro-Euro nexus both that exists within jazz and that jazz further promotes in the overall musical world—consistent with above commentary on the CICP process scope—is most aptly understood not as a horizontal confluence, but as a vertical blossoming between cultural streams that occurs atop African and African-American roots. In chapter 6, I elaborate on this through an analysis of blues as a distinctly black music phenomenon in which African/African American improvisatory, rhythmic, emotional, transpersonal/spiritual, and other facets serve as the basis for jazz's unmatched syncretism. The assimilation of European classical influences, as well as co-evolutionary relationships with that tradition, unfold atop these black music roots, which in turn promotes even broader connections in what I call an Afro-Euro-global nexus. In extending the continuum in this way, I do not suggest a linear pedagogical chronology, where the Afro-Euro must be in place prior to broader global pursuits. Rather, I seek to delineate a cultural topography, aspects of which can fall into place in any number of nonlinear ways, in which key landmarks in American music help its musicians, and music schools, navigate meaningful, manageable, and creatively fruitful pathways amid the infinite possibilities in today's world.

I also outline a creativity continuum in which improvising and composing are viewed as primary creativity modalities, interpretive performance is seen as a secondary form of creativity, and further areas of craft and inquiry are deemed ancillary creativity. As I explain through Leonard Meyer's taxonomy of syntactic (e.g., harmony, melody, and rhythm) and nonsyntactic (e.g., dynamics, density, tessitura, duration, silence) elements,[14] improvisers and composers may manipulate the full syntactic/nonsyntactic spectrum of elements, whereas performers may only create with a few syntactic parameters (such as timbre, dynamics, and tempo).[15] The point is not to delineate a values hierarchy, but rather to advance a more differentiated creativity spectrum in which all components may be organized into a coherent system in a jazz/CICP-based music studies model. Put another way: Whatever degree of creativity one might ascribe to performance or analysis will blossom on entirely new scales when situated within the systematic improvisatory development framework.

Moreover, when a consciousness component is added to the analysis, the power of the systematic improvisatory development framework as a richly differentiated soul pathway comes into focus. Key is that the framework, even with its broad horizontal scope, represents a vertical blossoming of the first-second-third-person/spirituality-art-science spectrum that is inherent in the integral worldview. Not only does the interplay of the three primordial impulses manifest itself on a macroscale in the emergent model, but it also takes hold on the most localized microscales (e.g., relationship between stylistically open and style-bound improvisatory strategies, improvisation-composition-relationship, etc.). Creativity and consciousness may thus flow from the innermost recesses of the soul and permeate all facets of the system. While all music is rooted in some kind of soul connection, distinctions between what I call self-confining and self-transcending soul pathways come into view. Self-confining soul pathways are creativity-deficient, in which transcendent connections are invoked largely within narrow epistemic horizons. The neo-Eurocentric framework, confined to interpretive performance, is a primary example, with the neo-Eurocentric-plus an expanded version. As I analyze in part II, such models are prone to musical fundamentalist tendencies that rival their religious counterparts in force and impact. Self-transcending soul pathways, by contrast, are creativity-rich, enabling primordial first-second-third-person impulses to permeate and not only inform a rich tapestry of localized differentiation within the system, but also open up connections to the broader musical landscape and beyond. In chapter 2, distinctions between self-confining and self-transcending soul pathways are among a host of parameters by which I differentiate between multicultural and transcultural diversity paradigms.

I further discuss the ramifications of the above account for a new understanding of rigor that is based in the all-important interplay of exploratory and emulative experience.[16] Exploratory approaches are those undertaken with little or no constraints established in advance, as in free improvisation (with no preset harmonic or rhythmic parameters). Emulative approaches involve pre-established constraints for the respective kinds of creativity, as in improvisation within the set harmonic, rhythmic, and stylistic parameters of jazz. Emulative engagement also entails the all-important disciplines that comprise musical craft, from focused development of instrumental technique, to theoretical and aural grounding and activities such as transcription and study of the work of master practitioners. Both exploratory and emulative approaches are necessary and, when sustained in tandem, give rise to an entirely new conception of rigor that grounds technical or analytical focus in interior, intuitive, and expressive experience. The most diligent assimilation of skills in craft and systematic conceptual inquiry cannot be deemed rigorous if divorced from creative application and imagining.[17] The emergent conception of rigor, inherent in the above systematic approach to improvisatory development, thus promotes, as AACM trumpeter Lester Bowie puts it, capacities for artists not only to express themselves "in any idiom, draw from any source, deny any limitation,"[18] but also to embark on further kinds of navigation that extend far beyond music.

Important ramifications come into view for distinctions between conventional and emergent musical identities. Immediately apparent is that the Interpretive Performance Specialist, at the heart of the conventional, neo-Eurocentric paradigm, is largely devoid of the exploratory-emulative interplay given the absence of improvising and composing, hence primary creativity. That this is no small deficiency is nothing new; it is the reason for a half-century-plus of efforts to change that paradigm. The exploratory-emulative interaction sheds new light on the egregious nature of this deficiency. The jazz CICP identity, on the other hand, when construed integrally and thus to contain the systematic improvisatory development spectrum, is rich in exploratory and emulative engagement. Here it is important to emphasize that the exploratory is primordial to the emulative in the jazz CICP identity— meaning that the integral jazz artist identifies as creative musical explorer first, with a kind of music called "jazz" happening to be the primary channel from which his/her excursions are launched. While jazz purists may decry this portrayal, I believe it is entirely consistent with the commentary, as well as creative output, of the great jazz innovators.

Moreover, the situating of jazz within the expanded identity that transcends category enables deeper and fuller penetration into the treasures within this cultural site. Think, too, of broader parallels: The kind of societal citizenship needed in our times requires individuals to identity first as human beings and members of global society, and then as members of nations. Extending this thinking further from a nondual, integral standpoint, planetary human identity might be grounded in yet more expansive cosmic identity. The self-transcending CICP-plus profile, mentioned in the introduction and to be discussed more fully shortly, grounding its rich creative foundations in consciousness-based development, might be thus seen to exemplify the integral evolutionary spectrum that proceeds from egocentric to ethnocentric to worldcentric to cosmoscentric.[19] Of further significance is that this expanded epistemic scope not only radically broadens the horizons of self-identity but also inheres powerful capacities to sustain ongoing cycles of identity construction and dissolution. Meaning that the very processes that promote vertical depth and horizontal expanse also promote capacities for individuals to critically interrogate this terrain, and thus render its instantiation less prone to the inertia of conditioning and more the result of dynamic creativity/consciousness unfolding.

What about the Interpretive Performance Specialist-plus identity, central to lower order reform discourse, who adds improvisation and composition to the conventional interpretive focus? Here, the confinement of improvising and composing to curricular embellishments, as in pedagogical aids, or occasional departures, typically means that the exploratory-emulative interplay is weak. Accordingly, without that key synapse to the systematic improvisatory development spectrum, the IPS-plus (or neo-Eurocentric-plus) musician will lack the necessary epistemic infrastructure whereby creativity and consciousness may flow throughout the system and inform the totality of components. The IPS-plus musician, thus identifying first as an interpretive performer within a tradition, thus remains prone to viewing the musical world through that narrow lens. Along the above integral evolutionary scale, both IPS and IPS-plus identities—even with the latter's multicultural experiences to be considered more fully in the next chapter—are lodged at the ethnocentric scale, which is almost as self-critically bereft, and thus paradigm blind, as the egocentric.

In sum, the jazz CICP paradigm is unmatched in its grounding in the systematic improvisatory development continuum, thus uniquely capable of harnessing its scope, integration, rigor, and self-transcending/transformative properties. The next realm of inquiry involves the self-organizing aspects of this paradigm. When artistic development is experienced as connection with, and unfolding of, the soul level, there is no stronger impetus for intensive pursuit of skills to fashion a channel for this blossoming. Inspired by the psychologist C. G. Jung, I call this vertical unfolding over time "musical individuation."[20]

INDIVIDUATION: SELF-ORGANIZING CREATIVE DEVELOPMENT OVER TIME

Every individual has a unique story to tell, a distinct pathway to walk through life, a highly personalized way of being in the world. Just as every culture has unique contributions to make to global culture, every individual has unique contributions to make to his/her community and the world at large. The psychologist C. G. Jung referred to this personal unfolding as "individuation," which he defined as the integration of interior dimensions of the psyche with the exterior dimensions of experience.[21] The jazz-based CICP-plus identity embodies these principles in music, thus giving rise to musical individuation—the evolution of a distinctly personal artistic voice. Recall the principle of individuality and freedom of expression as among the key features of black music. "You figured out how you wanted to sound," Art Farmer reflected, "and then you went and worked on it."[22] Or, to put it as succinctly as only Thelonious Monk could, "Play yourself."[23] Moreover, Alice Coltrane directs the inquiry inward when she states that "you're not manufacturing someone else's plan. . . . Your creating comes from within you," the level of "the soul."[24]

Following is an account of how individuation unfolds over the course of a musical career, and the ramifications thereof for a music studies paradigm based thereupon.

Creativity-consciousness development, consistent with the above analysis, is key: the broader the creative infrastructure, and thus epistemological scope, the greater the integration of wide-ranging musical and extramusical influences, overall life experience, and the innermost dimensions of consciousness in the personal artistic voice. Because connection with the level of atma, or soul, is the driving force, individuation—and the broader navigation it entails and enables—is optimally self-organizing. Conversely, the more limited the creativity/consciousness infrastructure, as in the Interpretive Performance Specialist identity (confined to secondary creativity), the more limited the degree of individuation and self-organizing development. While the IPS-plus process scope is broader, and improvising and composing serve more as pedagogical aids, or perhaps musical hobbies, the inner conduit for evolution of a creativity-based individual voice is nonetheless lacking.

A look at CICP-based musical individuation in terms of three interweaving, yet also discrete, aspects of engagement—direct creative experience, reflection, and craft—illuminates the above points and the centrality of jazz to the individuation process for twenty-first-century American musicians. Direct creative experience (DCE) entails the actual creative episodes, the acts of improvising and composing (or performance, or analysis), which I view in this context from an exploratory standpoint, meaning improvising and composing with no constraints set forth in advance (e.g., jazz time feels and changes, or composition in classical, fully notated style). Inasmuch as the deeper and broader creative experiences lead to greater prospects for individuation, improvising, and composing, these experiences will therefore be central to DCE in the integral, higher order scheme. Reflection happens in a more formal manner apart from DCE, where practitioners—perhaps while walking down the street, along the seashore, or lying awake at night or in the wee hours of the morning—ruminate on the significance of a given creative episode, and/or their overall creative experience and growth. Here practitioners fathom the meaning of the experience as related to their work and lives, and also assess the progress of the work, and determine areas to be pursued for further development. Hence, a craft component unfolds organically from DCE and reflection.[25]

Direct Creative Experience

The significance of the improvisatory/compositional episode for individuation lies not only in its expressive qualities, where it provides an outlet for the primordial impulse to create, but also in its transformative and noetic properties. By *transformative*, I mean penetration to deep levels of creativity and consciousness, the integration of which renders creativity and creative development as forms of yoga, or spiritual/religious/mystical union. By *noetic*, I mean a kind of musical understanding that spans outer and interior dimensions, and that is simply not possible without this creativity/consciousness epistemic expanse.[26] The central locus for musical understanding resides not in overlying, language-bound disciplinary genre categories, but in contact with a realm of experience that is transcendent of category. Below I consider how this interior knowing is key to optimal understanding of exterior musical reality.

The philosopher Suzanne Langer points us in this direction when she extols music's capacity to lead us "beyond the pale of discursive thinking . . . and be true to feeling in a way that language cannot."[27] Improvising and composing—again, viewed at the moment from an exploratory, not emulative lens—penetrate to a stratum of creation in which basic musical elements are experienced in abstract, fluid, malleable, and undifferentiated form. Musical ideas originate as deeply intuitive and abstract facets of a creative flow, fathomed not through conventional terminology and analysis, but through subtle dimensions of feeling, intuition, prior to coalescing in differentiated, manifest form—hence, undifferentiated wholeness giving rise to differentiated form.

Invoking another facet of Jungian thought, which from an integral perspective intersects with various spiritual worldviews, this interior penetration broaches the realm of the "archetypes."[28] These are understood here not in terms of discrete, metaphysical forms but as dynamic, primordial impulses that originate deep in consciousness and infuse creative expression with richly transcendent, and transformative, impact. Over time, and with requisite study and practice, creative access to undifferentiated musical (syntactic/nonsyntactic) elements and an expanded array of extramusical forces—personality traits (including interior archetypal features of the psyche), exterior influences from one's life circumstances—coalesces in differentiated, personal style structures. Improvising and composing, particularly when grounded in the emulative and exploratory approaches mentioned above, as well as when complemented by meditative practice, are therefore uniquely equipped not only to promote penetration to the primordial, archetypal dimension, but also to the integration of primordial influences, musical influences, and extramusical influences into the resultant personal voice and identity. I go further into the mechanics—and ramifications for self-organizing development—of this deep access and integration below. Most important at the moment is that this renders the resultant personal voice at once richly grounded in transcendent as well as relativistic dimensions of an artist's life. No more powerful coupling exists for artistic expression to transmit a transformative impact to listeners and society as a whole.

Reflection and Craft

Reflection is where creative artists fathom meaning and direction in their work. If the impulse to create is intrinsic in human consciousness, let alone cosmic intelligence, so is the tendency to ruminate on the place of creativity in one's work and life, and also to consider how this creativity can evolve. Therefore, when aspiring (or established) CICPs reflect on the kaleidoscope of musical elements that are glimpsed in direct creative experience, they will likely single out one or more moments that are particularly poignant, perhaps due to personal sense of beauty and resonance with that moment, and/or the challenges it posed to the artist's current skill set. This might involve encounter with tonal or modal pitch environments, or rhythmic frameworks, that are perceived as expressively powerful in the improvisatory or compositional flow yet also stretch the CICP's technical, aural, and/or theoretical limits. These represent optimal conditions for a given area to be imbued with meaning and personal relevance, and thus serve as the basis for the deeply intimate relationship that informs subsequent development in the craft phase. As elements begin to coalesce in the individual improvisatory-compositional voice, they are established as part of one's musical identity. As examined above through the lens of primary and secondary creativity, no such relationship to knowledge areas and identity formation is available to Interpretive Performance Specialists given the absence of improvisatory and compositional outlets for knowledge and influences to be infused, and thus to drive further development. Nor is the same kind of intimacy likely with IPS-plus practitioners, even if improvising and composing, mainly emulative, are part of their process scope. CICP identity is not only more expansive but also more vertically grounded as thus capable of harnessing the self-organizing thrust inherent in the roots of creativity and creative development in the psyche—individual and cosmic. CICPs are thus capable of embarking on not only far broader but also far more integrative, rigorous, and self-organizing craft expeditions.

Two Aspects of Craft Development: Self-Motivational and Self-Navigational

Craft involves pursuit of technical and conceptual skills and understanding. Two facets of self-organizing development are noteworthy—one is "self-motivational," the second "self-navigational."[29] By *self-motivational*, I mean the intense internal drive that is enlivened upon experiencing creative expression and the emergent personal voice as a direct reflection of the totality—the innermost and outermost—dimensions of one's being. *Self-navigational* entails enlivenment of capacities to independently fathom areas of pursuit for the blossoming of the personal voice.

On the first, self-motivational account: No more powerful incentive is aroused to invest the time and energy on a regular basis to the rigorous skill development required of creative artistry than the recognition of the individual creative voice as not only a direct reflection of one's inner and outer worlds, but also a catalyst for integrating these worlds. As aspiring CICPs see creativity and personal style development as the result of penetrating deep into consciousness, artistic growth is revealed as inextricably linked to the quest for differentiated wholeness, or inner-outer unity—as noted, synonymous with yoga/religion—that is the fundamental purpose of existence. While, as noted, not all readers may be inclined to embrace my assertion of an improvisatory cosmos, in which human beings are co-evolutionary participants, the much more manageable notion that the creative impulse is inherent in the human psyche is but a small step short of the idea of an improvisatory core to this creativity. The coupling of improvisation and composition as the basis for the broader set of skills and understanding that extends from this core only adds to the self-motivational impetus for growth. External rewards (e.g., recognition, or monetary gains) pale in comparison to the sheer force of the internal motivation possible in the creativity-driven individuation process. To paraphrase an earlier axiom, we improvise and compose because the cosmos improvises and composes through us.[30]

Second is the enlivenment of self-navigational faculties, where students develop the ability to discern, independently of teachers and other institutional resources, areas needing attention and avenues for addressing them. Key here is that the creative expression of any kind of musical terrain constitutes the integration of that terrain, and its primordial underpinnings, in consciousness. When a given primordial thrust is sufficiently expressed and thus integrated, which may take days, weeks, months, or years, the aspiring artist senses this instinctively, very much like one feels satiated by eating a sufficient quantity of a certain kind of food even if a larger appetite remains. Upon satiation with a certain musical expression, awareness is then drawn to new realms of inquiry and expression. Here is where the need is essential for institutions to shift from top-down, teacher-driven pedagogy to bottom-up, student-driven learning environments rich in exploratory creativity yet also as wide an array of emulative resources as possible. The exploratory experience enlivens the self-navigational instinct; the emulative provides structural outlets. Chapter 3 presents a model predicated on harnessing this self-driven thrust with carefully considered surface curricular and organizational outlets.[31]

This underscores the point that, even in the most powerful instances of self-navigational growth, this does not deem irrelevant institutional resources—instructor expertise, educational materials, curricular models—but, in fact, underscores how valuable these resources may be. Here, however, the relationship can be flipped, where self-driven growth becomes the driving force, and exterior instruction and resources serve as tributaries that inform that growth as opposed to serving as primary (and limiting) catalysts. The greater the enlivenment of the interior impetus for development, the more students will be able to take advantage of exterior resources. Put another way, learning begins with quests and questions; self-driven learners who come to the classroom with questions/quests that are elicited in the creative process and reflection on that process bring unmatched receptivity to the full scope of what the institution has to offer.[32]

Individuation, Musical Understanding, and Circumventing the Central Impasse

What are the ramifications of musical individuation for the jazz-driven transformation? To reply with a summation of key principles and preview of those to come: First is that the self-transcending jazz CICP framework and its parts-to-whole/whole-to-parts trajectories that uniquely promote the blossoming of the individual voice also support the wide-ranging musical development necessary in today's world. Creativity, consciousness/spirituality, culturally and epistemically diverse engagement, integrative and rigorous development, self-sufficiency, critical vitality, embodied musicianship, syntactic (melody, harmony, rhythm) and nonsyntactic (timbre, density, silence) fluency are among the aspects that not only constitute the emergent scope but are also organically integrated within that scope. Indeed, to even invoke the term "integration," long a prominent theme in reform conversations, risks conflating common aspirations to rectify the fragmentation of the conventional neo-Eurocentric model through piecemeal linkages—typically between performance, theory, and history—with the fundamentally new kind of synergistic interconnectedness inherent in the jazz CICP paradigm. Not only does overarching unity amid infinite diversity become the norm in the emergent model, but the exquisite circuitry of the jazz CICP framework also allows the flow of creativity and consciousness from the soul level to inform all aspects of the system and uphold further unifying and self-organizing functions. There is no greater impetus for self-driven growth than when artistic realization is rendered a quest for soul realization.

The analysis also spawns important diagnostic ramifications. Likely obvious is that the moment improvisation disappeared from common practice in the European classical tradition was the moment the breadth and integration inherent in CICP artistry would be extinguished as even a distant hope for music studies. Perhaps less obvious is that because most change advocates have not been CICPs, they have been oblivious to the vertical dimensions of the crisis and thus prone to pursuing largely horizontal solutions. Here it is important to emphasize that the very same inner mechanics that drive personal individuation, which can be thought in terms of personal disciplinary and genre formation, also drive what might be called collective individuation, as in the formation of overarching disciplinary and genre categories in the broader field. Recall how CICPs experience basic musical elements in fluid and abstract forms and how these elements interact with extramusical influences to yield enduring structures that take hold on an individual scale; this also underlies the evolution of overarching disciplines and genres, and thus curricular models in the field at large. Therefore, in a musical culture in which improvisation is absent or subordinate, the curricular landscape will not only be narrow but also fragmented within that scope—of which conventional foundations that are confined to performance, theory, and history, typically approached separately, are a clear example. In a community of CICPs, the curricular landscape will be not only broad but organically interconnected from its foundations on up. Without grounding in the inner mechanics that underlie sequential differentiation within wholeness, change advocates have failed to recognize the disappearance of improvisation in the European tradition as a vertical crisis, where the very foundations of creative artistry and understanding were removed from the heart of the system. Instead, the situation has been construed primarily as a horizontal lapse—whereby improvising and composing were lopped off a broader process scope—as a result of which reform would be sought through efforts to insert the processes within the existing framework. Directly related efforts to link performance, theory, and history, even if these have not significantly taken hold, would conceptually reify the conventional foundations at the expense of the improvisatory. A closer look at the division of labor between creation and performance sheds further light on why only foundational overhaul of the system atop the CICP framework at the heart of the Afro-Euro-global nexus will suffice if music studies is to individuate and realize its full potential.

Diagnostic Deliberations: Division of Labor as Central to IPS and IPS-Plus Dissociation

To begin with a quick recap of commentary from the introduction: Up through the early nineteenth century, the majority of musicians in the European classical tradition functioned, albeit to varying degrees, as Contemporary Improvisers Composers Performers. After that time, musical practice, as

Christopher Small illuminates, would roughly mirror the division of labor occurring in Western industrialized society and become more specialized.[33] Composition would be relegated to a distinct minority, improvisation rendered almost entirely extinct, and interpretive performance deemed the primary task of the majority. From an integral standpoint, the division exemplifies the tendency in the evolution of knowledge systems whereby the thrust of organic differentiation, involving the emergence of increasingly detailed parts within a complex yet unified whole, is sometimes punctuated by periods of dissociation—where parts become severed from the whole and take on a life of their own. In music, this is precisely what happened when primary creativity fell by the wayside and interpretive performance became central.

A more complete analysis, moreover, would reveal the dissociation not only to be horizontal, where performance and creation lines split off from one another as part of a lateral decimation, but also, in the almost complete deletion of primary creativity from the resultant system, to consist in a vertical disconnection—in which music in the European tradition, for the majority of practitioners, would split apart from the creative foundations of human art making. With the repertory viewed as the pinnacle of humanity's musical achievement, the very notion of being a musician would become synonymous, and this thinking prevails to this day, not with the artist who creates his or her own music, but with the practitioner who focuses on performing music created by others—often a continent and centuries removed from the artist's time and place. The fact that the model represented a radical departure from the creative foundations of the very tradition to which it ostensibly paid homage would become more of a historical curiosity than a key diagnostic indicator, let alone aperture to new possibilities. As already glimpsed, and further elaborated upon in forthcoming chapters, the casualties extending from the prevailing model include limited channels of artistic expression and understanding, ethnocentric/racialized biases, inhibited pedagogical development, and impaired critical thinking and self-organizing capacities.

In order to invoke foundational (rather than ornamental) change, it is imperative to recognize that both the reigning neo-Eurocentric framework and neo-Eurocentric-plus reform efforts alike are constrained by the inertia of the division of labor. Two developments are key. First involves the centrality of performance, theory, and history in the conventional model. I call these the three "false pillars"[34] in that they masquerade as foundational at the expense of creative foundations. In other words, if the purpose of being a musician is to perform music created by others, and increasingly over the decades and centuries at other times and places, it would appear that analysis of these works, engagement in coursework that helps sharpen the ear to internalize their syntactic components, and study of their historical contexts make for a complete program of study. I characterize these as false not because there is no place for them in the curriculum or culture of music studies, but because they preclude the improvisatory/compositional foundations that are central to the European classical tradition, and are also entirely inadequate for underpinning the kind of navigational and noetic abilities called for in today's world. Performance, theory, and history have thus assumed the status of ontological givens—as if they are primordial to any further realms of musical reality. It is as if, to characterize the situation with a bit of theological satire, when God created the heavens, the earth, and the various realms of human endeavor, music burst forth—across the globe, no less—in the form of European repertory and musicians who played and studied it. Therefore, to paraphrase biblical admonitions about worshipping false idols, the neo-Eurocentric model can be seen as engulfed by worship of the false ideological and curricular pillars of performance, theory, and history. Having erroneously assumed centrality, these pillars have imposed an objective, third-person orientation on a field whose prominent role, as with all of art, within the first-second-third-person structure of human consciousness—the integral trinity—is to uphold second-person, creativity-based experience and growth. As explained in prior commentary, performance, theory, and history are not discarded in the emergent integral CICP framework, but rather resituated in significantly expanded form.

A next key development would only further the object-mediated inertia of the division of labor. This involved the appearance of the fields of music education and ethnomusicology. Music education is the area in music studies devoted to preparing public school music teachers and conducting corresponding research on music teaching and learning. Ethnomusicology is the study of the relationship between music and culture. While ethnomusicology was from its inception predicated on a musical worldview that extended beyond European classical music, it would not be until the 1960s that music education would significantly embrace, at least in rhetoric, a more diverse vision. Nonetheless, both fields remain constrained by the object-mediated thrust of the division. I elaborate on this in the next chapter as I distinguish between multicultural and transcultural diversity paradigms as straddling both epistemological and ethnological dimensions. In approaching improvising and composing as largely curricular add-ons and pedagogical aids, music education falls short of the CICP identity shift noted above. Ethnomusicology falls short in confining improvising and composing to culture-specific applications. While all these approaches have a place, they fall far short of the broader creative vision.

Moreover, prevailing advocacy—often coming from music education—for integrative learning models further reifies the neo-Eurocentric underpinnings that stem from the division and the three false pillars. At first glance, my assessment may seem ungrounded, as the common exhortation that "music theory and history classes study the repertory played in ensembles" would appear to be exemplary of integrative pedagogy. At closer inspection, however, this may be recognized to only perpetuate the prominence of the false pillars and marginalization of true pillars of primary creativity. Again, because improvising and composing are understood as but components to be added atop the existing core, their foundational capacities remain unrecognized and unharnessed. Until change conversations recognize improvisation—and more specifically, systematic improvisatory development—as the basis for both broader scope *and* integration, the prevailing foundations that, in fact, are neither designed nor equipped for scope and integration will only be reified.

At which point, the question arises—how to break free from these lower order reform tendencies? A first step is to recognize the ramifications of those voices that have predominated change conversations and those that have been excluded. Music education and ethnomusicology disciplines and perspectives have dominated, while the jazz-based CICP voice has been conspicuously absent both demographically and conceptually. While jazz education itself must accept some of the responsibility for this in remaining confined to a narrow conception of the idiom, it would be naïve to ignore the broader discriminatory patterns at play that have failed to insist on the jazz voice in change deliberations. In fact, the conservative orientation of jazz education can be seen as rooted in the same object-mediated roots that gave rise to neo-Eurocentric and neo-Eurocentric-plus platforms, and thus inherited from the division of labor. While the exclusion of jazz warrants further discussion, the following observation speaks volumes about the lower order trajectory of music studies change deliberations: most participants in the conversation, being largely products of the prevailing creativity-deficient model, while—to their credit—recognizing the system as in need of repair, would nonetheless lack the direct navigational and noetic foundations of the integral jazz CICP identity to penetrate to foundational premises that would yield paradigmatic, rather than ornamental, change.

A second step is for change agents to critically interrogate the change conversation through the closely intertwined lenses of epistemology and ethnology, a relationship that tends to elude lower order visioning and identify common cut-off points along each line that, once reconceived integrally, may be transformed into gateways for new visioning. An example of an epistemic cut-off point is Small's much-heralded notion of musicking. While helpful to liberation from conventional object-mediated patterns, this precept must now be reexamined for its ambivalence, at least as it is commonly invoked, to foundational musical topographies that might uphold a broader epistemological spectrum. Primary examples of such topographies are the systematic improvisatory development framework and the creative identity shift, both of which have the capacity to promote an unmatched range of musical engagement. Common references to musicking thus perpetuate the lower order tendency to "flatline" the process scope, a tendency that must be recognized as directly inherited from the very neo-Eurocentric framework that lower order reform advocacy seeks to change. The change conversation may thus be assessed as caught in a self-perpetuating tailspin where the very epistemic crisis that undergirds the original model also impedes capacities to critically examine both that model and efforts to reform it. This epistemic lapse in turn fuels, and is exacerbated by, parallel tendencies to flatline the ethnological scope. Here, multicultural aversion to key cultural topographies, in reaction to the longstanding monoculturalism, obscure important cultural contours for broader navigation. Primary casualties of the multicultural gaze include failure to recognize black music and its massive place in contemporary musical practice, and to thus pursue corresponding curricular implementation. Therefore, in addition to depriving music students of important skills and understanding, musical multiculturalism, despite its intentions to rectify hegemony, perpetuates among the most egregious of hegemonic patterns brought to light in social justice discourse—whereby seminal contributions of African American culture are rendered invisible. As I elaborate in the coming chapter, the transcultural foundations of the self-transcending jazz CICP framework render it a site where both epistemological and ethnological lines unite and coevolve synergistically. Until the jazz CICP is placed front and center in change visioning, epistemic lapse will reify its ethnological counterpart.

I thus propose that change agents embrace the notions of "beyond musicking" and "beyond multiculturalism" as catalysts for reconceiving and critically examining common reform themes and thereby unearthing new guiding premises. The above critique of piecemeal attempts to link the three false pillars of theory, history and performance, and recognition that these attempts reflect weak epistemic penetration into both classical and jazz CICP frameworks, may further aid in this process. The importance of this kind of diagnostic work cannot be overstated—the inertia of the neo-Euroentric paradigm, and neo-Eurocentric-plus/multicultural efforts to reform it, is of such force that without clear articulation of new epistemic and ethnological parameters, a litany of unexamined assumptions inherited from prevailing practice will continue to undermine change efforts. On this account, the fact that the multicultural imprint runs as deep as the monocultural in impeding paradigmatic change cannot be overstated. A primary task, therefore, of change agents is to commit to a kind of "rehab" in order to counteract the indoctrination that has beset change advocacy. As urgent is the need to reform the conventional framework, equally urgent is the need to "reform the reformer."

CLOSING THOUGHTS

Music studies change advocacy has seen no dearth of items to be added to an ever-expanding curricular assembly line. Aside from the obvious (though all-too-relevant) absurdities of comparing artistic development to a factory paradigm, the combination of logistical (available curricular space), philosophical, and political impediments to change have yielded but ornamental modifications of a model requiring foundational overhaul. To paraphrase an earlier point, any conversation about a music studies paradigm that aspires toward wide-ranging creative navigation, broader and deeper understanding, organic integration (rather than piecemeal linkages), rigor, critical thinking, pedagogical optimization, and student-driven growth, and in which the word *jazz* does not come up early and often, is fundamentally flawed. As the embodiment of a higher order, integral conception of musical creativity and its roots in consciousness, jazz offers a template for the preparation of entirely new paradigm of musical artistry, pedagogy, scholarship, and societal leadership. The integral framework not only expands the visioning lens but also brings a powerful diagnostic thrust to the inquiry. While one does not need Integral Theory to recognize that music studies is beset by a creativity crisis, the integral model offers a powerful lens for penetrating deep into the roots of the crisis, fathoming its broader ramifications, critiquing patterns in change discourse that seek to reform the model, and also—perhaps most significantly—radically expanding the horizons of future possibilities.

Insights into jazz as transformative catalyst, and exclusion from the change conversation, from a creativity vantage point are but part of a bigger story that remains to be told. The next chapter in this story examines the idiom's contributions, as well as chronic exclusion, through the lens of diversity and race.

Chapter Two

Multiculturalism, Transculturalism, and Race

If it is not startling enough that the majority of music majors in America graduate with little or no experience, let alone substantive skill development, in the primary creative processes of improvisation and composition, the closely related scenario whereby these same students also graduate with a lack of engagement or proficiency in music of their own American culture, or other traditions beyond European classical music, must be equally disquieting. Indeed, at a juncture in human history when the need has never been more urgent for development of a culturally diverse awareness, music studies—a field that could, and should, assume diversity leadership—perpetuates a social justice transgression that can only be characterized as among the most egregious in all of education.[1] While lower order change advocacy has been oblivious to neither creativity nor diversity deficiencies, it has fallen short in penetrating to their shared roots, and also fathoming the extent to which their limiting impact permeates the entire spectrum of music studies and beyond. By contrast, higher order, integral visioning, which is predicated on an epistemology/ethnology nexus, illuminates how creativity and social justice crises are inextricably bound, with each fueling the other, and are thus only rectifiable when approached as part of an intricately interwoven, creativity-consciousness matrix. Jazz, due to its creativity-rich foundations and seminal yet precarious ethnocultural status in American society, factors prominently in both the analysis of, and solution to, the crisis. To be sure, the irony of the situation could not be more striking: the very genre that is uniquely equipped with the creative, integrative, rigorous, self-organizing, and self-transcending tools for twenty-first-century musical navigation has also been conspicuously marginalized in lower order curricular deliberations.

Having examined the conundrum from an epistemic/creativity standpoint in chapter 1, this chapter probes the ethnocentric/racialized biases that work in tandem with the creativity crisis and that, because they are typically unexamined, constrain even the most robust appeals for diversity.[2] I begin with distinctions between multicultural and transcultural diversity frameworks, which correlate, respectively, with lower and higher order reform approaches. As intimated previously, multiculturalism is predicated on a view of the musical world in terms of discrete, cultural compartments that are encountered one-by-one in aspirations to evolve an informed diversity awareness. By contrast, transculturalism views the central pulse of musical reality to reside in the self-transcending creative process and syncretic, hybrid structures that arise from that creativity, thereby situating cultural compartments as tributaries that inform the evolution of the personal artistic voice. A large inventory of distinctions between the models underscores the assessment that the paradigmatic distance that separates transcultural and multicultural diversity frameworks is greater than that which separates monocultural and multicultural models. I suggest, moreover, that multiculturalism may do more to impede the diversity quest than further it by identifying examples of what I call "ethnocentric blind spots"—areas that elude attention even amid fervent diversity appeals. Failure to recognize the African American roots of popular music in the advocacy of this area in music studies is one example. Another is frequent use of hegemonic language and labeling, such as the common use of the heading "Art Music" in reference to the European classical tradition, which essentially declares that music outside this tradition does not constitute art. Similar hegemonic impact, albeit less blatant, results from headings such as "New Music" and even "World Music" that exclude much music that is "new" and of the "world." Whereas other areas of the academy that are attuned to social justice devote vigorous attention to how things are named, this has yet to significantly transpire in music studies, underscoring yet another way in which the field, and its reform movement, fall short in fulfilling their potential.

I close the chapter with consideration of principles from overall racism research, which factors only peripherally in music studies diversity discourse,[3] to underscore a general trajectory in lower order reform conversations that conspicuously stops short of the highly charged black-white racial dynamics that are so central in contemporary society, and important musical ramifications thereof.

MULTICULTURAL AND INTEGRAL TRANSCULTURAL MODELS OF MUSICAL DIVERSITY

Overview of Distinctions

Both multicultural and integral transcultural frameworks are rooted in the imperative to develop an awareness of the cultural diversity in the musical world and society in which we live. The models differ fundamentally, however, in how they define diversity aptitude and approach its development. Table 2.1 inventories the many distinctions that I draw between multicultural and integral transcultural diversity paradigms. I use the qualifier *integral* to distinguish my conception of transculturalism from other uses of the term.[4] In no way should the inventory suggest that work that might be generally deemed multiculturalist or transculturalist aligns with all corresponding parameters; the diagram intends to delineate general tendencies, which in any case I believe are fairly consistent across various accounts.

To begin with principles that may be readily inferred in the headings themselves: Multiculturalism, as noted, is rooted in a view of the musical world as an infinite spectrum of generally discrete, cultural compartments to be approached—in the strictest application of the worldview—one by one in aspirations to evolve an adequate diversity awareness. From an integral transcultural standpoint, which does not lose sight of the place for culture-specific engagement, the central pulse of the musical landscape resides not in the established genre or cultural categories that dominate academic and commercial thinking, and whose status is reified through corresponding labels, but in the improvisatory and compositional creativity that transcends labels, and from which the terrain of the compartments took hold in the first place. Whereas multicultural engagement with improvising and composing is typically from an emulative, culture-bound perspective at the expense of the exploratory, transcultural pedagogy is grounded in the interplay of emulative and exploratory approaches in the establishment of a creative identity as an interior, self-organizing basis for highly personalized and intimate connections with the outer musical world. Recalling principles from chapter 1, aspiring creative artists experience basic musical elements in fluid and abstract forms, and how these elements interact with each other and extramusical influences to inform the individual voice. The individuation process is thus recognized as a kind of spiritual unfolding, whereby interior, primordial, and relativistic influences are integrated in consciousness. This enlivens powerful self-motivational and self-navigational instincts for further development of this voice and thus new levels of engagement with the cultural pluralism in the musical world and society in which we live that is important to this voice. While multicultural pedagogy is often confined to passive learning formats (e.g., ethnomusicology lecture coursework), even when it

Table 2.1. Multicultural and Transcultural Diversity Paradigms in Music

MULTICULTURAL	TRANSCULTURAL
Views musical world primarily in terms of discrete, cultural compartments/genres.	Views musical world primarily in terms of creative processes and cultural confluence.
Diversity as largely ethnological.	Diversity as ethnological and epistemological, inherent in systematic improvisatory growth.
Ambivalent to epistemology, in terms of mode of musical engagement and establishment of creative musical identity.	Epistemology central; hands-on, creative engagement and establishment of creative identity key to navigation and understanding.
Musical cultures as self-confining destinations.	Musical cultures as self-transcending tributaries.
Multimusicality as horizontal juxtaposition.	Multimusicality as vertical, creativity-based synthesis.
Linear, additive model: Engagement with cultural compartments/genres one-by-one (the more the better) in aspirations for diversity awareness.	Nonlinear model: Enlivenment of creativity-based, interior connections to outer world the basis for formal engagement with cultural regions. Connections to even a single new tradition can lay groundwork for further self-driven navigation and understanding.
Encumbered by challenges of scope.	Challenges of scope addressed through self-organizing dynamics of individuation process.
Emulative thrust guides practical application and inquiry.	Emulative/exploratory interplay guides practical application and inquiry.
Institution-driven pedagogy.	Self-driven, basis for institutional input.
Postmodern leveling and aversion to cultural core; no genre—even that of one's own culture—more important than another to diversity quest.	Integral musical topographies. Creativity-based, self-cultural grounding key to diversity awareness and broader navigation.
Oblivious to tools inherent in jazz/black music—including improvisation, rhythm and embodiment— for culturally diverse connections.	Recognizes improvisatory, rhythmic and embodiment tools inherent in jazz/black music for culturally diverse connections.
Some (not all) music is world music.	All music is world music.
Popular music viewed and approached separately from jazz and black music.	Popular music and jazz viewed as differentiated forms of overall black music wave; jazz recognized as rich source of tools.

Defines itself in response to monocultural paradigm.	Defines itself in response to monocultural and multicultural paradigms.
Devoid of exemplars who innovate across diverse cultural boundaries.	Exemplars abound who innovate across diverse cultural horizons.
Largely academic aims, oriented toward scholarship and music teacher pedagogy.	Oriented toward real-world creative musical navigation and new paradigms of research and music teacher pedagogy.
Static evolutionary account of musical landscape.	Dynamic evolutionary account of musical landscape, leading toward syncretic era.
Oblivious to hegemonic language and terminology.	Critically interrogates language and hidden multicultural/monocultural hegemonies.
Spirituality recognized but ambivalent to mechanism, let alone differentiation between types.	Spirituality viewed through multiple epistemic and structural lenses, with emphasis on richly differentiated circuitry inherent in creativity-consciousness foundations.

incorporates hands-on approaches (e.g., music education teacher training classes, world music ensembles), its epistemic scope nonetheless stops short of the creative identity shift considered in the previous chapter and thus remains confined to horizontal, category-bound understanding and approaches. Upon encounter with some baseline number of cultures, the thinking therefore goes, an adequate threshold of diversity awareness will be achieved, rendering the multicultural model highly institution-driven.

The transcultural model shifts the locus from number of cultures encountered in particular to depth of interior, personalized, creativity/consciousness-based connection to the outer musical world in general. Meaningful and substantive connections to even a single new culture or cultural influence, even if contacted as part of a highly personalized hybrid expression or creative trajectory, can serve as the basis for a lifetime of self-driven culturally diverse pursuit and awareness. While musicians who self-identify as Interpretive Performance Specialists or even IPS-plus practitioners for whom improvising and composing are largely additive, and thus confined to emulative application, may be able to cultivate a distanced, perhaps exoticized fascination with music of other cultures; the CICP artist—because the primary creativity of improvising and composing is central to his or her very sense of musical being—is able to establish heartfelt connections at the deepest stratum of consciousness: the level of *atma*, the soul.

Put most succinctly, the multicultural model is oriented toward *teaching about* kinds of music while ambivalent to epistemology, whereas the integral transcultural approach strives to *enliven within* student experience interior connections to the outer musical world through robust epistemic engagement and establishment of a creative identity. I shortly take up another key distinction, having to do with self-cultural grounding. Multiculturalism, perhaps ironically, remains ambivalent about the place of grounding in the music of one's own culture and its relationship to overall navigation. Transculturalism views self-cultural grounding as of paramount importance. The extent to which one can fathom the music-culture relationship, which is the basis for deep understanding, in music of other cultures is directly predicated on the extent to which one has fathomed this relationship, which again comes down to the establishment of a creative identity, in one's primary musical culture. I also address how the transcultural approaches culture-specific engagement when it comes to cultures other than one's own.

To be sure, my characterization of the multicultural paradigm, which again I argue is the prevailing conceptual guide in the music studies diversity quest, may at first glance appear excessively generalized and thus not representative of much work that may appear to approach my transcultural criteria yet that I nonetheless situate under the multicultural heading. I believe the following commentary nonetheless supports my distinctions and general argument of a prevailing multicultural orientation that may do more to impede diversification of the field than support it. Here the importance of the creative identity shift—exemplified by the jazz CICP—cannot be overstated in distinguishing between the models. I therefore characterize all approaches to diversity—including those that are placed under the headings "intercultural" and even "transcultural"—that stop short of this identity shift as multicultural.[5] If the inertia of neo-Eurocentric and neo-Eurocentric-plus thinking is to be overcome, the epistemological bar needs to be raised significantly beyond what commonly transpires in change conversations. From this standpoint, even Christopher Small's "musicking," at least in terms of how the idea is commonly invoked by change advocates, needs to be recognized as indicative of multicultural conception.[6] Therefore, even if a gradation of multicultural approaches might be identified, I believe the principle of a transcultural CICP creative identity shift as a key distinguishing principle between even the closest multicultural approximations (of the transcultural) emerges as a new criterion in the conversation that supports these distinctions.

It is also important to differentiate within the multicultural domain between what might be considered "conceptual," or "idealized," and "operational" multicultural models. Conceptual multiculturalism is what might prevail were lower order change advocacy not constrained by prevailing resistance to even moderate reform in the field. In other words, it pertains to what music studies might look like were change advocates given the provision to redesign the whole thing from scratch. Operational multiculturalism is defined as the kinds of interventions that are typically made (e.g., ethnomusicology lecture classes as electives and occasional core curriculum courses, teacher education methods classes) given prevailing conditions and constraints. Diagnosis of the assumptions underlying the conceptual, even if its full manifestations are rare, is nonetheless key to potential emergence of the integral transcultural paradigm.

Self-Cultural Grounding

At first glance, it may appear that the transcultural model I advance cedes little or limited space for culture-specific engagement. Nothing could be further from the case. Two forms of cultural engagement are, in fact, essential to the integral transcultural vision. One involves self-cultural grounding, the other contact with new cultures in culture-specific and syncretic form. A key transcultural principle unites the two: the extent to which a musician is able to meaningfully engage with, embrace, and understand the creative expressions of another culture is directly predicated on the extent to which he or she is creatively grounded in his or her own culture. Just as a strong sense of personal self is key to healthy relationships with others, a strong sense of cultural self is key to productive engagement with other cultures. Here I concur with Nzewi's emphasis that African music students gain grounding in their traditional music for the purpose of "mediating physical and metaphysical worlds, (or) harmonizing corporeal and spiritual experiences of life."[7] Self-cultural grounding is among the two primary ways transcultural verticality differs from multicultural horizontalism—the other being the transcultural establishment of an improvisation-based, CICP musical identity grounded in the exploratory-emulative interplay.

At which point the question arises: What constitutes the cultural core in a country as diverse as America?

The multicultural response to this question, from what one might reasonably infer from the limited extent to which the question is placed front and center, is that American musical culture, reflecting the culture at large, is best understood as a wide mix of influences. From this standpoint, the idea of a cultural core is subordinate to a preoccupation with the broader expanse. Indeed, I encounter among ethnomusicologists and music education colleagues, the two fields where multicultural predilections are most prominent, either ambivalence in response to the question, or even vigorous aversion to the identification of key cultural topographies, where one might be deemed more central, within the American musical landscape.[8] One gets the sense—unless (as per the above-mentioned operational multiculturalism) European classical music is uncritically regarded as the default cultural center—that it is more important to expose students to as great a range as possible than to provide grounding in a core cultural heritage.

The transcultural response to the above question shares a multicultural embrace of the pluralistic nature of American music, but also places high priority on grounding in a central cultural identity, which means delineation of important topographies in the overall landscape. In my view, the fact that African American music originated on American shores and represents the most distinct contribution from this nation to the global musical landscape represents a prominent ethnological argument for the central place of black music in the quest for self-cultural grounding in America. Moreover, from an epistemological standpoint, and thus the creativity premise noted above, jazz—within the black music pantheon—is a leading candidate for cultural centrality (but not exclusivity) in its unmatched integration of improvising and composing, and wide range of other features that are not only key to an American musical identity but also robust engagement and collaboration with music and musicians from other cultures. Michelle Obama's assertion "that we preserve, develop, and expand this treasured art form in every single school across America" is predicated on capacities inherent in jazz to invite creative engagement and synthesis among "all ethnicities, backgrounds, ages, and creeds."[9]

What about individuals who have little contact with or affinity for jazz, and for whom the genre may as well have originated in a different solar system? What about someone, like my mother, who grew up listening to Verdi and Puccini and evolved a musical identity with that operatic tradition at its center? Or Navajo, Hispanic, or Asian children who grew up in American households but were immersed in music from those respective traditions and whose musical identities blossomed accordingly? Would not the argument for jazz and black music as core to American cultural identity need to fall by the wayside in these instances?

Here a set of criteria by which individuals may more clearly define their respective identities, which is paramount to the transcultural framework, both illuminates the framework's capacities to embrace a wide range of identities, and also recognizes jazz, the site in America where CICP artistry makes its return to the West, as central to an overarching self-cultural core in the nation at large.

In Search of a Self-Cultural Center

First is that individuals identify that musical culture that most strongly resonates on the soul level, or however one might describe music to which one connects deeply on emotional and spiritual levels. Because the primordial, archetypal impulses that are, from a transcultural vantage point, important to the soul connection are embedded in the primary musical culture, the significance of this kind of self-cultural grounding cannot be overstated. As Nzewi emphasizes in the context of African music, "traditional practices make a human person human, make our modern communities human," as well as cultivate "world human tolerance."[10] Here, however, it is equally important to distinguish between what in chapter 1 I call "self-confining" and "self-transcending" soul connections. In the first, primary creativity—improvising and composing—is deficient and thus, while some degree of transcendent grounding may be possible, the intricate circuitry through which creativity and consciousness may flow and inform the entirety of the musicianship spectrum is limited. As discussed, the interpretive-performance-based neo-Eurocentric paradigm is a primary example, although any genre that is dominated by an emulative thrust may also be so characterized. By contrast, self-transcending soul connection is possible when engagement is rooted in improvising and composing from both exploratory and emulative standpoints and invites the flow of creativity and consciousness from primordial dimensions not only throughout the local musicianship system but also throughout connections made with the broader musical world that take hold in the emergent, syncretic voice. To recall an earlier transcultural principle: The central pulse of the musical world, and the emergence of the individual voice, lies not in intact cultural compartments, but in the syncretic processes and hybrid structures that result in and comprise overlying compartments. Style/cultural compartments are process-structure tributaries that flow into the overarching syncretic unity when the transcultural identity is in place.

From this standpoint, multicultural ambivalence to epistemology, and thus creative identity, confines the paradigm to piecemeal juxtaposition of, at best, monocultural, self-confining soul connections. But even this is problematic, as I discuss further, given the challenges of depth of connection with even one new musical culture. In other words, more likely than soul connection with a new culture in epistemically deficient models is a kind of distanced allure. Self-transcending soul connection with a primary culture, on the other hand, lays groundwork for a deep soul connection with other cultures—even when engagement falls far short of mastery and more entails inspired infusion of influences therefrom.

The point is not that individuals who identify a cultural core that is largely interpretive/emulative in nature should abandon that core, but rather—assuming there is interest in broader cultural navigation—that they integrate it within a self-transcending CICP identity, the most robust site for which is jazz, and thereby have the best of both worlds (jazz and some other cultural site). Imagine, for example, music studies models in which students are able to foster Native American/Jazz, Hindustani/Jazz, Mariachi/Jazz, Bluegrass/Jazz, and other identities. In all instances, musicians would be able to harness—to name two foundational tools jazz brings to broader navigation—the idiom's self-transcending improvisatory spectrum (consisting of stylistically open and style based) and globally resonant rhythmic foundations.

This enables, at once, vertical cultural grounding through whatever tradition one deems central and also its relationship with jazz-based creativity, and thus—as discussed in the context of the systematic improvisatory development framework—unprecedented horizontal access. It also enables genres that were previously engaged as largely emulative stand-alones to, at once, continue to function as such yet also to inform the evolution of the improvisation-based, syncretic personal voice. In other words, musicians engaged in this broader creativity need not alter traditional forms that may not be conducive to such—such as mariachi or European classical repertory—but these traditional forms will inevitably flow into and inform the CICP-driven individuation process. This conjoining of self-confining and self-transcending musical soul pathways will undoubtedly enliven conventional realms of interpretive performance.[11]

Therefore, even in instances where musicians have minimal or no contact with jazz, the moment they declare commitment to culturally diverse engagement, the word *jazz* must loom large in their developmental trajectories if that engagement is to be substantive. Moreover, if—as is likely in the majority of instances—such musicians resonate with American popular music, then at the very least this suggests that African American music, central to popular music, also shares a core place in their identities. At which point, it is but a small step to recognize jazz, as the site where key facets of black music have richly blossomed, as also a part of that identity—perhaps obscured as such due to educational lapse, and rectified through corresponding educational reform. I further believe a case may also be made that music that takes hold on a nation's shores also emanates deep in its soul, which lends further support to the need for education to enliven this self-cultural awareness. I take this up further in chapter 5 in discussion about the existence of a collective field of consciousness, which I believe offers support for the notion of a cultural soul. Meanwhile, in order for progress in this transcultural direction to take place, further identification of inherited obstacles in reform discourse is essential. A key example of prevailing multicultural orientation is what I call a "paradox of ethnomusicology."

Paradox of Ethnomusicology Illuminated and Resolved

The paradox arises from two major contributions ethnomusicology has made to our understanding of the musical landscape, and a contradiction in the application of this understanding.[12] One contribution involves the sheer scope of traditions that have been studied. Ethnomusicologists have done fieldwork, made recordings, and produced scholarship on music from most every corner of the planet, from Afghanistan, Bali, and Belarus to Alaska, Barbados, and Brazil. Second is the field's illumination of the inextricable link between music and the totality of influences that comprise the broader culture. One cannot understand the music of a culture without understanding the people who make and experience the music and the infinitude of forces that shape culture.

The paradox comes into view when the previous statement is taken to its next logical step: One can understand the music of another culture—to reiterate an above point—only to the extent that one has established a creativity-based, intimate relationship with the music of one's own. In other words, if music and culture are inextricably linked, how can one substantively apprehend the music of another culture if this link is not established to the music at the heart of one's own cultural identity?

Prior analysis of the jazz CICP identity, and its inherent Afro-Euro-global nexus, illustrates how the transcultural framework offers a resolution to the paradox. The transcultural model also sheds light on possible hidden hegemonies in multicultural/ethnomusicological discourse that sustain the paradox. Central is the absence of critical reflection on the issue of self-cultural grounding. To remain ambivalent about the question of a cultural center is to render music studies prone to the inertia of the neo-Eurocentric framework, which runs so deep in individual and collective awareness that only through clear articulation of an alternative cultural core will it be possible to liberate from hidden and inherited neo-Eurocentric musical assumptions. The argument that, in fact, no such cultural center exists in American music, and that the diversity aspirations of today's world may only be fulfilled by denying any kind of music curricular centrality, not only runs counter to the music-culture relationship that has been central to ethnomusicology, but also flies in the face of what it means to be a musical artist—at which point, the multicultural imprint must be recognized to be as deep, and rigid, and arguably as prohibitive to progress in the all-important quest to diversify music studies as the monocultural imprint.[13] Again, the point is not that musicians need to abandon any particular cultural or subcultural gateway but that those who aspire toward broader navigation can ground this gateway in the jazz CICP that I believe must be recognized as the cultural core to American music.

Having directly experienced the relationship between music and culture through the lens of creativity-based engagement in one's own culture, musicians now have an interior basis for optimally fathoming this relationship with music of other cultures.

Encountering New Musical Cultures

To reiterate, the extent of understanding and engagement with other cultures is directly dependent upon a creativity-based relationship with one's own. Here, however, an important criterion comes into play that is fundamentally different from self-cultural grounding and key to multicultural-transcultural distinctions. Whereas self-cultural grounding entails the interplay of emulative and exploratory engagement from early on, the basis for meaningful connections with new musical cultures will typically be in the infusion of influences of a given culture in the individual voice through exploratory creativity. In other words, an important aspect of self-cultural grounding is repeated exposure to, and practice and study of, normative features of the primary musical culture—hence, emulative experience. By contrast, personalized connection with a new culture is based in the merging of some new influence with some established style feature, which is thus at its core a syncretic phenomenon, and can happen from the earliest moments of cross-cultural exposure. Subsequent systematic, emulative engagement with the new culture thus has an interior basis to unfold in ways that are optimally relevant to a musician's personal trajectory. But without syncretic relationship between primary and new culture, which must take hold—or at least be perceived as possible—in the individual creative voice, the degree of intimacy will be limited. Shortly I acknowledge that this can manifest in radically different modes of engagement. This principle therefore calls for pedagogical models rooted in exploratory experience that, as discussed in chapter 1, underlies systematic, emulative approaches.

By way of illustration: Imagine a young John Coltrane, or contemporary counterpart, running a set of chord changes, or working on a particular scale pattern, or some other technical exercise. These are all-important, culturally grounded sources of tools that exemplify emulative work. However, inherent in both improvisatory activity and identity is the impulse to embark on spontaneous creative excursions that enable synthesis both of materials being worked on, and of influences from a broader cultural spectrum. Inasmuch as Coltrane's early music studies, not unlike that of many jazz musicians, included jazz and classical sources, and in his case even some exposure to non-Western scales, these creative excursions would sow the seeds for the blossoming of an individual voice informed by fairly diverse influences. His contemporary counterparts, moreover, inhabit a world in which diverse exposure is significantly more prevalent. What bears emphasis in all cases is that the emergent individual voice, or identity, is the lens through which one apprehends, and thus establishes personalized relationships with, the outer musical world. As noted above, these exploratory, syncretic foundations allow for systematic engagement with one or more cultures as appropriate to the individuation needs of each musician. Whereas multiculturalism is ambivalent about the epistemic/identity foundations necessary for these intimate, syncretic connections and leans toward some degree of systematic study disconnected therefrom, the transcultural paradigm is predicated on the establishment of these epistemic roots.

This, however, raises further questions that distinguish between the two diversity paradigms. Inasmuch as it is impossible for any given musician to systematically engage with all—let alone even a few—of the cultures from which influences might be derived, how can a pedagogical model circumvent tendencies toward superficial skimming, or perhaps co-opting of tools from another culture, while leaving its broader richness aside?[14] In other words, how can authenticity be sustained in culturally diverse navigation?

Key responses to these questions are found in a look at the work of artists whose work is exemplary of transcultural excursions.[15]

Authenticity and Exemplars

Once again, Coltrane comes to mind. Significantly influenced by, among other cultures, Indian music and thought, "Trane's" formal study of Indian music was limited, even as its influence resulted in expressions of great depth, power, and beauty. The same could be said of the more recent interest by many jazz musicians in Middle Eastern music, or for that matter, Ravel's and Debussy's encounter with Javanese gamelan in the late nineteenth century, or Stravinksy's with African music early in the next. Indeed, the past decade or so of other MacArthur Fellows—including Anthony Braxton, Vijay Ayer, Regina Carter, Steve Coleman, George Lewis, and Tyshawn Sorey—amply highlights this point. Contemporary artists such as Esperanza Spaulding, Jane Ira Bloom, Bobby McFerrin, Edgar Myers, Nicole Mitchell, and Jen Shyu are just a few of the many others who might be added to this list.[16] The fact that all of these artists are jazz CICPs is noteworthy, as is the general principle that—more often than not—the overarching creative trajectory involves rigorous grounding in a primary musical culture that is augmented by contact, often with limited systematic study, of secondary cultures. This is not to suggest that extensive study of secondary cultures is entirely absent among transcultural musical navigators, but that it is more the exception than the norm, and has little to do with depth of expression, nor interior connection with the outer musical world that is far more important than the number of traditions encountered to the diversity imperative.[17] A principle broached above thus makes its return—that the basis for authenticity lies not in the degree of grounding in, or exactitude of replication of practices from, new cultures contacted. Rather, it lies in the depth of integration of a given influence in the individual voice.

Multiculturalism is incapable of identifying any such pantheon of exemplars in support of its platform(s). The best it can do is identity tradition-specific practitioners, which while of course will always have a place in musical practice, are inadequate models when it comes to navigating across cultural boundaries. One would have to extrapolate, as might be inferred from idealized multiculturalism, the untenable scenario whereby students gain mastery in one tradition after another. At best, multiculturalism might identify practitioners who have achieved competency in two, perhaps three traditions. But even here, principles by which such practitioners might move beyond a horizontal view of the musical world as an endless sea of discrete categories to vertical apprehension of cultural sites from a creativity-consciousness vantage point elude multicultural discourse. Here Mantle Hood's notion of bi-musicality, where students are urged to gain competency in the music of at least one additional culture to that which is primary, may represent the beginnings of a response to my concern.[18] However, in terms of the kind of creativity-based vertical grounding that I argue is the key to twenty-first-century diversity aspirations, I believe a more expansive approach is needed.

A multicultural view that I also encounter is that first one attains some degree of mastery of a tradition, and then one creates within the horizons of this tradition. In its focus on emulative creativity, this view falls short in terms of the equally important exploratory component that is key to vertical depth and correspondingly new kinds of connection and understanding. As I argue shortly, it reflects confused or perhaps even misguided artistic aims in the multicultural paradigm, where pedagogy and research are disconnected from the central pulse of musical practice, which as I have been arguing is syncretic in nature. Here is where key distinctions between views of collision and teleology, or lack thereof, between multicultural and transcultural paradigms come into view.

Multiculturalism is rooted in a static teleological perspective—the musical world is comprised of largely discrete cultural categories and is understood by taking up one category after another. Not entirely oblivious to collision, multiculturalism views the phenomenon against this epistemically ambivalent, object-mediated (even under the musicking banner) backdrop. As Sarah Weiss concedes in her grappling with the complexities of hybridity and the challenges of authenticity, "Nothing is, and never has been, authentic, as in original and undiluted."[19] Therefore, collision—and thus syncretism—is not only inevitable but also intrinsic to the nature of musical reality.

However, instead of viewing this through the lens of discrete categories, transculturalism views it through the lens of the interior dimensions of the creative process, and also the evolution of knowledge systems toward differentiated wholeness. Collision is inherent in the tiniest instances of space and time, the most minute moments of the improvisatory flow, the self-referral reverberations in cosmic intelligence as it curves back on itself and gives rise to art from undifferentiated silence, and then science, and then the infinite manifestations of primordial spirituality-art-science interactions. Transcultural teleology is predicated on the steady progress—signs of which have long been evident—toward an overarching, richly differentiated yet organically interconnected musical ocean in which culture-specific tributaries, the primary locus for multicultural/ethnomusicological inquiry, coexist in robust integrity with the syncretic whole. While ethnomusicology is not entirely devoid of inquiry into hybridization, it remains constrained by the inertia of the field's culture-specific origins (how could it be otherwise?), which in turn obscures the direct relationship between the interior dynamics of hybridization in the creative process, how it informs at once the emergence of the creative artistic voice and collective style evolution, and the role of hybridization as evolutionary catalyst and norm, not curious by-product, in the overarching musical world.[20]

The task of the educational institution is therefore, first and foremost, to establish an environment in which a self-organizing, transcultural creative identity blossoms, and then to provide as much as possible in the way of exterior resources—including culture-specific pedagogy—that allows students to pursue the particular areas of study that facilitate the growth of this identity and corresponding skills and understanding.

Distinctions between multicultural and transcultural diversity paradigms are further illuminated by consideration of their contrasting aims.

Contrasting Aims of the Paradigms

It appears that multiculturalism's primary thrust is to prepare pedagogues whose teaching is informed by diverse traditions, and scholars who research these traditions, in a general aim to cultivate a kind of "global musical citizenship,"[21] as it is sometimes framed, in response to the long-standing focus of music studies in European classical music. Aspirations to promote creative musical artistry that is modeled after contemporary innovators, who as discussed above traverse diverse horizons, do not factor prominently in multicultural discourse. While it is not uncommon for ethnomusicologists to develop culture-specific competency in another musical tradition, this is more of a by-product of their initial interest in studying the music of a given culture. Such culture-specific musical grounding is far less common among music education colleagues who deploy multicultural strategies in their preparation of school music teachers. Accordingly, to whatever extent multicultural pedagogy and research might be seen as connected to musical practice, the development of contemporary musical artistry and innovation is clearly subordinate to the quest for understanding and pedagogical application. As I discuss in chapter 1, inasmuch as the first needs to be recognized as the basis for the second, concerns come to light about the degree of coherence in the multicultural model between its goals and corresponding practices.

I believe the integral transcultural paradigm not only exhibits strong coherence between goals and means for their realization, but also lays groundwork by which multicultural aspirations for culture-specific understanding might be fulfilled within an expanded epistemic context. Five transcultural aims might be identified that are coherent with its artistic, pedagogical, research, and activist vision.

First is artistic, involving infusion of influences from diverse cultures in the individual creative voice, a purpose that is central not only to artistic evolution but also to the evolution of deep connections to the cultural diversity of the musical world around us. With the establishment of this generalized relationship to musical pluralism, individual artists will then be able to determine the nature and extent of systematic culture-specific study, possibly including extensive in-residence immersion.

Second is to provide tools that enable collaboration with musicians from diverse traditions around the world. The jazz-inspired CICP skill set is of adequate rigor and flexibility to enable its practitioners to not only penetrate beyond their localized style parameters but also move past a cultural middle zone and find meaningful engagement with practitioners from other traditions. Cross-cultural encounter is rarely a completely egalitarian, two-way affair, where musicians meet in common terrain that is roughly equidistant from their respective cultural points of departure. Rather, it more typically involves one or more of the participants traversing further from their home base and into new territory than their cross-cultural partners. I have found that jazz CICPS are equipped with skills that enable them to go further into the newer cultural terrain than musicians from most if not all other traditions.[22]

Third, the integral transcultural paradigm lays groundwork for corresponding pedagogy. The integration of diverse influences in the emerging creative voice not only fosters deep connections and self-driven growth but also prepares pedagogues who will seek to create the same kinds of learning environments for their students. As I discuss in chapter 3, carefully selected transcultural gateways that connect creative exploration with cultural resources underlie more systematic, culture-specific engagement. Such strategies parallel approaches to musical disciplines.

Fourth, and closely related, the integral transcultural framework promotes corresponding research models. These models may look quite different than their multicultural counterparts, focusing first on key landmarks for artistic navigation rather than embarking on analytical survey, or perhaps later even in-depth analysis, driven by conventional academic interests. Examples of these transcultural landmarks might include culturally mediated and contrasting conceptions of the relationship of tradition and innovation, as already glimpsed in the exploratory-emulative interplay, and also conceptions of the relationships among time, form, creativity, and spirituality/consciousness, as I explore in chapter 6. To reiterate, this kind of inquiry need not be construed as replacing conventional historical and cultural studies, but rather viewed as organically related to creative experience and development, a link that when in place can then promote new levels of engagement and achievement in conventional areas.

Fifth, the transcultural paradigm aims to prepare integral arts visionaries who will exemplify in their work and thought the highest ideals of diversity to the society at large and emerge as powerful change agents. Their music will organically and magically infuse elements from varied sources, and their teaching, writing, and visioning will redefine what it means to truly be a "global musical citizen." While multiculturalism is driven by an activist thrust, its musical roots are, generally speaking, confined to culture-specific engagement, whereas the transcultural situates the culture-specific within a syncretic cultural confluence that enables activism to gain a kind of interior grounding.

In sum, the lower order, multicultural approach to diversity, similar to multicultural approaches to creativity, can be understood more as reaction to the prevailing neo-Eurocentric paradigm than as a viable paradigmatic alternative that is built on new roots. The higher order, transcultural diversity platform, central to which is the establishment of a creative identity, represents an entirely new model.

Several questions come to the forefront as the analysis continues. Is multiculturalism simply incomplete? Or is it fundamentally flawed, with shortcomings that call for wholesale overhaul in diversity thinking and pedagogy? While the slogan that I occasionally invoke, that "anything multiculturalism can do, transculturalism can do better," may suggest the first, I believe a stronger case may be made for the second, and the even more sobering assessment that multiculturalism may do more to impede than promote diversity progress, particularly when it comes to black music.[23] Following are examples of what I call "ethnocentric blind spots" that support this assessment. In other words, within overarching, politically correct appeals for the broadening of the cultural horizons of music studies, important areas are overlooked due to lingering ethnocentric/racialized biases. First is found in the advocacy of popular music, a relatively recent area in music studies reform deliberations, where acknowledgment of the black roots of the music is conspicuously scarce. In addition to the obvious social justice casualty are artistic/pedagogical shortcomings that undermine efforts to advance this area.

POPULAR MUSIC ADVOCACY: MULTICULTURAL AND TRANSCULTURAL APPROACHES

Music education, ethnomusicology, and music theory—albeit with the latter's polarized views on the topic—are among the areas at the forefront of efforts to establish popular music as a bona fide academic discipline. According to John Covach, a prominent spokesperson in these efforts, "music schools (typically) teach a curriculum primary focusing on classical and jazz traditions," leaving students interested in popular music studies with limited options.[24] Even from a multicultural standpoint, this statement is deeply problematic in suggesting that jazz enjoys some semblance of equal curricular status with classical music. When an enormous percentage of music majors graduate with little or no experience, let alone substantive skills, in jazz, nothing could be more misleading.[25]

From a transcultural standpoint, however, the statement is even more problematic—and consistent with tendencies that prevail in popular music literature.[26] The problems are twofold. First it reifies the disconnection between popular music and its African American foundations, a relationship that assumes front and center stage when jazz and popular music are not compartmentalized but recognized as manifestations of an underlying black music unity. Jazz musicians since the 1970s have broached a range of terrain that falls under any reasonable conception of what constitutes popular music, even if jazz musicians would not characterize the terrain as such, in highly innovative and organic ways. By not only separating jazz and popular music, but in fact also positioning the two realms as quasi-oppositional (space for the first precludes that for the second), Covach—consistent with prevailing patterns in the field—succumbs to a particularly egregious form of multicultural assembly-line thinking. Without black music, there would be no Elvis Presley, Beatles, Beech Boys, Grateful Dead, Rolling Stones, and all the way on up through Madonna and Adele. This severing of popular music from its cultural core is yet another example of the important contributions of African Americans being rendered invisible.

Serious artistic and pedagogical casualties also stem from this limited perspective.[27] Consider this in terms of the relationship between jazz composition, which includes small and large ensemble composing, and the songwriting foundations of popular music. Small jazz ensemble composition is a highly advanced form of songwriting that involves melodic fluency, includes rich harmonic structures and progressions, organically integrates strong grounding in contemporary rhythmic languages—thus, Black Atlantic Rhythm—as well as incorporates improvisatory prowess. Large jazz ensemble composition brings highly developed arranging and orchestration skills to the mix. Jazz composers-performers view popular music not as a separate musical compartment but rather as a facet of a seamless black music tapestry. Exemplifying the transcultural vision, moreover, that seamlessness does not stop with popular music but extends to all music.

In a single stroke, popular music advocacy—reflecting the largely horizontal nature of multicultural discourse—ignores these roots and precludes harnessing the important tools jazz has to offer popular music curricular models and potential artistic innovation. A transcultural understanding of popular music circumvents both this social justice transgression and its closely related pedagogical/artistic limitations by recognizing the common African American foundations of jazz and popular music, both allowing the powerful tools of the first to enhance studies in the other, which has a reciprocal effect, and also further celebrating the centrality of black music in American and global culture.

The prevailing multicultural conception of popular music may be seen as a subset of a more pervasive and overarching ethnocentric blind spot involving the use of hegemonic language in lower order, multicultural reform circles.

HEGEMONIC WORD GAMES: EXCLUSIONARY LANGUAGE IN INCLUSIONARY GUISE

Anyone who has given serious consideration to the literature on diversity, or conversations on the topic happening in other areas (i.e., other than music) of college/university campuses, will likely notice the often-intensive scrutiny given to terminology. This holds whether the issue at hand is race, gender, sexual orientation, or disability awareness. Put another way, to invoke a central theme in diversity discourse sometimes referred to as "raciolinguistics,"[28] words are powerful—they have the capacity to perpetuate stereotypes, or begin to dissolve those stereotypes and catalyze the critical interrogation of deeply conditioned assumptions that is essential for more inclusive and equitable learning communities. However, I am continually astonished at the extent to which not only conventional music studies but also more notably music studies change visioning—including that which ostensibly places diversity front and center—remains oblivious to this principle.

A primary example is the heading "art music," which is almost always used to refer to the European classical tradition.[29] While I fully realize why colleagues seek an alternative to *classical*, which technically denotes a period in the European tradition, the term is largely used by musicians and scholars in informal and formal settings (e.g., Robert Freeman's book *The Crisis of Classical Music in America*[30] or *New York Times* music reviews) and rarely is there confusion over its intended meaning. Moreover, any problems inherent in use of the term pale when compared to those posed by "art music."

To probe this more deeply: When the heading "art music," or "Western art music," is reserved for only one musical culture, the statement is made loud and clear, even if this is not the intention, that other musical cultures are not worthy of consideration as art. To reference European classical music as "art music" or "Western art music" is to say that the music of John Coltrane or Bobby McFerrin or Jane Ira Bloom does not constitute art. If one ascribes to the view, as discussed above, that art and music are inextricably linked to the totality of life, then it is but a small step to infer from the denigration of a musical tradition the denigration of the people that make that music. I would even argue that, in fact, this form of "ex-nomination"[31] is actually more egregious in its racist impact than explicitly derogatory language. Why? Because it advances the unspoken assertion that *the inferior status of what is excluded is so self-evident that it need not even be directly named.* In other words, as objectionable as it may be for someone to declare that music X is inferior to music Y, at least the intention is clear and some kind of reaction to the words used might ensue. However, when a seemingly inclusive term is used in an exclusive manner, the impact runs all the deeper in individual and collective awareness. In fields as paradigm-blind as conventional music studies, and lower order reform conversations (where this language abounds), occasions to challenge the more subtle exnominatory expressions are far more elusive. This problem is significantly compounded when conversation about language and terminology are absent, whereby even many of the most fervent change agents are oblivious to these practices.

Another example in music is the common reference to contemporary European-based (but that might be composed anywhere) concert music as "new music." Once again, amid the infinitude of musical expressions happening around us every day that might be categorized as "new," the exclusive reservation of this term for an extraordinarily tiny slice of musical practice has a pernicious and dismissive impact. The fact that one will be hard pressed to hear much hip hop at an academic "new music" concert underscores this point. To cite a further instance: Musicians with expertise in both jazz and classical music are often said, when it comes to the classical side of their skill set, to have great "legit" chops, perpetuating the idea that classical music is legitimate, and jazz is not. Less common now, though still in the collective memory and largely unquestioned, is the reference to classical music as "serious music." Consider the condescending and misguided remarks made by John Cage, largely hailed as among the great twentieth-century musical emancipators, in response to concert music composers in the twentieth century partaking of jazz influences. "Jazz per se derives from serious music. And when serious music derives from it [jazz], the situation becomes rather silly."[32]

Epistemology, Ethnology, and Language

In addition to the more blatant forms of exnomination noted above are those that might appear more innocuous yet, upon closer inspection, are no less egregious in their hegemonic impact. Here, building upon prior commentary, the close relationship between epistemology, ethnology, and language comes to the fore. In short: Any given process (epistemology) has ethnological correlates. When these correlates are left unexamined, or shrouded in exnominatory/exclusive terminology, ethnology succumbs to ethnocentrism.

Even a term as seemingly neutral as *performance* is a good example. While there are many types of performance, the term in musical academe is typically assumed to mean interpretive performance of European classical repertory and its contemporary offshoots (including what is called "new music!"). The reasoning is not entirely invalid: The European tradition is where the art of interpretive performance, particularly in its most specified form where performers are given no latitude for improvisatory embellishment, has most fully blossomed. Hence a vivid example of the epistemology-ethnology relationship. However, and here is where language comes into play, ethnology succumbs to ethnocentrism when the term *performance* is not qualified, and just presumed to be centered in European classical performance. One need not even ask whether a degree in violin or clarinet performance might involve let alone focus on Klezmer, Turkish, North or South Indian, or Jazz traditions—all of which include rich forms of performance on those instruments. Accordingly, the seemingly neutral epistemic label reifies the exclusionary, ethnocentric impact—again, not by what it states, but by what it even more powerfully omits by inference. Every time this term— from this standpoint—is uttered in conversation, mentioned in promotional materials, or listed in degree requirements, the impact is perpetuated and imprinted in individual and collective awareness.

The same holds for history, musicology, and theory, study of which again is uncritically presumed to be centered in European roots. Within musicology, moreover, the term *ethnomusicology* is reserved for non-European traditions, with the heading "historical musicology," a potently charged form of exnomination that includes not just one but two words that uphold the subordinating impact, reinforcing its distance from ethnomusicology. The implication is that only the European tradition, despite the fact that most of what is studied within it dates back only a few centuries, includes a history worthy of attention by musicologists.[33] Or, conversely, that Europe is devoid of ethnologic features worthy of study.

Direct correlates are evident with patterns Jay Garfeld and Bryan Van Norden lament as typical practice in academic philosophy departments. While the emphasis is typically on Western thought, the area offering the coursework is typically named the Department of Philosophy. [34] The message, loud and clear, is that even with the rich wisdom of philosophical traditions from around the world and time immemorial, only Western philosophy is considered as a reliable source or means for seeking truth. The authors suggest at the very least a renaming—to Department of Western Philosophy—in order to convey more accurately and honestly what is valued, and to not continue the marginalization of non-Western culture inherent in the absence of such naming. In music studies, the parallel to this renaming would pertain to not only most music schools and departments but also most every discipline within them.

Composition provides another example, even if substantive (or in many cases any) engagement with the process is foreign to the majority of participants in most music schools. Because the art of fully notated composition, like interpretive performance, blossomed in the European tradition (with composers across the globe working in this framework), rich epistemic-ethnologic connections are clearly evident. However, because composition also occurs outside that tradition, with popular music songwriting and small and large ensemble jazz as but two examples, failure to specify the particular compositional cultural aesthetic renders the ethnologic ethnocentric. A related manifestation of this effect is the prevailing tendency that I take up in chapter 7 to view improvisation as a subspecies of composition, which essentially then reifies the already-marginalized improvisatory epistemic-ethnologic line as subordinate to the dominant compositional line. Although improvisation, of course, was central in the European tradition in earlier times and transcends virtually all cultural boundaries, the improvisatory connecting thread that is increasingly prominent in today's world was delivered through the African American tradition.

The use of the term *jazz* to designate a department or area within a music school illustrates another facet of the language/terminology problem. Jazz is labeled by genre, while the conventional disciplines of performance, theory, and history are not; this kind of linguistic double standard stigmatizes jazz—as if to say, "This music is different from how music is typically defined in our school and field." Moreover, jazz is process rich, while the conventional disciplines of performance, theory, and history are process weak, yet the respective designators mask the strengths in what is marginalized (jazz) and the deficiencies in what is privileged (Euroclassical).

The use of the heading "world music" to mean music beyond European classical, jazz, pop, and other Western idioms is yet another example.[35] This reifies the current place of the Western genres, which means the centrality of the European is all the more strengthened in relationship to the exoticized "other." Is not European classical music also world music? Of course, no one could deny this classification, but until this question is raised, it goes without saying that "world music" excludes this (European) tradition, thus underscoring, by verbal omission, the prevailing Euro-supremacy. Here an interesting variation of exnomination comes into focus. Whereas European classical music is explicitly privileged, as discussed above, through its synonymous and sole inclusion under the heading "art music," it is implicitly privileged by its *exclusion* from the heading "world music." From a transcultural perspective, all music is world music, rendering the heading unnecessary and irrelevant save for the present rectifying function.

What is the solution to these patterns? Do labels need to be adjusted in order to more adequately and honestly convey the terrain that they represent? Or does the terrain need to open up in alignment with the broader scope of today's musical world? In the next chapter, I argue that both wholesale renaming of conventional knowledge areas to more precisely designate the terrain addressed, and expanding what falls under labels that are retained in the new model, will be important to rectifying the ethnocentric/racist impact of prevailing terminology.[36]

Learning from Exemplary Diversity Discourse beyond Music

Indeed, other areas in the academy and society at large have provided leadership and help illuminate the extent to which music (and philosophy) lag behind. Gender studies, LGBT studies, social work, progressive schools of education, and other areas in which social justice is prominent devote considerable attention to how individuals and groups are named. At-risk youth are more appropriately referred to not as "underprivileged," but as youth from underserved communities, hence shifting the focus from what might be perceived as individual deficiency to circumstantial deficiency, or injustice. Beyond the academy, the professional sports world has demonstrated important leadership, as seen in reactions to the demeaning mascots and logos of the Washington Redskins in the National Football League, or the Cleveland Indians in baseball.

As creativity-driven activists individuate, sensitivity to the use of language as paradigm reifying or transforming, as well as capacities to transcend prevailing usage, grow apace. The fact that this issue continues to elude music studies change conversation, with diversity advocates still referring to European classical music as "art music" or "Western art music" in addition to the further patterns identified, is consistent with my distinctions between multicultural and transcultural paradigms, and that the first continues to dominate. Perhaps ironically, key resources for the very diversification sought, such as jazz, are marginalized as a result of politically correct, multicultural egalitarianism. The epistemology-ethnology-language relationship reveals that diversity platforms that fail to shift the ontological switch from structure to process, and in so doing fail to center creativity-rich models as key to the pluralistic quest, are not even remotely egalitarian. From the standpoint of musical correctness, not all musical categories are equally significant when it comes to broader navigation! This has nothing to do with inherent artistic or cultural worth, and everything to do with inherited, and profoundly misguided, tendencies to view the musical landscape through an epistemically tainted lens—and then to cement one's skewed findings through labels.

The impact of this failure to critically examine common patterns in language and labeling in music studies directly exemplifies what Kristin Anderson has called "benign bigotry," referring to those patterns that remain hidden from view yet perpetuate exclusionary tendencies just as pernicious as those resulting from overtly denigrating language.[37]

Consistent with this social justice and critical inquiry lapse, change visioning is minimally informed by racism research that might help counteract these tendencies.

INSIGHTS FROM RACISM RESEARCH

Several lines of inquiry from research and literature on racism corroborate with prior discussion in this chapter and set the stage for drawing musical/music studies correlates to overarching patterns in the field. Much of what follows falls within the broad scope of Critical Race Theory, an analytical framework that seeks to ground activism in the world in social sciences and humanities scholarship.[38] Among the many strands of Critical Race Theory, particularly relevant to the topic at hand is the situating of individual racist thinking and behavior within overarching, systemic patterns. Racism, in other words, is deeply etched in educational and societal systems, and thus even without overt racist acts, the phenomenon is nonetheless pervasive. This is borne out by research on degrees of racism that differentiate between everyday racism, which might involve classroom instructors calling on or responding to students of color differently than students not of color, and more egregious acts of racism, which might involve racist epithets or violence. Research on stages of racism identifies a progression that extends from the holocaust of slavery to Jim Crow/segregation policies to institutional racism.[39] Conversance with literature on the topic—a rarity among most music faculty[40]—is an essential part of a broader healing process that also includes deep introspection into one's thinking, speech, action, and engagement with diverse epistemologies that ground both diagnosis and healing of the patterns in the innermost recesses of consciousness. Unfortunately, race and overall diversity discourse, consistent with overarching patterns in the academy, remains generally averse to inquiry into spirituality and consciousness, particularly from the nondual mystical perspective of the integral approach that powerfully cuts across cultural borders. Later I reflect on the self-inflicted social justice transgressions perpetuated when notions such as "soul," "spirit," and "God" are excluded from the conversation, particularly when it comes to black-white racial dynamics. I believe a jazz-inspired integral paradigm of social justice scholarship has the capacity to rectify the problem in a personally meaningful and academically rigorous manner.[41]

Meanwhile, identification of musical parallels with important overarching themes in race discourse provide means for direct application and strides forward in music studies. The commonly cited pattern of "white privilege" finds its correlate in what I call "white musical privilege," manifesting itself not only in overt forms—for example, curricular priority, salary (classical colleagues typically earn more), professional symphony orchestras with salary scales and benefits packages where no such institutionalized benefits exist in the jazz world—but also in less subtle ways, as indicated in prior discussion of language and terminology and organizational structures that reflect neo-Eurocentric privileging. Thus, to reiterate, correlative with raciolinguistics is musical raciolinguistics.[42] Closely related is Robin Diangelo's notion of "white fragility," which identifies subtle and sometimes more dramatic reactionary patterns in the white community upon confronting the topic of race.[43] A common example is to deflect conversation to a subordinate point, even if disproportionately relevant to the topic. For example, a white person, in the context of epidemic violence and discrimination against blacks, might go to great lengths to emphasize that racism is a two-way affair, and even cite instances of being a victim of racism, both of which are valid but can shroud the more pressing issue that is being broached. Even more distressing is when appeals for equality are misperceived as the denigration of the dominant culture. An example of "white musical fragility," then, involves conventionalists, and even lower order change advocates, construing arguments for foundational positioning of jazz as a reverse kind of hegemony, as if inclusion of one music necessitates devaluation of another.[44]

These contribute to the significant problems that W. E. B Du Bois identified in the pattern of "double consciousness," by which he meant the necessity for African Americans to view themselves, and thus their construction of self-identity, through two lenses.[45] One was that of their own ethnocultural blackness, but only as filtered through a second lens, that of white America. What in turn might be deemed "double musical consciousness" entails the apprehension of African American music through both neo-Eurocentric and black music lenses. Even if musical academe is largely populated by white colleagues (including the subsection of those who teach black music), the impact holds, and perhaps may even be exacerbated given the notable absence of substantive conversation on race in the field. Lower order reform approaches that overlook the foundational tools inherent in black music represent but one casualty of the phenomenon. The dissociation discussed earlier of popular music studies from its African American foundations, as a result of which jazz and the powerful tools for cutting edge innovations in pop and much other music are rendered invisible, is another.[46] Yet another example, perhaps at the other end of the academic aesthetic spectrum, is the stereotypical marginalization of black experimentalism, for which, as George Lewis illustrates, the AACM legacy is exemplary. Double musical consciousness, at once, perpetuates such stereotypes in the white musical majority and disempowers the establishment of these powerful contributions in the self-identity of the black music minority.[47]

Lingering Aversion to Musical Blackness

I have coined the phrase "lingering aversion to musical blackness," or LAMB for short, in order to bring attention to these tendencies and the overarching resistance to the foundational place of black music in American musical culture and in music studies.[48] While it might not be surprising to encounter this pattern in conventional music studies, to witness it in change circles, particularly those predicated on diversifying the cultural horizons of music studies, involving colleagues that lay claim to a social justice commitment, is particularly disturbing.[49] A diversity continuum underscores this point: At one end is the monocultural framework that prevails, with a multicultural reaction occupying the first increment of progress. However, there is a sharp drop-off when it comes to discourse on race, which is the next increment in the scale. Key to this increment is recognition of what Deborah Bradley, Juliet Hess, and others characterize as a pervasive "musical whiteness."[50] But yet another drop-off is evident, which is where I believe the present discussion makes important contributions. This involves not only the situating of music studies diversity and race discourse within the overarching conversation on black-white racial dynamics, but also bringing into view "musical blackness" from both social justice and artistic/pedagogical standpoints. I am talking, of course, of not only adding black music to prevailing curricular models but also foundational overhaul with African American music occupying a central place—not as multicultural destination, but as transcultural gateway.

Nonetheless anticipating resistance to this viewpoint even within progressive circles as a kind of reverse hegemonic privileging, the significance of this increment in the continuum as not just a horizontal expansion of current thinking, but a vertical turn, cannot be stressed strongly enough. In other words, to reiterate a principle from chapter 1, what, if anything, is being "privileged" is an unmatched process scope—one that also happens to be inherent in the cultural core of American music—that has the potential to undergird a music studies paradigm capable of unprecedented musical navigation and understanding. The separation of ethnology and epistemology that has plagued both the conventional neo-Eurocentric framework and (albeit to a lesser degree) the multicultural diversity paradigms may therefore be healed.

The time has come to stop thinking primarily in terms of *kinds* of music, and instead to shift the initial focus to the creative processes, and thus self-transcending musical gateways and navigational vehicles, that comprise the basis for an interior relationship with the outer musical world. This is the heart of the transcultural vision. Only through this lens is it possible to return to and navigate the realm of overlying musical categories from an adequate interior vantage point. While all music is created equal, not all musics are equally robust gateways to the world, and until this politically incorrect yet artistically incontrovertible principle is recognized, music studies change discourse and action will never escape the multicultural morass and its hegemonic limitations. Reform advocacy needs to overcome tendencies to flatline the process scope, which means expanding prevailing horizontal conceptions of "musicking" to include its vertical foundations, if it is to productively broach the realm of genre/culture and identify key landmarks for navigating twenty-first-century musical topographies. To reiterate a prior point, the transcultural vision does not reject musical categories, but rather shifts the lens through which they are understood to the creativity by which genre and disciplinary categories take hold and evolve.

From a multicultural vantage point, jazz is a kind of music that exists within an infinitude of other genres. From a transcultural vantage point, jazz is not primarily a kind of music, but a mode of musical being and navigation that is uniquely endowed, through its CICP foundations (and systematic improvisatory continuum) with powerful self-transcending capacities that open up connections from a point of departure to the musical whole. From this standpoint, any conversations on the topic of creatively and culturally diverse musical expeditions, at least that are to embark from points West, in which the word *jazz* does not come up early and often can only be dismissed as impoverished; relics of a neo-Eurocentric-plus, multicultural perspective that has done more to impede the diversity imperative than resolve the crisis.

CLOSING THOUGHTS

It cannot be overstated that liberation from ethnocentric/racialized biases that constrain diversity discourse requires heavy lifting, meaning digging deep into inherited patterns and how they become manifest in untold forms of thinking, speech, and action. Indeed, if lingering aversion to musical blackness is alive and well even in the most progressive music studies circles, one can imagine the extent of the imprint in general multicultural discourse, let alone the neo-Eurocentric framework. An important first step in music studies is to recognize that the conversation in the field lags far behind general race discourse. A common trajectory among those who have committed to this work is instructive: Initial proclamations about "not having a racist bone in my body" tend to abound at the outset of the journey. Upon engaging in conversation and reading literature on the topic, and beginning to examine personal patterns through this expanded lens, one's awareness begins to open up to the deeply entrenched nature of racist pathology. No one is without a racist bone. At which point, another pitfall awaits the committed seeker—the notion of "mission accomplished" following the initial breakthrough. Here individuals, having attained what appears as some sort of high ground, may even be prone to proselytizing with friends and family that "you need to do this same kind of work" to attain the same kind of liberation from the scourge. However, this lasts only as long as the next instant when the individual discovers yet another layer of racist conditioning. At which point the realization sets in—that this is a lifelong endeavor.

To be sure, this can be daunting as well as demoralizing. Here, though, the integral perspective brings several important facets to the healing equation that could not render it more hopeful. One is that the very creativity and consciousness epistemological scope that is the driving force of artistic development is, at once, a source of tools that are essential to liberation, and also a channel for personal development that is directly enhanced by this liberation. Put another way, clearing away conditioned ethnocentric/racialized tendencies directly contributes to the richly differentiated interior circuitry through which creativity and consciousness, and thus the soul connection, may flow and flourish. In sum, individuation is not only a matter of creative expression and expansion but also a matter of diagnosing and removing obstacles. When healing of deeply rooted ethnocentric/racist tendencies is viewed from this perspective, the motivation to commit to such could not be stronger.

The ramifications for music studies could not be more inspiring—a musicianship paradigm of unprecedented creativity, diversity, integration, rigor, and self-organizing vitality, uniquely capable of uniting contemporary and conventional exploration and understanding, with African American music at its core, lies waiting to be recognized in the musical world around us and serve as the basis for wholesale redesign of twenty-first-century music schools. This in turn lays groundwork for a broader arts-driven revolution in creativity and consciousness in education and society at large.

Chapter Three

Music School for a Transcultural Age

What would a music school look like that was built upon a jazz-based, higher order transcultural vision, and its paradigmatically new approaches to creativity, diversity, consciousness, and other lines of musical, educational, and human development?

This chapter responds to this question by delineating key features of a new model, and also grappling with important obstacles in the very conversation itself that will need to be addressed with great skill. If Thomas Kuhn's observations about the turbulence inherent in scientific revolutions is any sort of guide, the obstacles escalate significantly when—as in music studies—deeply rooted and often hidden ethnocentric and racialized biases work in tandem with philosophical conflicts within a field. The fact, as I argue, that these biases constrain the music studies reform conversation as much as the conventional model whose reform is sought only underscores the complexity of the task at hand.

Extending from prior commentary, the chapter argues for a music studies framework that harnesses the self-organizing properties inherent in the creativity/consciousness-based individuation process. As exemplified in the jazz-based CICP identity, the self-organizing spectrum includes self-artistic, self-transcending, self-diversifying, self-integrative, self-pedagogical, self-noetic, self-rigorous, self-critical, self-motivational, and self-navigational features. A higher order, integral model seeks to enliven these interior, self-driven impulses within students and provide institutional strategies and resources for systematic further growth that can optimally blossom atop heightened student receptivity and self-organizing momentum. Five new curricular and organizational pillars for a twenty-first-century school of music are central to the emergent vision: music creation, music inquiry and craft, music pedagogy, music and consciousness, and music and society.

To provide a brief overview:

Music Creation includes the primary creativity of improvisation and composition, each of which is approached through multiple constituent languages, and the secondary creativity of performance, which happens largely in private instruction and ensembles, foundationally new models of which are advanced.

Music Inquiry and craft takes two of the conventional pillars of the core curriculum—theory and history—and situates, renames, and redefines them within a much-expanded context. Music inquiry encompasses cultural, aesthetic, theoretical, cognitive, critical thinking, historical, and transpersonal (consciousness/spirituality) studies. Craft includes studies in melody, rhythm, embodied musicianship, harmony, and aural musicianship—but a portion of these fall within the generally narrow horizons associated with the music theory realm. Note the inclusion of embodiment, which as I explain below is directly integrated with rhythm and aural musicianship, and also links with music and consciousness, within this category.

Music Pedagogy includes classroom pedagogy, preparation of school music teachers, and corresponding research on music learning and teaching.

Music and Consciousness combines direct engagement with meditation and methodologies for evolution of consciousness and corresponding theoretical studies.

Music and Society encompasses a range of outreach initiatives—including entrepreneurship, musical ambassadorship, arts activism, and consciousness-based transformative leadership—that may be viewed as a direct extension of the pedagogical continuum, but as it takes hold externally, beyond the classroom.

The five pillars are conceived as tightly interwoven, intersecting channels that facilitate the interior blossoming of the broader musicianship paradigm discussed in the preceding chapters in the self-organizing, jazz CICP model. Prior to examining the pillars in depth, however, I believe it is imperative to lay some groundwork for the conversation that will need to transpire not only with conventionalist colleagues but also with colleagues, such as multiculturalists as considered in the previous chapter, who are disposed to change, but nonetheless may be challenged by the vision I set forth. If the force of the monocultural imprint is not problematic enough in change deliberations, that of the equally limiting multicultural imprint, also having eluded attention, must also be placed front and center.

PRELIMINARY CONSIDERATIONS

I begin with an overview of what I view as hot-button issues, with glimpses of how jazz-based approaches provide new foundations upon which important connections to European classical resources and strategies are made. First involves musicianship studies, which has typically come under the heading of music theory and aural skills. Appeals for reform of this aspect of the music core curriculum have largely been closest to the heart of the reform conversation from its inception over a half-century ago.[1] As noted above, I place musicianship under the new heading, "music inquiry and craft," and entirely redefine the content and pedagogy of the area around the needs of the jazz-based CICP. Aspects of European classical music and common practice harmony, which has served as the basis for musicianship foundations, are carefully integrated within a considerably expanded approach. The fact that the modal-tonal-transtonal spectrum of jazz encompasses the overarching progression from diatonic to nondiatonic harmony in European classical music provides a key intersection that, I have found from personal experience, at least elicits preliminary receptivity to the model I advance. While there are, of course, in addition to commonalities, important differences between jazz harmony and European classical harmony, and thus trade-offs, I believe the incorporation of improvisation, composition, and engagement with globally resonant contemporary rhythmic practices yields a creativity-based, diverse, integrative, and rigorous alternative that is far more aligned with the needs of today's musicians—even including those who may be symphony orchestra bound.

I also propose an entirely new framework for ensemble experience in which prevailing emphasis on large ensemble participation is restructured within a model in which the small creative music ensemble, in which students improvise and compose, occupies the center. This carries with it an entirely new kind of dynamic in the reform conversation. Why? Because whereas many music faculty harbor deep concerns about the viability, effectiveness, and relevance of the music theory and aural skills paradigm, concerns about the place of large ensembles in the curriculum are more due to the quest for curricular balance than to the perceived quality of the ensemble experience itself. In other words, faculty would rather see a better distribution between large conducted ensembles, in which students are nestled among large sections of musicians (think string players in the orchestra, woodwinds in the band) playing the same part, and chamber music. But the driving force for change appeals is not due to perceived shortcomings in the actual large ensemble experience. This coupled with the stature of the large ensemble in music studies culture, with bands, orchestra, and choirs typically an important part of music school/department identity, is likely the reason why large ensemble requirements have not significantly budged.

Perhaps the area most immune to even discussion of change, let alone reform measures, has been the private lesson. Indeed, no pedagogical format is more emblematic of the neo-Eurocentric paradigm than the one-on-one, master-apprentice relationship that comprises studio instruction.[2] Accordingly, my advancing of a jazz-based alternative—even if it, as in my new approaches to musicianship studies and ensemble, integrates aspects of European practice—is likely to elicit concerns. Nonetheless, I believe my model is capable of yielding levels of virtuosity that equal, if not surpass, those of prevailing neo-Eurocentric approaches and also preparing students for the far broader musical navigation that is called for in our time.

The new approaches to all of the three above areas are important examples of the Afro-Euro-global nexus, in which jazz-based foundations underpin overarching integration of European classical approaches and open up new levels of achievement and understanding in classical music and broader musical exploration.

A closer look at the five new curricular and organizational pillars illuminates these points. I then reflect on the political complexities inherent in the idea of a jazz-based music studies paradigm, even amid arguments for what it has to offer achievement and vitality in European classical music and beyond.

PILLAR #1: MUSIC CREATION

Music creation consists of the primary creative processes of improvisation and composition and the secondary creative modality of interpretive performance. Implicit in this continuum, and in fact directly encompassed in the systematic improvisatory developmental framework considered in chapter 1, is a broader spectrum of rigorous and integrative engagement in ancillary creativity areas: harmony, melody, rhythm, aural awareness, music embodiment, cultural, historical, cognitive, and transpersonal/spirituality studies. These comprise a particularly robust parts-to-whole epistemic scope that opens up to heightened consciousness—or as I termed it earlier, a richly differentiated soul pathway, for which jazz is an unmatched exemplar. This creativity-driven thrust invites complementary engagement in whole-to-parts practices such as meditation, which anchors its own systematic development continuum, to be explored more fully in chapter 6.[3]

Primary Creativity: Improvisation and Composition

Improvisatory and compositional foundations encompass multiple constituent languages. The improvisatory line includes style-specific (centered in jazz) and stylistically open improvising. The compositional line includes small and large ensemble jazz composition, popular music song-form, and concert music/classical approaches. Reflecting the establishment of a creative identity that is essential to the higher order, integral vision, improvising and composing occur throughout the curriculum—in private lessons, ensembles, and a range of coursework. However, underlying these applications must be robust grounding in contemporary, syncretic creativity that is not confined to preset disciplinary or style boundaries.

Secondary Creativity: Performance

Performance occupies a central place in the conventional model, taught primarily in private lessons and ensembles, and confined largely to interpretive performance of European classical repertory and contemporary offshoots. In the emergent model, performance is situated within the Contemporary Improviser Composer Performer identity and corresponding curricular redistribution. Though performance moves from its current position of exclusive centrality among modes of music making, this is not to suggest a devaluing of performance skills development—if anything, an even higher degree of virtuosity is sought in the higher order integral framework. However, a more differentiated conception of virtuosity that expands conventional notions of the term guides performance pedagogy. This is illuminated by a reconceived notion of the private lesson.

Private Instruction Reconceived

Conventional, neo-Eurocentric approaches to private instruction are fairly straightforward, focusing on European classical repertory and development of corresponding instrumental technique. Neo-Eurocentric-plus efforts at change take two forms, in my experience. One is to include, for expansion of this model, a broader range of music in private lessons, and other areas of the curriculum. Another, pursuing a contrasting line of thinking, calls for less emphasis on developing performance skills in order to make room for other areas. Virtuosity, associated almost exclusively with European-based interpretive performance skills, is often held in suspicion.

A higher order, integral conception of private instruction yields a vastly expanded, multidimensional paradigm of private lessons for today's musicians. Today's musicians need greater virtuosity, not less, and today's music schools need an expanded conception of what this means.[4] Four principles central to a higher order, integral approach reveal a new set of purposes for private instruction that situate the conventional impetus in a considerably broader framework. From an integral standpoint:

1. The primary purpose of mastery of a principal instrument is to develop a channel for one's own improvising and composing.
2. A secondary purpose of mastery of a principal instrument is to develop means for performance of compositions of, and improvisatory interactions with, musical collaborators.

3. A third purpose is to develop a performative channel by which one can learn repertory, from a range of traditions as relevant to one's artistic development, for creative, technical, and conceptual enrichment. For some, but not all, musicians in the West (if not elsewhere), learning European classical and jazz repertory will be important to fulfilling this function.
4. A fourth purpose of mastering an instrument in the twenty-first century is what represents the beginning and end of conventional approaches, to prepare students for professional careers as Interpretive Performance Specialists, but which in the new approach is deemed appropriate for only a small percentage of students. In other words, in an emergent pedagogical environment in which mastery of an instrument is primarily to serve the needs of the CICP, capacities for conventional focus on European repertory still exist. However, now students so inclined will arrive at IPS destination from an informed and broader vantage point. I estimate that no more than 5 percent of music students, having access to a broader slate of options, will nonetheless choose this specialized career path.

This in no way should suggest devaluation of that particular avenue; it is simply to underscore the natural tendency in human art-making to create (via primary creativity as central) and diversify. If anything, moreover, the idea that but 5 percent of musicians coming in through a CICP culture might still gravitate toward specialized interpretive performance may even bestow newfound respect for that pathway—not as superior, but as an avenue that is suitable only for a small percentage of musicians. I wonder how many faculty members in today's music schools, including those who are inclined to impose the Interpretive Performance Specialist pathway on all or most students, would actually—given expanded CICP options—have arrived at the IPS framework.

Might the model I propose threaten levels of achievement and vitality in European classical music? Absolutely not; I believe the opposite holds. The preservation of this tradition does not require the vast majority of practitioners to develop the rarified and domain-specific recitalist and audition-ready skills of the fourth purpose above. Rather, it will be amply upheld by the significant numbers of musicians who realize strong but more generalized performance skills that are applicable to that tradition and beyond, corresponding to the third purpose above, with the small percentage achieving abilities in purpose 4 (which again are not more advanced, but are more localized around professional style criteria in classical music). Purpose 3 abilities will ensure levels of performance in regional and school orchestras that more than amply uphold the place of European classical music in communities large and small. Because these musicians will be engaged in a broader scope of work, moreover, the prospects for magical and inspired performance, let alone expanded programming, may be quite high. The smaller percentage of purpose 4 musicians, again who attain rarified skills in classical performance, will be sufficient to populate major orchestras. This redistribution will also address the ever-increasing pool of musicians that graduate from music schools each year who must compete for decreasing positions in such orchestras. This leads to distinctions between approaches to ensembles in the curriculum according to the various worldviews.[5]

Ensembles Reconceived

The central ensemble in the conventional neo-Eurocentric model is the large ensemble—orchestra, choir, wind band. Lower order, neo-Eurocentric-plus conversations recognize the need for a broader ensemble experience and the limited expressive capabilities inherent in the large ensemble format. Compare, for example, the experience of the section violinist doubling the same part with a half-dozen or (often) more other violinists, with whatever expressive decisions that might be made largely dictated by the conductor, and the experience of playing in a string quartet. From a higher order integral standpoint, both conventional and lower order perspectives fall short in moving past default centering of interpretive performance. In other words, even if the string quartet circumvents reliance on a conductor, it is still constrained by the notated score, typically created by someone else. The purpose of achieving better balance between large and small ensemble experience is not so students will spend less time with a conductor in front of them, but so they will spend less time with a music stand in front of them.[6]

Therefore, the central ensemble framework in the integral model is the small, creative music ensemble in which participants improvise and perform compositions of group members—hence, direct alignment with the primary purposes of private instruction, construed integrally. However, consistent with integral paradigms across fields, this does not replace conventional chamber music or large ensemble participation. Rather, it rebuilds the entire ensemble edifice around the creativity-based, small ensemble core. To be sure, this will require *redistribution* of curricular requirements, and the number of hours students spend per week in large ensembles, which are typically privileged in this regard. But I believe the broader, more integrative, and creativity-driven musical artistry that will be cultivated will more than compensate and give rise to unprecedented levels of vitality and passion, if not performance excellence, in the entire ensemble spectrum.

To reiterate, the restructuring of music studies atop creative foundations, while calling for redistribution of conventional areas within a far broader, yet more integrated scope, aims at a considerably broader conception of human creativity and consciousness development. The new conception of performance, with correspondingly revised approaches to private instruction and ensembles, represents a more differentiated parts-to-whole framework that will then more powerfully elicit, and integrate, complementary whole-to-parts consciousness-based engagement.

PILLAR #2: MUSIC INQUIRY AND CRAFT

Music inquiry and craft, the second pillar, vastly expands the prevailing notion of what constitutes a core curriculum, which, as noted, is normally centered in theory, history, and performance. A typical semester for first- and second-year music majors will look something like this:

- 2–3 credits music theory and aural skills
- 2–3 credits music history
- 1–2 credits keyboard harmony
- 2–4 credits private lessons
- 2 credits ensembles
- 6–8 credits electives or other requirements

As an alternative to the first two categories, I propose the Integral Learning Environment (ILE), an eight-credit, creativity-based, highly diverse and integrative paradigm that unites these and other areas atop improvisatory/compositional engagement and development within a single class. ILE functions at once as a musicianship class that broaches craft, performance ensemble, laboratory for creative exploration, and forum for wide-ranging conceptual inquiry.[7]

Integral Learning Environment

ILE is far more than the combining of conventional core areas in a single class. Rather, ILE turns the whole musicianship enterprise on its head: the driving force is improvisatory and compositional development, with theoretical, historical (both of which are renamed and reconceived, as noted above), and a wide range of other studies, serving to promote this creative development. The purpose of including improvisation and composition in the curriculum, unlike lower order change advocacy would have it, is *not* to enhance achievement in theory, history, and other areas of musicianship development. Rather, the purpose of including theory, history, and other areas of musicianship in the curriculum is to enhance improvisatory and compositional development, a by-product of which will be levels of conceptual understanding (theoretical, cultural, cognitive, historical, transpersonal/spiritual) that dwarf what is possible in conventional models.[8] The significance of this conceptual turn is underscored by the epistemic continuum and its sequence of identity shifts: the neo-Eurocentric identity is Interpretive Performance Specialist, instantiated from the time of the division of labor. The lower order neo-Eurocentric-plus identity is Interpretive Performance Specialist-plus, the musician who still views the musical landscape through a neo-Eurocentric interpretive lens but engages in a broader slate of activity. The higher order, Contemporary Improviser Composer Performer identity represents a foundational shift in sense of musical being. The Integral Learning Environment and its vastly expanded and richly unified spectrum is predicated on this identity shift.

Elsewhere I provide an elaborate account of the trajectory of the model and will only give a synopsis here.[9] In essence, ILE includes the entire scope of the systematic improvisatory development spectrum: multiple improvisatory and compositional languages, new and expanded approaches to aural skills (involving both principle instrument and voice), rhythmic training, embodied musicianship, melodic fluency, harmonic studies, keyboard, and openings to a range of conceptual areas, as noted previously. ILE functions both as musicianship skills laboratory and as ensemble, within which students improvise and for which they compose. Further, all students in ILE participate in small creative music ensembles, again involving improvising and composing, from within the larger group. Students also work on other musicianship projects, including rhythm and aural skills in small-group formats. Lucy Green has written extensively and insightfully on how the informal, student-driven learning in popular music, much of which takes place in groups, differs significantly from the institution-driven formal learning of the academy.[10] The ILE small ensemble format straddles both of these worlds.

In terms of logistics, ILE is a four-semester sequence that occupies the first two years of a music degree program. Each semester is an eight-credit class, which is typically half of the roughly sixteen credits students would take in each of those first four semesters within a 120-credit degree program. In addition to ILE, students would take private instruction on their principal instrument, ensemble, and one or two electives. They would not take separate coursework in theory, aural skills, or history during these first two years.

Low Overhead–High Yield Pedagogy

An important aspect of the class involves key gateway activities that connect improvisatory and compositional work with rigorous pursuit of craft skills. I characterize these as "low overhead–high yield"[11] pedagogical strategies in that they require minimal instructor intervention, yet consist in intensive, rigorous engagement that delivers powerful skills. Examples include melodic aural transposition, involving working out by ear patterns given in one key in all keys. Starting with simple folk songs and melodic cells (e.g., scales in thirds), progressing to more virtuosic melodies and scale patterns (permutations of seventh chords), this is intensive work that yields indispensable tools for CICPs. Another example is solo transcription, which is common in the jazz tradition, in which one emulates the work of master improvisers. ILE deploys an approach inspired by David Liebman in which students first sing the solo, then learn it on their instrument, then notate it. The purpose of transcription in ILE is not to stockpile a reservoir of idiomatic phrases that are to be regurgitated, to put it crudely. It is to internalize deeply rooted—what I would from an integral standpoint call "archetypally rich"—style features that inform melodic, harmonic, and rhythmic skill development. Indeed, solo transcription is as much rhythmic training as it is melodic or harmonic. Again, this is an intensive practice that requires minimal instruction intervention yet yields optimal results for musical practice and understanding. I regard aural transcription and transcription as among the most rigorous forms of both aural and technical development available, even if outside of jazz study they have been generally absent in overall curricula.[12]

A third example is keyboard realization, which warrants some elaboration given its relevance to intersecting terrain between ILE and the harmonic focus of conventional musicianship studies.

Keyboard Realization

Regardless of principal instrument, all students in ILE do considerable work at the keyboard, which is the primary (but not sole) vehicle for harmonic studies in the program. The basic concept of keyboard realization is that by translating chord symbol—whether from contemporary jazz/popular music lead sheets or baroque figured bass lines (precursors to today's lead sheets)—into sound, unmatched levels of fluency and command of harmonic structures are possible. This is very different than reading the notes of chords as spelled out in conventional notation, which might be done regardless of knowledge of the actual structures. Realization of chords from symbols requires a higher level of internalization. It requires minimal technical expertise at the keyboard, thereby being immediately accessible to students who have hardly even touched the piano prior to the class. However, this should not suggest diminished challenge to these students, let alone accomplished pianists. Working out harmonic progressions from an initial pattern in all keys, without the aid of notation (save for the initial key in which the pattern is presented), is a formidable task, particularly when the progressions span eight bars and include applied chords, modal mixture, altered chords, and chord extensions. Moreover, I have noticed through the years that students with minimal keyboard backgrounds, after an initial period of challenge, at times outperform piano principals in this kind of work. I surmise that this may be due to the fact that it confronts piano majors, whose entire musical lives are consumed with learning fully notated repertory, with entirely different ways of being at the keyboard.[13]

What about written harmonic work, which is the focus of conventional approaches?[14] ILE situates all written work in harmony along a continuum that always begins with keyboard application. The first written application involves students simply writing what they play at the keyboard. This ensures that students hear what they are writing, which is a significant challenge in conventional theory coursework. This is followed by approaches in which they can explore different kinds of spacing, voicings, and voice leading possibilities for which written application is more conducive. Five-part contemporary writing, based in jazz/pop keyboard work, where students play and thus write one note in the bass and a four-note structure in the treble clef, is the mainstay of ILE keyboard realization and written work. However, a unit on the four-part Bach chorale style writing that has long been part and parcel of conventional theory coursework is also included. Here, however, consistent with the ILE approach to jazz written work, a unit of figured bass realization at the keyboard precedes written application, which begins—unlike in conventional approaches—with "keyboard style" realization that is modeled directly after what students play. Bach-chorale style writing then follows.[15]

I would add that the overarching harmonic scheme in ILE is similar to that of conventional theory coursework, proceeding from diatonic to nondiatonic chord functions (applied chords, secondary dominants, modal mixture, altered chords).

Rhythmic Studies and Embodied Musicianship

When one steps back from conventional categories and inquires into what twenty-first-century musicians need for creative navigation, any informed account will not only place rhythmic skills high on the list, almost as essential as improvisatory skills, but also specify a realm within the contemporary rhythmic landscape that is of overwhelming significance: Black Atlantic Rhythm—meaning, rhythmic practices originating in Africa and assuming prominence and impact in musical cultures on both sides of the Atlantic, particularly in African American traditions, which then have been transmitted across the globe. Indeed, a strong case could be made for Black Atlantic Rhythm (BAR)[16] as a kind of "common practice" twenty-first-century skill area that equals the significance of European common practice harmony, which has long occupied the curricular core, in prior centuries. Because BAR is learned not in isolation but in conjunction with improvising and composing, and also pitch languages, in a single stroke the incorporation of an essential skill area also brings to the curricular mix powerful breadth and integrative properties that elude prevailing visioning let alone application.[17]

Moreover, BAR fluency strongly invites a musical embodiment component.[18] No aspect of music flows through the psychophysiology as does rhythm. Furthermore, different rhythmic languages, with their different cultural origins, flow through the body in different ways. I commonly instruct my classical students as they make their initial forays into jazz improvising to simply observe the contrasting ways in which classical musicians and jazz musicians move when they play. This is perhaps most dramatic on an instrument such as the saxophone, which while primarily a jazz/blues instrument in terms of its prominence in the musical world, has a bona fide classical tradition—in the sense of composed-notated repertory played by Interpretive Performance Specialists (as well as some saxophonists who are also jazz artists). With classical saxophonists, as with many other performers in this tradition, bodily movement tends to be more in the upper body, with dramatic and often choppy arm motion involving flapping elbows. With jazz saxophonists, there is more of a sense of full bodily flow, as if the music is a kind of current that emanates deep in the being of the artist and radiates through the body to the listener and environment. Whether my theory holds, that the differences in musical embodiment are rooted in the improvisatory/black music rhythmic foundations of jazz as opposed to the interpretive function and its white/European rhythmic foundations in classical performance, may be a topic for further research. Might, furthermore, the phenomenon of "embodied musical racism"—whereby culturally mediated physicality precludes engagement across cultural boundaries—be added to the litany of criteria that need to be addressed if music studies is to truly assume diversity leadership? While that topic warrants further attention, most important at the moment is that rhythm is arguably the domain in which the relationship with musical embodiment is most direct. Because Black Atlantic Rhythm seems to have global resonance, this points toward the importance of this form of embodiment for curricula and models that aspire toward transcultural navigation.[19]

World Music

Recalling discussion from the previous chapter, all music is world music, and musicians thus optimally forge connections with other cultures through creative grounding in that which is primary. The Integral Learning Environment lays groundwork for this by promoting a CICP creative identity, and also carefully selecting openings to diverse cultural practices that further elicit this kind of connection. Improvisation on drones, utilizing both Western and non-Western modal structures (Hindustani *raga*, Arabic *maqam*), and culturally informed rhythmic hybrids are primary examples. How, then, does more formal engagement with intact cultures occur? This takes place at the curricular upper-structure, through electives or requirements in ethnomusicology and other coursework that provide this experience. As emphasized in chapter 2, once interior, creativity-based linkages are in place, students are empowered to explore a range of possibilities, including in-residence immersion in another musical culture, according to their needs and interests.

Technology

The discovery of a flute, made from the hollow wing bone of a giant vulture that may date back over forty thousand years, indicates how far back technology goes in music. From an integral, transcultural standpoint, important underlying principles remain unchanged even if the technology itself has changed radically. The purpose of technology—whether in the form of the modern flute, midi, or interactive improvisation and composition software—is to provide an outlet for the flow of creative expressions from transcendent dimensions of consciousness through the personal voice of the artist to the world. Just as creativity and consciousness differentiate into untold new possibilities, so does technology. One of the challenges inherent in the incorporation of technology in music curricula is that the absence of creative foundations has rendered the field prone to reversing the relationship, where the technology itself becomes the driving force. For example, when music education students are required to take technology coursework or training because this is part and parcel of the current generation of students they will be teaching, confusion about the actual purpose of the instruction almost ensures that it becomes cut off from deeper artistic and aesthetic concerns, at which point, teaching about the transformative dimensions of the arts risks being reduced to gimmicks and gadgets. In chapters 5 and 7 I broach parallels with technological development and exploration in the world at large—as in genetic modification of life forms and the food supply, self-replicating artificial intelligence, increasingly destructive weaponry—and the ramifications thereof when separate from spiritual unfolding and intention. While an obsession with gimmicks and gadgets in music may not pose direct threats to the future of humanity, the same obsession in a broader context may indeed pose such threats.[20]

Helpful to the way forward is to identify contrasting functions of technology and to critically examine their contributions as well as drawbacks. Examples of pedagogical function include aural skills and music theory (construed conventionally here) software, and rhythm section backgrounds for jazz improvisation practice. One of the problems with the latter application is it can condition improvisers into playing with live musicians as if they were playing with machines. Notation software serves as an aid for composers in terms of legibility of scores and parts, although not so much the actual composition process itself. While the software is becoming increasingly sophisticated, there is still the risk of composers writing what they know can be readily notated and avoiding terrain that may pose challenges to the software. A music production function is fulfilled through recording software such as

Pro Tools.[21] Interactive compositional and improvisational software begins to move further into technology becoming an integral aspect of the creative process. While there is no denying that the integration of technology must be part and parcel to foundational overhaul of music studies, I believe there is an urgent need to ground this integration in emergent aesthetic principles and to carefully examine how underlying assumptions in conventional practice, and even neo-Eurocentric-plus/multicultural reform thinking, have contributed to confusion, if not a skewed relationship, when it comes to the potentially transformative function of technology. In this regard, music technology can be seen as a microcosm of the advent of technological advances in the world at large. To reiterate an above point: when technology, exemplifying the exterior dimensions of human creativity, becomes disconnected from the interior dimensions of consciousness, what could be an essential gateway to new evolutionary possibilities can become just as powerful a threat to survival.

Historical Understanding

The transcultural paradigm also approaches music history in a fundamentally different manner. Instead of conventional approaches that retrace the timeline of the European classical tradition over the past five centuries or more, or neo-Eurocentric-plus modifications that may identify alternative entryways and sequences, the transcultural approach grounds historical inquiry in the creativity/consciousness-driven individuation process. In other words, the self-historical trajectory that takes hold in the evolution of the personalized artistic voice serves as the basis for formal historical studies. Two practical manifestations are noted. First is that no formal music history coursework is required in the first two years of the model. Rather, historical connections are made as they relate to the contemporary improvisation, composition, and performance framework of ILE. From this standpoint, present-based entryways may spawn any number of spontaneously emerging connections, and some that are preordained, to aesthetic, theoretical, cultural, cognitive, transpersonal, and historical terrain. An initial phase of historical engagement, then, is situated within a broader, richly interwoven tapestry, at the heart of which is creative expression and rigorous engagement in aural, somatic, harmonic, melodic, rhythmic, and other areas.

At the level of the curricular upper-structure, students can then select from a range of formal historical coursework.

Further ILE Terrain

ILE, as noted, also creates openings to a range of other areas, including many that are not typically broached at the core curriculum level. As always, all conceptual terrain is accessed as it organically extends from direct creativity/ consciousness engagement. Inquiry into the improvisation process itself, for example, spawns cognitive, transpersonal, cultural, historical, and aesthetic connections that can be harnessed, even if this occurs only in introductory ways in the first two years of the ILE context. A similar cross-disciplinary continuum could be identified in respect to meditation practice. The basic idea is that organic links from hands-on, creative/transcendent experience through gateway analytical terrain establishes an interior conceptual synapse that is brimming with meaning and excitement and thus invites further studies at the appropriate time in a given student's development.

PILLAR #3: MUSIC PEDAGOGY

The third pillar is music pedagogy. While new pedagogical approaches to musicianship within a reconceived paradigm of what comprises the skill set of the twenty-first-century musician have already been discussed, the primary focus here is the advent of a jazz-based, integral (and thus transcultural) model for preparing music education majors to gain skills in classroom pedagogy for the public schools. It should go without saying that the impetus here is not to prepare music teachers with jazz pedagogy skills that might be added to their conventional neo-Eurocentric or neo-Eurocentric-plus pedagogical skill set. Rather, the impetus is to prepare teachers as Contemporary Improvisers Composers Performers, grounded in a paradigm of jazz as *writ large*, who are able to revolutionize public school music in alignment with the creativity and diversity of today's music world.

Therefore, conventional neo-Eurocentric approaches to teacher education coursework that are confined largely to European classical materials and their offshoots (e.g., children's songs) must be fundamentally reconceived. This must therefore go beyond lower order, neo-Eurocentric-plus approaches that recognize the need for cultural and epistemic diversity and thus augment the conventional foundations accordingly. It is also important, in delineating the new framework, to call attention to a glaring tendency in conventional teacher training programs. This involves students studying techniques of broaching musical terrain for which they have no musical foundations. A primary example is when music education students are required to take or elect coursework in jazz pedagogy with little or no background in jazz itself. Not only does this significantly limit the depth of instruction, if not essentially ensuring that confused and misguided concepts are disseminated as matriculating teachers enter the public schools, but it also perpetuates a particularly pernicious ethnocentric/racialized message: whereas aspiring music teachers take teacher education coursework related to teaching European classical music with significant grounding in that tradition, jazz—the thinking goes—requires no such prior grounding for successful teaching of this tradition to America's young people. This is not only denigrating but also pedagogically and artistically weak and incoherent—a perfect example of what has been called the "hidden curriculum."[22] In other words, while no course syllabus explicitly states that jazz is subordinate, the notion implicit in offering jazz pedagogy coursework to students without jazz foundations, and the same could be said for any musical genre beyond European classical, essentially drills home that message. Moreover, similar to the exnomination practices considered in the previous chapter, where European classical music is referred to as "art music" or "Western art music," thereby proclaiming without stating it explicitly that other kinds of music do not constitute art, the effect may be ever more damaging than the explicit denigration of the genres in question.

Here a general principle and two subsets bear emphasis: It is imperative to establish a creativity-based identity in music education students prior to their taking teacher education methods coursework; any benefits to be derived from this coursework prior to such identity formation will pale to what may be gained afterward. Inasmuch as jazz will be central to that identity for twenty-first-century American music majors, this will fulfill two constituent principles—first is that prior to learning about techniques of teaching jazz, students will have embarked on serious study of the art form. Second is that prior to taking ethnomusicology coursework or so-called world music methods coursework, establishment of the CICP identity is paramount. Otherwise, there is no interior mechanism for anything beyond distanced fascination and scattered bits of information and perhaps some practices from other cultures.

PILLAR #4: MUSIC AND CONSCIOUSNESS

The relationship between music and consciousness spans multiple dimensions. One involves the process-mediated transformations in consciousness characteristic of peak improvisatory, compositional, and performance engagement. These parts-to-whole epistemologies, which find their fulfillment in part of the systematic improvisatory development continuum central to the integral music studies model, are central to the evolution of creativity and consciousness over time in the individuation process—the blossoming of a distinctly personal artistic voice that is uniquely possible among CICPs. The second entails complementary meditation-based, whole-to-parts engagement, to be discussed in detail in chapter 5. There I delineate a systematic meditation continuum that parallels the improvisatory framework. Jazz, as the twentieth-/twenty-first-century reincarnation of the CICP-plus musical identity, brings the parts-to-whole/whole-to-parts improvisation/meditation relationship to the epistemic mix, revealing in this idiom the exquisite interior circuitry that I call a uniquely differentiated soul pathway.

A third area involves inquiry into the nature of consciousness, which as I also explore in chapter 5, and considers a range of views on the topic. With the nondual integral perspective placed front and center, a wide-angled lens is available that sheds light on the range of perspectives, including dualism, materialism, and—closely aligned with the integral—panpsychism and idealism. Directly extending from this approach is a fourth realm of consideration, involving the music-consciousness relationship. From a process perspective, the improvisatory core of human creativity is seen as a manifestation of the improvisatory core of cosmic creativity. From a structural perspective, correlations between primordial frequencies that result from the self-referral reverberations of eternal consciousness, the source of all being, and musical sound—including pitch and rhythmic languages—come into view. The Time Theory of Indian music, for example, posits specific correspondence between the intervallic structures of ragas and frequencies in the daily cycle, thus indicating that the transformative impact of the raga is optimal when they are performed at specific times of day.[23] Parallel ideas can be traced back in the West to Plato and Pythagoras, with Plato emphasizing attention to the effect of specific modes on human behavior for the sake of social harmony and progress.[24] Pressing's notion, mentioned above, of Black Atlantic Rhythm, whereby he correlates the ubiquitous nature of rhythmic practices that originated in Africa and further evolved through its diasporic extensions, and the spiritual impact often associated with these practices, to deep dimensions in human consciousness, is an important contemporary example.[25] The fact that jazz combines primordial improvisation processes and primordial rhythmic processes, and that the jazz tradition includes a long legacy of leading innovators that were significantly engaged in consciousness-based inquiry and practices, renders the idiom a particularly fertile lens into the nature of consciousness.

PILLAR #5: MUSIC AND SOCIETY

The fifth new pillar is music and society. This encompasses the range of areas that might fall within outreach, or arts ambassadorship, that extend directly from the enlivenment of self-organizing impetus for artistic individuation to the world at large. This includes embrace of, and engagement with, music and musicians in the immediate community of a given music school. It includes programs in the schools, as well as outreach programs for adults and the general population that are directly predicated on raising awareness of the emergent paradigm of music studies in the broader population. The celebration of the African American roots of American music, both from the standpoint of self-cultural identity and broader navigation and syncretism, is an essential aspect of the aesthetic dimensions of the music and society pillar. Also important, related to the prior pillar, is a consciousness-based transformative thrust that harnesses jazz's unique capacities to deliver a spirituality paradigm that, at once, transcends denominational categories yet also embraces denominational tributaries.

The music and society pillar can thus be thought of as an extension of the music pedagogy pillar, whereby the very preparation for the emergent artistic profile preparation that happens in the classroom becomes a parallel kind of preparation for emergent audiences. From this standpoint, the realm of entrepreneurship, among the most recent change themes in prevailing reform discourse, takes on new dimensions. While initially driven by the need to help musicians find professional outlets in a highly competitive world, typically approached through neo-Eurocentric and neo-Eurocentric-plus lenses, entrepreneurship from an integral vantage point opens up to broader transformational dimensions that are grounded in the idea of a creativity and consciousness revolution. A distinction between lower order and higher order conceptions of the theme follows.

Entrepreneurship: Lower-Order and Higher-Order Conceptions

It is important to recognize at the outset the origins of the entrepreneurship area as a response to a long-standing promise that a degree in music would, for the majority of music students, ensure employment in at least one of two primary areas that are related to the neo-Eurocentric framework.[26] Music education majors would find teaching positions in the public schools. Classical performance majors would find seats in symphony orchestras, with those few graduates who were particularly gifted perhaps embarking on careers as solo recitalists. While the job market for music teachers seems to be fairly robust, the financial hardships of many symphony orchestras, combined with the glut of qualified candidates pouring into the job market every year, has caused the classical music career bubble to burst. As a result, the central orientation of music studies, if not justification for its very existence, would come under scrutiny. The emergent discipline of entrepreneurship, predicated on the need for musicians to develop skills for forging their own pathways in the professional world, is one line of response to this scrutiny.

Because of these origins, entrepreneurship would thus be yet another example of a lower order change pursuit that fails to recognize itself as an extension of, and therefore as inheriting significant aspects of, an inherently limited paradigm. Instead of seeking to transform the foundations that perpetuate the specialized skill set, entrepreneurship has instead sought largely to render specialists better able to market their specialty. Just as multiculturalism appears to be a corrective antidote to monoculturalism, but in fact inherits a significant facet (epistemic ambivalence when it comes to the personal creative voice) from its perceived oppressor, entrepreneurship can also be seen as a seemingly progressive corrective measure that, while not viewing the entrepreneurially deficient roots from which it sprang as oppressive, also inherits significant limitations from those roots. Although it goes without saying that it is far preferable to have skills in marketing what one does than not, professional opportunities—let alone creative expression, artistic fulfillment, and the host of criteria that characterize creativity-based musical understanding—will always remain limited as long as the baseline profile remains confined to the IPS, or even IPS-plus.

A further, even more distressing casualty of neo-Eurocentric and neo-Eurocentric-plus approaches to entrepreneurship is that they perpetuate the prevailing worldview of musical academe to society at large. It must always be kept in mind that the ongoing search for, and landing of, employment opportunities is far more than a values-neutral endeavor, involving what seems to be the perfectly justifiable quest for a musician to make a living. Indeed, inherent in this quest is the direct transmission of musical value systems to the community—which when these are mired in hidden (or overt) ethnocentric/racialized biases, is deeply troublesome. Consider as an example the following scenarios involving chamber ensembles and their work in the community.

A common manifestation of the neo-Eurocentric approach to entrepreneurial arts ambassadorship might involve a chamber music ensemble, say a string quartet, that plays standard classical repertory and perhaps new, commissioned works that are largely based in the contemporary extension of that compositional stream. The group receives funding to help cover commissioning costs as well as performances in a range of settings, including underserved communities. The thinking is that the arts can be a powerful tool for empowering individuals of all backgrounds. Little regard, however, is made toward the need for culturally relevant artistic expression that is directly connected to the communities encountered. Thus, the neo-Eurocentric result involves yet further efforts to colonize all cultural locations with a single cultural worldview. The point is not that there is no place for European classical music in any given community, but that the empowerment of the artistic richness of those communities, through performances that directly link to that tradition, is central to actually upholding this broader arts-driven transformative mission.

Whereas the neo-Eurocentric approach to entrepreneurship, and broader arts-driven transformation, is—consistent with its monocultural and monoepistemic underpinnings—to augment interpretive specialist studies with marketing training, the lower order neo-Eurocentric-plus approach to this problem is—consistent with its mission—somewhat more expansive. In addition to adding coursework in entrepreneurship, attention is also devoted to preparing musicians to traverse broader terrain. Therefore, the neo-Eurocentric-plus string quartet can, like its neo-Eurocentric counterpart, play Hayden, Beethoven, and Bartok, and can also do more current, contemporary work that may infuse influences of jazz, popular music, and perhaps broader global influences. There might even be some improvising involved in some of the pieces. However, because this typically means not a shift in musical identity from interpreter to creator, but rather interpreter who may do some creating, this is incomplete. In other words, musicians remain grounded in a worldview that peers out onto the broader landscape through a neo-Eurocentric lens. While a step in the right direction, it thus still falls far short of what is needed because it reinforces the notion that European classical repertory, or at least interpretive performance (which can be applied to virtually all music), occupies the aesthetic/pedagogical/cultural center. Once again, the sheer force of the monocultural imprint that constrains even multicultural efforts at expansion cannot be underestimated. Until a wholesale shift in musical foundations and thus musical identity transpires, the situation will remain unchecked: entrepreneurial progressivity will masquerade as artistically viable and socially just, when it is far from either.

By contrast, the deepest connections with communities are found when artists exhibit genuine grounding in, if not the music of the community itself, connecting terrain that is at the heart of our own American culture. Grounding in Black Atlantic Rhythm, to once again reinvoke Jeff Pressing's heading that encompasses a seminal rhythmic stream in the twenty-first-century musical ocean, is a particularly powerful tool that, from my own experience, I see lacking in neo-Eurocentric-plus entrepreneurial visioning. Inasmuch as improvisation is the primary delivery system for BAR, roots in jazz emerge as central to this kind of authenticity. It is one thing to play an arrangement for string quartet, or bassoon or brass ensemble, of a Beatles tune or James Brown song. It is another to actually be able to express oneself with authentic grounding in the black music roots from which this material originates. There is a parallel here to the gateway principle considered earlier in the context of the Integral Learning Environment. Just as conceptual knowledge, as well as engagement with music of other cultures, needs to be connected to hands-on, creative engagement, the same holds for engaging communities with music that might not be at the forefront of their cultural experience. It is imperative that musicians are able to create music that bridges terrain of the culture in which they perform.

Which is precisely where the higher order, integral approach excels. Now an ensemble of Contemporary Improvisers Composers Performers who possess strong jazz grounding comes into view as exemplary; it could be a string quartet, woodwind quintet, or any combination of instruments, providing participants gain the paradigmatically new grounding inherent in the proposed vision. As I emphasized earlier, the envisioned shift in music schools from large conducted ensembles as the central performance format to small creative music ensembles, which considerably extends the growing emphasis on chamber music, is invaluable to musicians who later become members of chamber music ensembles with conventional instrumentation but that combine standard repertory with broader explorations. This grounding enables greater authenticity and personalized expressivity in that all members will be proficient improvisers/composers. Nothing is more powerful to listeners than hearing musicians tell personalized stories on their instruments/voices. Furthermore, the higher order ensemble, representing the higher order worldview and corresponding entrepreneurial framework, is actually far more capable of collaborating with musicians from the communities encountered, another powerful feature of the emergent approach.

AACM as Embodiment of Integral Entrepreneurship and Transformative Leadership

It is difficult to imagine a more direct embodiment of the integral entrepreneurial paradigm than the Association for the Advancement of Creative Musicians. In George Lewis's view, development of "strategies for individual and collective self-production and promotion that both reframed the artist-business relationship, and challenged racialized limitations on venues and infrastructure"[27] provides but a glimpse of this model's scope. The fact that the entrepreneurial facets of this model cannot be separated from the creative, experimental, and collaborative nature of the music itself, the need to render self-governing and self-deterministic faculties among the musicians who create it, the pedagogical incentive to develop forthcoming generations of musical artists/visionaries, the societal imperative to enliven a corresponding artistic awareness in the community, and the spiritual dimensions of the entire enterprise points to yet another emergent theme in music studies that may be reconceived through the lens of black music. Few among even the most progressive music entrepreneurship programs, because they typically exist in conventional, neo-Eurocentric or neo-Eurocentric-plus environments and are immediately constrained by outmoded curricular models that undermine creativity and self-organizing foundations, can lay claim to anything remotely resembling this organic interweaving of entrepreneurship within a broader transformative vision. Although one might argue that economic challenges as well as those of racial prejudice confronting many musicians were among the primary initial catalysts for the founding of the AACM, these issues were never separated from the even more foundational premise that artistic creativity is the key to addressing these issues and broader societal transformation. Recalling commentary from chapter 1 about the formidable array of areas of musical development that are rendered self-driven in the integral model—from self-transcending, self-diversifying, self-integrative, and self-pedagogical to self-critical and self-navigational growth, now a self-entrepreneurial facet may be added to the list.

Unfortunately, as I discuss below, the AACM has scarcely registered in the culture of academic jazz studies, let alone mainstream practice in music studies at large.

Improvisation across Fields

Another aspect of the music and society pillar is the recognition of improvisation as a core aspect to creativity across wide-ranging disciplines. Architecture, business, education, law, medicine, and sports are among the many examples of fields that have begun to look to jazz's improvisatory roots for inspiration and innovation pathways. This kind of work is sometimes characterized as New Jazz Studies.[28] Whereas conventional jazz studies aims to prepare present and future generations of jazz artists, New Jazz Studies harnesses principles from the music as they apply across fields. What I have proposed as "Integral Jazz Studies"[29] takes the further step of situating improvisation within the broader context of consciousness, making possible further vistas of transformation.

Deep Inquiry Group

A further aspect of the music and society pillar involves the formation of frameworks for jazz-based discussion, practice, and visioning that broach the furthest reaches of ultimate reality and meaning. In chapter 7, I discuss a framework that I call the "Deep Inquiry Group"—which is oriented for the general public and provides a systematic means for guiding thinking from third-person, conventional terrain to second-person, creativity-based considerations to first-person, consciousness-based inquiry that invites individuals to explore ideas at the edges of the human imagination. This is yet another facet of the broader creativity and consciousness revolution that will illuminate the function of the arts, and particularly improvised musical art, as transformative catalyst. Just as CICP-based musicianship extends the roots of twenty-first-century musical artistry deeper than ever and yields unprecedented horizontal navigation, the jazz inspired Deep Inquiry Framework extends the roots of reflection deeper than ever into the innermost dimensions of consciousness, shedding new insights on educational, social justice, environmental, artistic, spiritual, and other realms that will be key within the broader creativity and consciousness revolution. The Deep Inquiry Group harnesses capacities inherent in jazz to swing freely between the most localized, third-person attention to detail and the biggest questions of human nature, purpose, evolutionary potential, and the relationship between humanity and cosmos.

The Deep Inquiry Group is also where the five pillars of the emergent jazz-inspired music studies paradigm can be seen most clearly as interwoven points within the arts portion of the spirituality-art-science trinity that undergirds the jazz-driven creativity-consciousness revolution. Indeed, each pillar—music creation, music inquiry and craft, music pedagogy, music and consciousness, music and society—can be seen as an aperture to the entirety. The five pillars can thus be thought of as channels—perhaps comparable to the meridians in psychophysiology that are central to traditional Chinese and other forms of medicine, or even the notion that rivers function the same way in the "psychophysiology of the Earth"—through which the improvisatory essence of the cosmos flows from deep within the soul level through the educational system, is instilled in individuals coming through that system, and in turn is transmitted to the world.

JAZZ PRIVILEGING? OR JAZZ AS TRANSCULTURAL GATEWAY?

Jazz, particularly when construed as self-transcending, and thus as writ large, embodies the higher order, integral vision and provides a conceptual, cultural (transcultural), and pedagogical template atop which the entire field of music studies may be rebuilt. Whereas the premise, either stated explicitly or not, that underlies lower order, neo-Eurocentric-plus approaches is that music studies will be reformed atop European classical foundations (strict multiculturalists may not admit to this, but nonetheless often default to it via unexamined epistemic assumptions), I believe the time has come to turn this thinking on its head and rebuild the field atop African American musical foundations. As shown above along a number of parameters, this does not mean the imposing of a self-confining jazz-centric orientation in which—succumbing to the same lapse that dominates the prevailing neo-Eurocentric orientation—all other music is cast to the periphery. Instead, it means the establishment of a process-rich self-transcending core, along with key structural elements that promote the same goal, that enables wide-ranging musical navigation and substantive engagement in the various points of contact, including European classical music, along the route. When I speak of a jazz-driven Afro-Euro-global nexus that poses important ramifications for private lessons, musicianship, and ensembles, I am not only arguing that, as one occasionally hears, jazz skills can benefit classical performers, but also taking the further step of arguing for new levels of virtuosity on a principal instrument, harmonic, melodic, rhythmic, and other kinds of fluency, and understanding of the fundamental workings of music that can be applied across genres and disciplines. In a single stroke, by grounding music studies in America in its own cultural roots, European classical music takes its next evolutionary strides, and foundations are established that enable deep connections across cultural boundaries.

Inasmuch as this perspective is nonetheless likely to elicit concerns about replacing one hegemony, that of the prevailing neo-Eurocentric framework, with another that is centered in jazz, I believe the following strategies are key to productive discourse on this point.

The first is to step back from the term *jazz* in hopes of circumventing the above reactions. This entails simply articulating at the outset that if an important curricular aspiration is to prepare musicians who are able to traverse culturally diverse horizons, and it is difficult to imagine a more pressing twenty-first-century imperative, then it is essential to prioritize the skills and understanding needed. Formidable improvisation skills and establishment of a creative artistic identity immediately catapult to the top of the list. Closely related, moreover, is that this improvising must be grounded in contemporary rhythmic foundations, paramount among which for global infusion and excursion are African American time feels. It must also be grounded in fluency with pitch languages, particularly modality, given the prominence of improvisation in some sort of modal format across the globe. As emphasized in the previous chapter, the aim is not to prepare musicians with sufficient expertise to play traditional music in cultures across the globe, which in any case is not possible. Rather, it is to prepare musicians to establish a creativity-based relationship with the contemporary musical world and its rich diversity through infusion of influences in the individual voice, and to also engage in productive and meaningful collaborations with musicians from diverse cultures who share these aims. This means that all participants in these collaborations commit to finding some kind of common ground, rather than expecting their collaborators to achieve mastery in their particular musical lineages.

At this point, concerning the question of where these key tools may be most directly accessed, ideally in integrative form as opposed to in isolated, piecemeal compartments, the conversation can then return to the realm of genre through this expanded lens. Even from a marginally informed perspective on what it means for musicians—and, again, my focus is on musicians from America (and perhaps other regions in the West) embarking on global excursions from their self-cultural point of departure—to navigate across cultural horizons, a strong case for jazz as a primary source, without a remote second, begins to come into view. With a more complete account of what jazz brings to the enterprise, including specific kinds of culturally diverse collaboration (e.g., Jazz-Hindustani, Jazz-Arabic, etc.) and examination of the pathways of real-world artistic exemplars, the case only gains in strength. Therefore, from the standpoint of cultural diversity alone, residual objections about jazz-centric privileging may be countered with a powerful rejoinder: jazz foundations make possible a scope of navigation that dwarfs what is typically achieved, let alone imagined, from the multicultural perspective.

When the conversation takes the further step of situating jazz-based diversity tools with the broader disciplinary expanse also encompassed in the systematic improvisatory development framework, the argument for jazz occupying a central place in the curricular, cultural, and organizational structures of the music school of the future in America, and possibly far beyond, approaches inevitability. I believe, moreover, that the argument for a music studies paradigm in America that is constructed atop self-transcending jazz foundations gains further strength when situated within the context of an overarching revolution in creativity and consciousness in education in society. The richly differentiated soul pathway of the jazz CICP framework not only represents a cutting-edge development in music studies, but one that spawns important ramifications across wide-ranging fields.

Nzewi's powerful argument for the importance of traditional music in music studies in Africa both parallels and sums up my argument for the foundational role of African American music in music studies in America. "Traditional musics (of Africa) contain all that are needed in philosophy, theoretical content and principles of practice for culturally meaningful and independent modern music education at any level in Africa and perhaps, elsewhere."[30] By replacing the term *Africa* with *America*, and specifying that—in bringing the terms together—African American music constitutes "traditional music" in America, the same statement offers key wisdom to the way forward. This is all the more so upon elaboration of Nzewi's intriguing words "and perhaps, elsewhere."[31] Here is where the nexus between African American and European classical traditions, from which extend further global connections, can be readily inferred as a further parallel. A powerful framework emerges that is, at once, distinctive of American culture and also exemplary of broader twenty-first-century musical leadership.

CLOSING THOUGHTS

Elsewhere I argue that key to ushering in the emergent paradigm is a jazz/music education alliance.[32] No area more directly embodies the emergent musical paradigm than jazz, providing the idiom is construed transculturally and thus as writ large, while no area more directly straddles conventional practice, and yet is increasingly receptive to new horizons, than music education. Furthermore, music education, as the domain in music studies that prepares public school music teachers, is uniquely positioned to directly impact the broader world, as these teachers serve as the most plentiful ambassadors for whatever paradigm prevails at the respective institutions at which teachers, and administrators, receive their training.[33] Teacher education grounded in jazz-based, integral transcultural principles would not only yield new generations of extraordinarily creative, effective, and socially relevant pedagogues but also, through their work, fulfill Michelle Obama's vision for jazz to occupy an important place in all public schools. While the progressive wing of music education remains constrained by a multicultural orientation, emergent critique of multiculturalism in that field [34]—even if stopping short of a transcultural alternative—suggests receptivity to an expanded diversity vision along the lines of what I propose.

In order for this alliance to bear fruit, however, two further conversations need to transpire. One is within the jazz education community. When all is said and done, conventional jazz studies has not delivered a transcultural, integral paradigm that colleagues might look to for the new foundations. I do not make this statement oblivious to the challenges jazz educationalists have had to overcome at every stage in their efforts to bring serious study of this music in an academic environment predicated on the inherent superiority of the European tradition. Moreover, one might even argue that the conservative horizons of jazz education, whereby an inherently transcultural idiom is confined within multicultural boundaries, are largely due to these challenges. Nonetheless, I do not believe that it is unreasonable, as I and others have argued, to also conclude that jazz studies itself has become engulfed in its own kind of inertia that may fuel the resistance.[35] Overemphasis on the big band at the expense of small ensemble experience, emulative improvisatory work at the expense of the exploratory, reifications of rigid boundaries between what comprises jazz and what does not, and limiting influence of a burgeoning jazz education industry on the interactive and inventive aspects of the music are among the features of a field that has fallen far short of its potential. Here it is also important to point out that many colleagues formulate their conceptions of jazz from the approaches that prevail in their respective music schools, which is yet another factor in perpetuating the multicultural aversion to consideration of jazz's foundational properties. Imagine what a jazz education model—and overall music studies paradigm—might look like if grounded in, to reinvoke Lewis's celebration of the AACM vision, exploration of "new and expanded ideas about sound, relationship between improvisation and composition . . . interpenetration with other musical art worlds, and breakdown of genre definitions or the mobility of practices that informs the present-day musical landscape."[36] Only when this transcultural paradigm takes hold in jazz studies itself is there any chance that it might be embraced by music studies at large.[37]

A second conversation that is key to the jazz/music education alliance involves adherents of the conventional music studies model. If resistance to jazz-inspired transcultural principles is at times formidable among multiculturalists, one can only imagine the struggle to be confronted among the monocultural community, to which music education remains largely accountable.

Chapter Four

New Conversations with Conservatives

I commonly open my addresses at various conferences with the quip that "if I really had guts, I would give this same talk at my own institution,"[1] meaning that it is one thing to advance ideas that depart radically from the norm at symposia that are framed around future visioning and attended by colleagues generally disposed toward such; it is quite another to deliver the same message in one's home community, where—as is the case with most music schools—a conservative orientation tends to prevail. Though I have not entirely shied away from this kind of presentation at my own institution, I have learned over the years that it needs to be framed carefully if productive conversation is to transpire. Notions about "blowing up the curriculum and rebuilding from scratch," while increasingly entertained in reform circles (even if, as discussed, rarely unaccompanied by well-developed alternative visions about what a new model might look like), are not likely to elicit receptivity to productive conversation in conventional ranks.[2]

I also commonly emphasize that if music studies is to significantly advance, not only is there a need for a stronger progressive voice, which correlates with my idea of higher order change discourse, but there is also a need for a stronger conservative voice, by which I mean not only passionate advocacy for the prevailing model of music studies, but also an advocacy that is grounded in compelling, informed, and sophisticated rationale. In my experience, prevailing conversations fall short of these criteria. Conservative sentiments either tend to be voiced largely behind closed doors, partly due to the dictates of political correctness, or they enjoy a kind of unexamined privileged status in public settings. In other words, the onus is on advocates of alternatives to go to great lengths to make their case, while corresponding rationale for prevailing models is rarely if ever required or even expected. The situation is reminiscent of what Thomas Kuhn observes in his study of paradigmatic change in science, where the critical scrutiny bestowed on an emergent model subsides once the new model is in place.[3] In my view, among the most important contributions to be gained from a robust, unapologetic conservative voice, even if driven by little interest in change or innovation of any kind, that it may help illuminate ways in which emergent models will integrate aspects of conventional practice that might not otherwise come into focus. To reiterate an earlier point: the integral jazz CICP paradigm, while calling for wholesale overhaul of music studies from its curricular and conceptual foundations on up, does not exclude studies and practice in European classical music, but rather reintegrates key aspects of that important lineage in a contemporary context. Inspired by Christopher Small, what I call the Afro-Euro nexus will factor significantly in the deliberations and design surrounding this shift. Inasmuch, however, as the nexus will occur atop African American foundations, a principle that even challenges lower order, multicultural change visioning, one can only imagine the challenges this presents to the conventional, monocultural constituency. Accordingly, a first priority for higher order integral change agents is to establish conditions for an entirely new kind of conversation in which a range of perspectives is welcome, but in which the bar is raised for all participants—conservative and progressive alike—to frame their visions with a degree of critical integrity that has not yet prevailed.

I believe a pedagogical/aesthetic inevitability underscores this point—that when all is said and done, the twenty-first-century classical musician (performer, scholar, pedagogue) faces but two options in response to the parameters I set forth. One is to issue a declaration—perhaps a manifesto of sorts—as to the inherent supremacy of European classical music that clearly provides compelling reasons in support of this assertion, reflects an informed grasp of important other lineages (e.g., perhaps those that may be deemed Europe's closest competitors), and places front and center an argument why the improvisatory and compositional foundations of European classical music need not be foundational in a twenty-first-century music curriculum predicated on the preservation of that tradition. Any such statement might be seen as a rejoinder to the 2014 College Music Society "Manifesto"[4] that is among the most recent appeals for change in the field.

A second option, albeit radically departing from the first, is to reclaim the improvisatory and compositional foundations of the European tradition and rebuild it—consistent with the epistemological impetus central to European (and most) improvisers-composers—in a contemporary context. This, of course, would bring jazz to the fore, as both self-cultural (for Americans) core and global gateway. I do not believe there is any middle ground, and that skillful leadership among jazz CICPs can elicit a kind of critical inquiry within conventional circles that exceeds what may be elicited by multicultural advocates.

The chapter seeks to lay groundwork for this kind of conversation. It begins with a brief overview of critical thinking from the perspective of Integral Theory in order to lay groundwork for subsequent commentary. I identify a three-tiered critical inquiry model, with the tiers related respectively to first-, second-, and third-person domains of Integral Theory, to support this point and lay groundwork for the broader conversation. I then identify twelve misconceptions that I commonly encounter among conventionalists that will help disarm kneejerk reactions and initiate a kind of self-critical dynamism in conservative ranks. A primary example is what I call the "change as devaluation fallacy," which pertains to entirely unfounded tendencies to view reform appeals as reflective of diminished appreciation for European classical music. As I emphasize, the problem is not the canonic repertory, the greatness of which is beyond debate, but the paradigm that has emerged around this repertory.

I follow with what I call the "multiple paradigms principle" as another device for elevating critical discourse. In requiring all participants to articulate an informed account of not only their own platform, but also at least one contrasting platform, significant progress is made to neutralize the tendency for uninformed kneejerk reactions to models that contrast with one's own. This sets the stage for framing and resolving a dilemma that confronts the twenty-first-century classical musician. The dilemma—which I call the worldview/workplace paradox—stems from the conflict between the progressive social justice vision harbored by many classical performers, and the ethnocentric/racialized foundations of their professional discipline. By placing the paradox front and center, reconciliatory pathways begin to come into view.

RETHINKING CRITICAL THINKING: AN INTEGRAL PERSPECTIVE

Recall two primary features of integral approaches to all fields—that they span exterior and interior dimensions, and that they place great emphasis on engagement with diverse epistemologies, or ways of knowing, being, and creative expression. Critical thinking is no exception and may be uniquely conducive to the integral approach. This is illustrated in the self-referral core of human creativity and its foundations in consciousness. The curving back of consciousness onto itself, in other words, not only generates differentiation—and thus creativity—within undifferentiated wholeness, but also constitutes a self-critical thrust that is inherent in the psyche. The task of educational systems is to cultivate this self-referral, self-critical activity, through epistemically diverse pedagogical and curricular models, in order that it may blossom and promote capacities to critically interrogate not only one's own thinking and action, but also that of others. Just as self-organizing, self-diversifying, self-pedagogical, and the host of other self-based properties are the basis for exterior manifestations (outer diversity, pedagogy, etc.), self-critical grounding is also the basis for evolution of robust critical inquiry capacities.[5]

Three-Tiered Integral Critical Inquiry Model

The three tiers correspond to the first-, second-, and third-person perspectives (spirituality-art-science/I-We-It/subject-process-object) of integral theory. I analyze these in reverse in order to underscore correlations with conventional lower order reform and higher order reform perspectives, and notions of critical thinking.[6]

Object-mediated critical inquiry is third-person and typically prevails in lower order change conversations, where attention and analysis are directed at some idea or practice that change advocates seek to reform (or conservatives wish to defend). From this standpoint, critical thinking can be thought of in terms of an *intention* to examine some idea from a more distanced or objective standpoint that is minimally constrained by subjective bias. In its most robust form, this stratum of critical inquiry is animated by juxtaposition, or perhaps more aptly described as collision, of contrasting perspectives, whereby familiar convictions are examined anew just in virtue of encounter with differing and potentially competing ideas. The idea of "cognitive dissonance" pertains to this tier of critical thought, as does the common popular culture slogan "Think outside the box." However, in order to think outside the box, it is essential to transcend the language-bound conceptions that give rise to the box in the first place. This cannot be done by intention, or juxtaposition, alone. It requires expanding the epistemic scope, in which conventional, third-person modes of perception open up to second-person and first-person experience.[7]

Process-mediated critical inquiry, driven by creative experience, is the second-person expansion of the critical inquiry continuum. This correlates with the creative identity shift, or creativity turn, that is characteristic of the first of the two higher order reform frameworks. While many thinkers draw close parallels with critical thinking and creative thinking,[8] the actual mechanics by which the second enhances the first elude attention.[9] The guiding principle in the integral model—with extensive elaboration in chapter 6 as it tackles the question "What is improvisation?"—is the dislodging of attachments to familiar modes of thinking that is catalyzed by the act of creation itself. Recall Suzanne Langer's insights about music taking awareness beyond "discursive," or language-bound conception, and my analysis that the primary creative modalities of improvisation and composition excel in this regard. From an epistemic angle, the moment-to-moment creative turbulence of collective improvisation, where both generation of ideas and the need for spontaneous adaptations to ideas generated by others can help jar loose long-standing assumptions or convictions about a given field, or reality as a whole. "The interplay of individuality and unity," states Cornell West, "is not one of uniformity and unanimity imposed from above but rather of conflict among diverse groupings that reach a dynamic consensus subject to questioning and criticism."[10]

From a structural angle, the same self-transcending creative thrust also helps practitioners penetrate beyond localized boundaries—either disciplinary, stylistic, or cultural—that may have been rigidly in place at the outset of engagement in the particular domain and thus constrain understanding within prevailing assumptions. In other words, there is a stratum of awareness that transcends category to which robust creativity opens up access.

Self-mediated critical inquiry further extends the vertical dimensions (which contributes to horizontal expansion) of the critical inquiry scope. Whereas creativity-driven critical inquiry is parts-to-whole, self-mediated is whole-to-parts. If critical thinking discourse only peripherally broaches the creativity-driven realm, consciousness-mediated discourse—particularly from an integral understanding of consciousness—occupies even more remote fringes. Central here is the experience of pure consciousness, or the transcendent self, that is often associated with meditation practice. Meditation involves stepping outside the field of activity (mental, physical, or creative) and taking recourse to a level of awareness, or consciousness, in its purest form. As I explore more fully in chapter 5, pure consciousness is the experience of a silent, undifferentiated mode of awareness that is completely devoid of attributes except for awareness, or consciousness itself. Whereas process-mediated critical inquiry promotes dislodging of assumptions through engagement in action, self-mediated catalyzes this dislodging through silence. As a subset of the above axiom, one could reasonably assert that only by transcending the very phenomenon of thought itself is it possible to critically examine mental constructs. This stratum of critical inquiry model correlates with the fully integral, consciousness-based higher order change vision, which subsumes the prior two strata (but the reverse does not hold, particularly when it comes to the object-mediated tier).[11] In the next chapter, I discuss the importance of second-person creative engagement in conjunction with first-person, transpersonal engagement as an antidote to fundamentalist tendencies, including musical fundamentalism.[12]

How can one be confident that the integral model of critical inquiry is more viable than alternative models? Might, in other words, the above three-tiered framework be the result of an overarching bias that favors the jazz-based, transcultural CICP paradigm, while compelling frameworks might be delineated that reveal monocultural or multicultural paradigms to be equally or more critically robust?

While it goes without saying that readers will come to their own conclusions in response to these kinds of questions, I suggest a criterion that I rearticulate in part II of the book when it comes to the critical vitality of models of consciousness. Epistemologically diverse paradigms are more critically and self-critically robust than those that are epistemologically narrow. The integral transcultural framework not only spans a broader scope of musical engagement, but also is by the same premise most conducive to practitioners stepping outside its boundaries and critically interrogating the endeavor. Recall discussion from chapter 1 regarding the progression from egocentric to ethnocentric, worldcentric, and cosmoscentric identities as not only more expansive, but also more conducive to ongoing cycles of identity construction and dissolution. The creative process, and complementary engagement with meditation, upholds the dissolution phase; reflection on those experiences and pursuit of skills in craft and understanding in the quest to individuate uphold the construction phase. An important result when these cycles are sustained is heightened self-critical capacity. I will explore in chapters 5 and 7 that the same holds for an integral model of consciousness as opposed to dualist and materialist paradigms.

In regard to music, however, I do not suggest that jazz CICP practitioners are inherently endowed, due to their broad process horizons, with heightened critical inquiry capacities, but rather that they have access to unmatched tools—should they commit to utilize them—to sustain robust critical/self-critical inquiry. Neither is the point, moreover, that non-CICPs have no place in the change conversation. While, as noted in previous chapters, lower order change advocates tend to be products of the epistemically narrow horizons of the conventional model, even if—to their credit—they recognize the need for its reform, colleagues of such backgrounds still have the capacity to dig deep into their reservoirs of musical instincts and *imagine what it is like* to navigate the musical world and envision a future music studies paradigm as a jazz CICP.[13] This is as new to lower order, multicultural change advocates as it will be to neo-Eurocentric advocates who wish to enter the change conversation.

Identification of twelve prevailing patterns in conversations with neo-Eurocentricists provides further guidance in the quest for critically robust dialogue.

TWELVE CONVENTIONAL FALLACIES

Inasmuch as music studies is a particularly insular field, many colleagues are largely oblivious to the overall change conversation, even though it dates back over a half-century. They may come across the occasional essay, or curricular proposal, but unless they are in an area that places the flow of ideas front and center, they will generally not be abreast of literature or thinking that prevails. If, then, the multicultural imprint runs deep within, and constrains, prevailing change discourse, one can only imagine the depth of the monocultural imprint in circles that are devoid of reform deliberations. Such colleagues are therefore prone to prevailing assumptions that underlie the conventional model as well as impulsive reactions to reform appeals. A powerful means for defusing these patterns is to simply identify them at the outset—not in a pejorative way, but with a matter-of-fact demeanor that is clearly driven by aspirations for nothing more than a more productive dialogue. From this standpoint, I identify the following twelve common fallacies that I commonly encounter in change conversations, formal or informal, with hopes that the slate can be cleared at the outset for entirely new levels of exchange.

1. *Musician as interpreter fallacy*—that the very idea of being a musician is synonymous with interpretive performer, as opposed to primary creator, as in the improviser/composer/performer.
2. *Trading hegemonies fallacy*—that ceding jazz a foundational place in the curriculum is to replace one hegemony with another, that of European classical music for jazz.
3. *Core curriculum relevance fallacy*—that the conventional core curriculum rooted in interpretive performance, theory, and history studies serves the needs of twenty-first-century musicians.
4. *Core curriculum effectiveness fallacy*—that conventional core curriculum pedagogy results in enduring assimilation of skills and knowledge.
5. *Diversification as dilution fallacy*—that broadening the skill set of music studies will necessarily dilute the overall level of attainment, sacrificing scope for depth.
6. *Impaired ecosystems fallacy*—that redefining musicianship and curricular requirements, particularly large ensembles, will threaten the integrity of the music learning system by upsetting the essential balance between instrumental categories.
7. *Coexistence as coevolution/equality fallacy*—that the fact that most music schools/departments include faculty and coursework in jazz, music technology, and diverse musical cultures indicates that these newer areas are integrated into the cultural fabric of the schools/departments.
8. *Coexistence as access fallacy*—that the fact that most music schools/departments include faculty and coursework in jazz, music technology, and diverse musical cultures means students have equal access to the newer areas.

9. *Mission accomplished fallacy*—that sufficient addition of coursework in jazz, culturally diverse music, technology, and other areas that is characteristic of the lower order vision has already been sufficiently achieved, even if the conventional core remains intact.
10. *Denigration of classical music fallacy*—that appeals for reform inevitably constitute a devaluing of the European classical tradition.
11. *Creativity flatland fallacy*—that all aspects of music and musicianship are creative, and therefore that improvisation and composition ought not be privileged.
12. *Eurosupremacy fallacy*—that European classical music represents the zenith of humanity's musical achievement.

HIGHER ORDER RESPONSES TO THE FALLACIES

Let's begin with the first conservative reaction to change—that being a musician is synonymous with the specialized interpretive performance skills that are at the core of the neo-Eurocentric paradigm. Here it is interesting to note that even within neo-Eurocentric practice, one regularly encounters this presumed correlation, whereby music department websites will state something along the lines of boasting a robust faculty of "conductors, composers, singers, and musicians" (meaning interpretive performers). Humorous concerns aside, the lower order change platform, while calling for an expanded view of musicianship, nonetheless reifies this musician-performer fusion by merely augmenting the interpretive paradigm to comprise a neo-Eurocentric-plus model, instead of the foundational rethinking that is inherent in the higher order, Contemporary Improviser Composer Performer paradigm. In other words, interpretive performance still occupies the central practice and identity marker. By contrast, the higher order integral vision situates interpretive performance within the broader CICP framework—which is regarded as the central identity.

Second is the idea that shifting from a European-based framework to one in which jazz is central inevitably constitutes the replacing of one "closed system," as a colleague has put it, with another,[14] or in other words, the trading of one hegemony for another. Here is where conventionalists and lower order change agents alike need to shift the locus of conversation from language-bound genre categories, which dominate conventional and lower order thinking, to the category-transcending realm of epistemology. In other words, the jazz-based CICP paradigm exemplifies the very notion of an open, self-transcending system, and thus spawns rich connections to European classical music and the broader musical world. This sheds light on typical paradigm-blind tendencies among conservatives and lower order circles to equate European classical music with its neo-Eurocentric offshoot—which indeed is a closed system.

A third objection to change, that students will be deprived of essential foundations, needed to succeed in the musical world, is rooted in the assumption that the conventional core curriculum is as relevant in today's world as it was when it was designed (many decades ago).[15] In fact, the conventional core curriculum was never designed with diverse epistemic or cultural aims in mind, and this problem will not be remedied by superficial or even more substantive modifications that leave prevailing foundations largely or completely intact. The situation is tantamount to trying to build a fifty-thousand-square-foot library atop a foundation designed for a three-thousand-square-foot duplex. Recognition of this all-important point, and arguments for wholesale rebuilding, therefore, need not be taken as a critique of the inherent worth of the conventional model, but simply acknowledgment of contrasting intentions that separate it and possible alternatives.

Closely related is a fourth common objection to change, based on the assumption that the present core is effective even within the areas it does cover, and therefore core curricular change will deprive students of skills and understanding that are presently reasonably ensured. From a higher order standpoint, the complexities of enduring assimilation in conceptual areas, such as theory and history, as opposed to hands-on approaches, such as performance, improvisation, and composition, need to be placed front and center when it comes to *both* the conventional and alternative core curricular paradigms. As I have stated previously (in chapter 3), there is ample reason to question the effectiveness of the conventional music theory and aural skills paradigm, lower order modifications thereof, and any educational intervention in which hands-on pedagogy is not central.[16] Creative artists do not assimilate, in a meaningful, enduring manner, theoretical and historical knowledge disconnected from creative engagement and growth. The fact that the higher order approach does not presume hands-on pedagogy is impeccable, but at least it represents a move toward greater effectiveness.

The idea that expanding the profile of musicians will comprise achievement, privileging scope over depth, is another common conventional objection to change, what I call the "diversity as dilution" assumption.[17] The lower order response is limited by the fact that this change platform remains confined to the assembly-line framework that underpins the conventional model, just seeking a larger assembly line. In other words, the lower order approach fails to deliver means by which music curricula may circumvent the Central Impasse—the need to address an expanded knowledge base—that depart from the strictly horizontal nature of the problem. The higher order shift in creative identity to CICP brings fundamentally new organizing principles, of a vertical nature, to the mix in addressing the impasse. Synergistic relationships between a wide range of components now come into view, whereby in a single stroke, expanded scope and heightened, organic integration within that scope are possible. Instead of diluting an already excessively narrow skill set in which interpretive proficiency masquerades as depth, entirely new vistas of musical artistry become possible.

Sixth is the "artificial ecosystems" objection to change. I encounter this concern primarily from conductors, who—consistent with concern number 1—view musicianship as essentially interpretive in nature, and large ensemble performance as the central vehicle for the expression of that musicianship. To seek a broader kind of musicianship than the interpretive focus, which likely raises concerns about dilution of interpretive performance skills, as well as about curricular distributions that involve decreased time in large ensemble rehearsal, is to "upset the ecosystem." While this argument may have some cache given its ostensibly progressive parallels to environmental causes, closer inspection reveals its grounding in the fundamentally flawed assumption that interpretive performance, and the large ensemble experience, constitute organizing principles in the evolution of musical artistry. Growing numbers of colleagues, even if their worldviews remain centered in interpretive performance, express concerns about the amount of time students spend in large ensembles. While lower order change arguments move further in a quest to expand the interpretive focus, the best they can do in countering the impaired ecosystem argument is to propose reducing large ensemble requirements in order that students can devote more time to chamber music. From a higher order perspective, this does not shift the paradigm one iota because interpretive performance remains central; whether the ensemble is large and conducted or small and unconducted is moot from the standpoint of the Contemporary Improviser Composer Performer requisite for twenty-first-century musical navigation.

From a higher order vantage point, moreover, the conventional artificial ecosystem is examined from a more complete complex systems perspective that reveals it as particularly shaky. Principles such as self-organization, feedback loops, and micro- and macrohierarchical structures cannot be sustained through interpretive performance foundations. I will go into this further in part II.

Next are objections based on the assumption that just because most music schools/departments include faculty and coursework in jazz, music technology, and diverse musical cultures, this means that the newer areas are integrated into the cultural fabric of the schools/departments. In fact, more typical is a cultural divide between conventional, neo-Eurocentric areas of music schools and those, of non-European origins, on the outskirts. Closely related is the idea that students have equal access to the newer areas. The fact that these areas are usually offered as electives, with conventional curricular requirements already packed to the brim, indicates otherwise.[18]

Ninth is the argument that adequate change has already been achieved—in other words, the addition of coursework in areas such as jazz, world music, and technology over the past few decades renders schools of music sufficiently diverse and aligned with contemporary practice. I call this the "mission accomplished" syndrome, satirically inspired by the words on a banner behind a former U.S. president atop an aircraft carrier as he prematurely proclaimed that the above-noted Iraqi invasion was successfully completed. The fact that the reform mission is far from accomplished, and in fact has scarcely yet begun, is evidenced by the fact that, while indeed many schools have diversified in the range of areas they include within their buildings, they have most emphatically not diversified in terms of curricular access—with the majority of students engaging with the newer (to musical study) areas only peripherally. In other words, beyond the occasional elective in these areas chosen by the interpretive performance majority, jazz coursework is taken largely by jazz majors, technology offerings by technology majors, composition by composition majors.

Oblivious to the capacity for improvisation and composition to serve as new foundational pillars, lower order reformers will at best issue weak counterarguments that simply state the obvious—that the majority of students have limited capacity to partake of these offerings. Foundational rebuilding is reduced to a kind of "curricular horse trading," where colleagues try to swap one course for another, and where every little scrap of space in the present model is examined as a potential site for superficial additions to an already-overflowing framework.

Tenth is the conventional objection whereby change appeals are taken as a devaluation of the European classical tradition. In other words, one cannot—the conventional thinking goes—simultaneously cherish the music of Beethoven, Chopin, and Debussy yet harbor and express deep concerns that the creative processes that gave rise to this exquisite music are absent from the curriculum, let alone the identity of most music students. While lower order conversation may offer a kind of politically correct or superficial reminder that engagement with new developments and past treasures may indeed coexist, limited commentary occurs on how this actually might happen. Again, horizontal thinking prevails. Higher order visioning shifts the thinking, thereby circumventing the impasse, from horizontal inventory (the ever-larger assembly line) to vertical roots (creative CICP identity) as a new organizing principle.

The higher order perspective, with its more robust grounding in diversity discourse, also reveals the reaction to appeals for change as a form of white fragility, if not white privilege.[19] In other words, the view of arguments for musical equality as denigrating the privileged musical center directly parallels views encountered in some majority population circles of the quest for equality among oppressed groups as denigration of majority populations. To place the conversation in a yet broader context, the situation is somewhat reminiscent of the artificial patriotic fervor that U.S. governmental leadership stirred up in support of its invasion of Iraq following the 9/11 terrorist attacks. Opposing the invasion invited accusations of being unpatriotic, and in extreme instances even being accused of siding with the terrorists. Similar parallels might be noted in critiques of scientific materialism in philosophy-of-mind discourse, where rejection of that particular paradigm is erroneously, and egregiously, misconstrued as a rejection of science itself.[20]

A next limitation is in response to the contention voiced by conservatives—to the effect that interpretive performance is a form of creativity, and therefore there is no need for improvisation and composition, or least for improvising and composing to be privileged in the creativity spectrum. Here several points are to be made. First is that central to the higher order platform is a view of creativity as *writ large*, thus not inconsistent with the conservative quest for an inclusive view of creativity. However, within this higher order account, improvisation and composition are regarded as primary forms of creativity that promote creativity throughout the entire music studies spectrum. In other words, the positioning of improvisation and composition as central in the higher order vision does not constitute privileging but simply the identification of foundations that promote optimal creativity in all phases of musical artistry—hence, the systematic approach to improvisation studies considered earlier. Unfortunately, this eludes the lower order perspective, which while tending to privilege improvisation and composition does not take the further step in identifying the broader creative spectrum that may be enlivened when these modalities are central.[21]

A twelfth and final tendency among conservatives is typically implicit but rarely stated or articulated in prose. This is the view that European classical music represents the pinnacle of humanity's musical achievement and therefore unequivocally warrants occupying an exclusively central place in musical study. As intimated above, the problem is not that some—and likely more than a few—colleagues harbor this viewpoint; they are as entitled to their perspectives as are colleagues along all points of the visioning spectrum. The problem is that the archconservative, Eurosupremacist musical worldview is rarely if ever subjected to critical examination, rendering it an unquestioned ideological background that continually informs the prevailing paradigm, yet eludes recognition as such even as a hubbub of activity swirls around the curricular surface. As stated, the position is likely impossible to prove, nor is an adequate assessment mechanism even conceivable, in that it would need to be calibrated in a way that took into account the totality of aesthetic/artistic paradigms across the globe, and then measure them against one another on some sort of culturally neutral scale. Moreover, as difficult as it is to imagine what that sort of scale might look like, particularly given that the design of which would require intimacy and expertise with all the world's music—the acquisition of which contradicts the very purpose of the project—the broader ramifications, including implicit valuation/devaluation of not only musical forms but also corresponding cultures and human beings, of such an endeavor are even more problematic. Yet such is the ideology that reigns supreme and underpins the conservative voice and prevailing curricular and organizational structures in music studies.

Again, even more problematic than the ideology itself is that it largely remains hidden from view, lurking in the shadows and wreaking havoc from a place of privileged seclusion. Even much change discourse, which is driven by egalitarian perspectives that counter the dominant ideology, fails to place it front and center in ways sufficient to assess its impact. The situation is a bit like a medical biopsy that fails to fully probe the depth of the tissue in which an abnormality is lodged, even as all sorts of treatments are considered that, at best, remedy symptoms, but at worst, may be predicated on a fundamentally flawed analysis of the disease at hand. The task of the change agent is to establish a culture of critical discourse in which Eurosupremacist ideology moves from the shadows to the spotlight, at which point participants in the prevailing model no longer have a place to hide.

Multiple Paradigms Framework

The basic idea is that critical vitality is optimal when arguments for change and conservation are grounded in substantive understanding of contrasting perspectives. I am talking about more than anecdotal, generalized descriptions of one's inclinations, or the viewpoints being opposed. Rather, I am talking about highly informed, peer-reviewed (or peer reviewable) accounts in which underlying assumptions are related to overlying practices, thus comprising paradigms. It is not enough, therefore, to advance and frame one's own perspectives in as sophisticated a manner as possible; it is equally important to exhibit conversance with models with which one might take issue. When this criterion is applied to both one's own perspectives as well as those of others, one not only raises the critical bar but also elevates the backdrop of professional courtesy and collegiality. Now minimally informed, kneejerk reactions can give way to the healthy juxtaposition of contrasting worldviews and philosophically robust exchange.

While one might well wonder if something along these lines is not already in place, a closer look at typical faculty deliberations quickly dispels any such illusions. For one thing, while the conservative voice inevitably assumes prominence in any deliberations about change, the onus is typically on advocates of some new idea to make their case; it is rarely on adherents of convention to justify their position in any sophisticated manner. Accordingly, while change agents must routinely provide a rationale for their ideas along the above lines, conservatives are rarely required to do the same. It is simply not part of curricular discourse for advocacy of reigning paradigms to be grounded in compelling rationale; instead, the fact is that a given approach has long been in place, coupled with presumptions that corresponding rationale exists somewhere in the academic committee archives or research literature. But think about it—where is there a peer-reviewed or reviewable case for the conventional curriculum, particularly as assessed against even what I call neo-Eurocentric-plus, let alone integral alternatives? One is hard-pressed to not only identify such a case but also even imagine what it might look like.

The inertia of the status quo reigns supreme in academic discourse, and I believe the multiple paradigms criterion has much to offer breaking out of this pattern.

For change advocates, moreover, I add a further criterion to the framework—the need to provide an informed account for not only a conventional and preferred new model, but also at least one *alternative to that reform model*. This will help change agents who, at least in principle, resonate with the idea of paradigmatic change, yet remain entrapped in the inertia of the prevailing paradigm, break free from its binding influence. My delineation of lower order and higher order change advocacy, both of which are framed in distinction to a neo-Eurocentric conventional model, is an example of this requisite fulfilled. My identification, moreover, of two higher order models, one creativity-driven, the other consciousness-driven, extends this fulfillment idea.[22]

Here I might further note a parallel that I have observed among change advocates to the above-mentioned absence of critically robust rationale for the conventional model. As noted in previous chapters, I am continually struck by the fact that most reformers have not articulated a musical worldview of their own, but rather are more driven by reaction to the prevailing neo-Eurocentric worldview. Arguments that music studies needs to incorporate improvising and composing and encounter with diverse musical cultures without identifying the foundationally new pillars, as well as pedagogies, that will accommodate this expanse, do not constitute a new worldview! Criteria for worldview delineation include clearly identified cultural/ethnological, epistemological, artistic, pedagogical, and transpersonal considerations among others. The incoherence of multiculturalism, the prevailing ideology in music studies reform, along both ethnological and epistemological lines underscores my assessment that worldview delineation is lacking. Once again, the fact that most change advocates are not CICPs but rather products of the Interpretive Performance Specialist model who have partially liberated from its shackles looms large as a limiting constraint in change conversation.

The multiple paradigms principle will therefore also help reformers articulate their personal worldviews. When, moreover, this articulation is grounded in the three tiers of integral critical inquiry, and its diverse epistemic scope, the worldview construction endeavor can also be complemented by an equally important worldview dissolution cycle. It is not, in other words, that one defines a worldview that is to hold from here till eternity. Rather, one sustains ongoing cycles of worldview formation and dissolution, a process identical to artistic identity formation and dissolution. In addition to being personally meaningful, no gesture is more powerfully inviting of productive exchange with colleagues, particularly those of contrasting viewpoints, than the indication of commitment to self-critical interrogation, nor that one has invested the time and energy to grasp opposing arguments. Immediately even the most hardened hearts of colleagues who harbor the most polarized ideas from one's own begin to soften, making possible a kind of nuanced harvesting of the fruits stemming from the juxtaposition of the contrasting platforms that would not otherwise be possible.

The multiple paradigms framework also helps bring to the fore facets of European classical music that tend to remain obscured in the conversation.

THE WORLDVIEW-WORKPLACE PARADOX: THE TWENTY-FIRST-CENTURY CLASSICAL MUSICIAN'S DILEMMA

The multiple paradigms principle illuminates a range of problems in the neo-Eurocentric paradigm—including its creativity-weak, diversity-weak, fragmented, and institution-driven orientation. Among these, moreover, a particularly disquieting dilemma confronts the thoughtful participant in this paradigm—the egregiously ethnocentric/racialized assumptions upon which the framework has been built and which thus are regularly perpetuated to the world by its practitioners, and on the other hand, the genuine social justice commitment held by many, if not most, classical musicians—hence, a paradox between worldview and workplace. Again, were the majority in the field to lean to the extreme right, as in harboring white supremacist inclinations, the paradox would not exist, even if a far worse problem would arguably prevail. In any case, one could see how the current orientation, even if confined to music studies, fuels the social manifestation.

As long as critical examination of the reigning model remains absent, conservative colleagues will be able to work under a spell of convenient silence in respect to the paradox. It is a bit like harboring intense concerns about the environment, yet working for a corporation that is known for this long track record of pollution and lobbying against environmental regulations. Most classical musicians will reject their ethnocentric/racialized version of this dichotomy as unacceptable, were they to stare it directly in the face. But this rarely happens. Therefore, directly paralleling issues of sustainability at large, where eventually the ecological reality will remove all places to hide, the same holds for the conventional neo-Eurocentric music studies paradigm in a world increasingly engulfed in an unprecedented celebration of creativity and diversity. The multiple paradigms framework helps the majority of classical musicians place this dilemma front and center and realize they are, as it were, living a double life—at which point, it is up to participants in this worldview to decide how they will proceed.

For extreme adherents of the supremacy thesis, the decision is easy—even deeper retrenchment in the reigning model. They are entitled to that choice, and are now invited to back it up in ways that the field has not yet seen.

For the majority that rightly reject this thesis, a continuum of alternative options presents itself. One might entail the moderate conservative notion that, even if other musical traditions are of equal value, music studies should continue its emphasis in interpretive performance of European classical music since the effectiveness of that model—at least in the eyes of neo-Eurocentricists—is clearly established. Why risk undermining something that is a proven success?

Others, seeing the lingering ethnocentrism/racism behind that option, and perhaps recognizing that the prevailing model might not be as impeccable as is assumed, will seek more substantive liberation. Here some form of multicultural expansion might appear as a logical pathway. Having focused in one tradition, practitioners thus proceed to gain exposure to other musical cultures and gain corresponding skills.

However, I believe the multiple paradigms principle has the power, if implemented to its fullest extent, to inspire and guide ex–neo-Eurocentrists beyond the multicultural option and embrace a jazz-based, integral transcultural vision. For one thing, having attained a formidable, if localized, kind of virtuosity on their principal instrument, and having established strong connections with the repertory of one single culture that they considered their home lineage, such colleagues may appreciate self-cultural grounding in jazz as a correlate. Alert to the limitations of a multicultural assembly line—which it is important to always keep in mind is not predicated on musical artists navigating creative pathways across traditions, but rather a received academic imprint—I can envision the integral, transcultural vision to be of significant appeal to "recovering neo-Eurocentrists." Perhaps most important is the idea of the jazz CICP as the return of the prior European-based CICP, now in more developed, globally informed manifestation. When exposed to these considerations and the multitude of ways, as I have spelled out in the previous chapter, that a jazz-based paradigm has the capacity to yield an Afro-Euro nexus that promotes an unprecedented set of skills and understanding, I believe important leadership may indeed come from the conservative constituency.

How Effective Is the Conventional Neo-Eurocentric Music Studies Model for Classical Training?

Another factor that points in a transcultural, jazz CICP direction may be among the most powerful principles unearthed by the multiple paradigms criterion. This has to do with expanding the criteria upon which the overall effectiveness of the prevailing model is assessed. Little elaboration is needed at this point in terms of the severe limitations of the neo-Eurocentric framework for contemporary musical exploration and engagement. But what about the effectiveness of the model in respect to classical training itself, construed here in terms of interpretive performance, and corresponding theoretical and historical inquiry? Once again, the inextricable link between ethnology and epistemology helps yield differentiation where vague homogeneity once prevailed. Immediately, an incontrovertible and affirmative fact comes to the fore when it comes to interpretive performance: on any given evening, formidable, often excellent—and occasionally magical—performances of European repertory can be heard in recital, chamber music, or large ensemble formats at music schools around the country and world. The significant casualties aside that result from the predominance of that mode of musical engagement, in itself it can only be viewed a success.

But might high levels of performative achievement have created a kind of smokescreen that masks deep deficiencies in conceptual understanding—conventionally labeled "theory" and "history," and part of broader conceptual scope that I call music inquiry?

I believe a strong argument may be made that this is indeed the case, and that this point must be placed front and center and critically interrogated. From the standpoint of broader contemporary navigation, I believe conventional theory and history models—even with lower order ornamentation—are almost as dysfunctional as interpretive performance specialization. Inasmuch as the frameworks were not originally designed around a musical world beyond European classical repertory, it may be unfair to assess them through this lens. On the other hand, this point in itself should be reason for wholesale rebuilding as opposed to surface modifications.

What are the grounds for this argument? I begin with personal experience. Over my many years of working with fine classical musicians in improvisatory settings, and as guest speaker and curricular consultant in music schools, I have conducted an informal survey of interpretive performers based on a simple question: To what extent does your undergraduate studies in theory and history inform your day-to-day music making and musical understanding? The answer among a solid majority of respondents: negligible. When, on the other hand, I diplomatically pose to colleagues in music history and theory questions about how effective they perceive the model to be, I encounter—at least at first, and particularly in collective forums—great enthusiasm for the foundational skills and understanding it offers musicians. When I intimate that a very different perception seems to prevail among performers, the vast majority of whom come through this very kind of coursework, the response is that, "well, they did not take the theory and history core at our institution." At the very least, there is clearly a conversation that needs to transpire between performers and scholars even within the neo-Eurocentric community.[23]

Among the contributions of the multiple paradigms principle to this conversation is that it will bring diverse parameters of inquiry into the mix. Perhaps most obvious is the long legacy of educational literature that illuminates the limitations of passive pedagogy, with corroboration in recent years from neurobiological research into human learning, and is consistent with concerns about theory and history.[24] Whereas interpretive performance pedagogy is hands-on, and thus yields enduring results, theory and history tend to be passive. One might bring into play issues such as contemporaneity—relevance to the musical world around us—and pedagogical interconnectedness—integration of theory and history with other domains. While it is important, as I have noted, to not conflate lower order appeals to link performance, theory, and history together as genuine integration, this approach at least recognizes the symptoms of fragmentation, if stopping short of acknowledging its roots in the creativity crisis. As I inquire in chapter 3, why is core musicianship pedagogy relegated largely to the discipline of music theory when any number of other areas are equally if not more equipped to deliver such pedagogy? Multiple paradigms criteria will place this question front and center for advocates of the conventional model, and alternatives, which will likely lay groundwork for receptivity to the extraordinarily broad and integrative musicianship tools offered by the jazz CICP. Conversation rooted in multiple paradigms principles will also bring into view qualitative and quantitative research that raises serious questions about the efficacy of prevailing models.[25]

The task of the change agent is to establish a culture of dialogue where these kinds of questions and self-evident solutions come as much internally, meaning from constituencies conventionally in charge of musicianship, as from the outside. Once conversation is initiated that places these kinds of questions and considerations on the table, advocates of convention will be able to entertain the broader educational and societal ramifications of the neo-Eurocentric (and neo-Eurocentric-plus) frameworks. While previously, the idea of the jazz CICP process scope as an unmatched conduit for flow of creativity and consciousness from the level of atma, or soul, and that neo-Eurocentric paradigm preempts this flow, might seem blasphemous, this idea may seem viable against a backdrop of robust dialogue.

Without this conversation, prevailing rhetoric about the transformative, unifying, healing, or other aspects of the arts will always be heard from a conventional neo-Eurocentric lens, and without any other sort of filter, perhaps reify the idea of European musical supremacy. In other words, "if only a larger portion of our country and world could hear and appreciate the beauty of European classical music, the world would be such a better place"—something like that. To which, a multiculturalist reply might read, "If only a larger portion of our country and world could hear the beauty of all the music across the globe, the world would be such a better place." To which an integral transculturalist reply might read, "If only a much larger portion of our nation would tune into the creative vitality of the African American musical stream that has originated on our shores, and in our soul, reconnects with the prior creative vitality of the European classical tradition and its structural richness, and offers powerful pathways to the global musical landscape, we would be doing our part to make the world a better place."

CLOSING THOUGHTS

One does not need Integral Theory to recognize that music studies is beset by severe crises in creativity, diversity/social justice, and pedagogical integration and effectiveness—to name among the most common rallying cries for change. Where Integral Theory can be of considerable help, however, is in revealing these crises as part of an interrelated web of pathologies whose roots extend deep into individual and collective awareness, and whose ramifications—and parallel manifestations—extend across wide-ranging fields. Integral Theory also excels in bringing into view a wider array of casualties, and solutions, that are not commonly linked to those that are typically viewed as primary. Severe deficiencies in overall musical understanding, critical thinking, self-organizing/student-driven development, embodiment, and self-driven pedagogical acumen are among the broader areas that, when fathomed through an integral lens and thus rectified, may serve as fertile avenues to a broader arts-driven transformation.

Therefore, while my focus in this chapter has been on patterns that are commonly encountered in dialogues with conservatives, I believe they further underscore the considerable self-interrogative work that needs to occur among change advocates. As I have argued, nothing short of a robust program of "rehab" among reformers will suffice if the field is to break free from neo-Eurocentric and neo-Eurocentric-plus inertia. Critical examination of common language and terminology may be a particularly fruitful place to start this process. The possibility that the word *jazz*, as I argue in chapter 2, may elicit radically different interpretations from multicultural as opposed to transcultural vantage points, even to the point where the paradigmatic gulf between these interpretations exceeds even that which separates monocultural (neo-Eurocentric) and multicultural visions, lays groundwork for critical interrogation of a far broader range of terminology. As discussed, this includes not only exnomination labeling patterns (art music, new music, early music, etc.) that perpetuate ethnocentric/racialized discrimination, but also names assigned to conventional disciplines (theory, history, performance), genres (jazz, world music, popular music, etc.), change buzzwords (creativity, diversity, integration, entrepreneurship, technology, etc.), and contrasting diversity paradigms (multiculturalism, transculturalism). This might be followed by identification of assumptions inherited from one's primary musical discipline (music education, ethnomusicology, performance, composition, jazz, etc.), prevailing tendencies toward endless horizontal expansion of the curriculum, and patterns such as "ethnocentric blind spots"—particularly when it comes to black music—that perpetuate hidden hegemonies amid an ostensibly progressive vision.

When all is said and done, and this is also where Integral Theory excels through its emphasis on attending to the repository of conditioned patterns that comprise the psychic shadow, all individuals need to decide from the innermost recesses of their hearts the extent to which they are willing to move beyond their comfort zones and engage in the broader transformation. From this standpoint, colleagues who deep down truly believe in the inherent superiority of European classical repertory, and perhaps European culture, and have minimal interest in ethnoracial social justice issues in the world at large, are most absolved of activist obligation, unless this entails efforts to guard against encroachment of other kinds of music in the curriculum. The interior-exterior activism bar is raised, however, for colleagues in European classical music who may or may not harbor musical supremacist inclinations but who are genuinely concerned about black-white racial dynamics in society; these colleagues need to decide if, and then how, they will resolve this workplace/worldview dilemma in their own lives and participate in the overarching healing. I hope commentary in this book is helpful to these ends.

The inner-outer activism bar is further raised for colleagues in a field such as music education who have, at least conceptually, resolved the worldview/workplace dilemma. Even if, in other words, such colleagues clearly aspire toward a culturally diverse curriculum that is reflective of the cultural diversity they cherish in society at large, the question then becomes the extent to which they are willing to look deeply into the residual racialized indoctrination, stemming from society at large—and as I suggest, unexamined multicultural ideology—that may constrain their individual growth, and are willing to be a dynamic voice for change. "History will have to record," stated Martin Luther King Jr., "that the greatest tragedy of this period of social transition was not the strident clamor of the bad people, but the appalling silence of the good people."[26] It would seem to me that Ruth Gustafson's assessment of an "attrition rate of close to 100 per cent among African American students"[27] in many school music programs might be among the many compelling catalysts that, perhaps inspired by King's words, stir the activist impulse among such individuals from deep in the heart—or the powerful critiques of prevailing musical colonialism issued by Juliet Hess, Deborah Bradley, Lise Vaugeois, and others. I hope my identification of black-white racial dynamics, and musical/curricular ramifications thereof, and the prospects of a self-transcending jazz-based transcultural paradigm as key to unprecedented navigational scope, at the very least elicits serious critical attention as a next key juncture in the interior/exterior activist conversation.

The most important contribution of Integral Theory, with further ramifications for interior-exterior activism in music and beyond, may lie in its grounding in consciousness—the exploration of which is increasingly recognized as key to humanity addressing the litany of challenges confronting the world and transforming them into gateways for unprecedented flourishing. Although music studies is conspicuously underrepresented in conversation—academic or otherwise—on the topic, a jazz-driven integral view of consciousness dramatically expands the horizons, transformative potentialities, as well as critical integrity, of music studies change visioning.

II

Jazz and the Consciousness Turn

OVERVIEW

The challenges of today's world will only be addressed through the probing of the innermost dimensions of the human being and the harnessing of resultant wisdom in new paradigms of educational and societal practice. Understanding and development of consciousness, then, must be embraced as the next frontier in education and society. Reflecting the inextricable link between creativity and consciousness, part I examined jazz as a uniquely robust parts-to-whole (PW), creativity-driven pathway to this interior source. Part II in turn pursues a complementary whole-to-parts (WP), consciousness-based line of inquiry and engagement that leads toward this same transformative unity, again through a jazz-inspired lens. The interplay of PW/WP pathways is key to the broader creativity-consciousness revolution that jazz has the capacity to catalyze in music studies and subsequently transmit to the world.

From a PW perspective, jazz is the site of the return of the Contemporary Improviser Composer Performer that prevailed in earlier times in the European classical tradition, thus helping restore creativity as primary means for interior artistic development and exterior musical navigation. This enables the bridging of divides between the monocultural/neo-Eurocentric paradigm, multicultural/neo-Eurocentric-plus efforts to modify that model, and the actual transcultural musical excursions of twenty-first-century musical innovators. This robust epistemological spectrum at once promotes transcendence of language-bound categories, thus exemplifying important critical inquiry capacities, and also openings to inner experiences of heightened consciousness. It would be a natural extension of this epistemic spectrum for a long legacy of jazz artists to have engaged with formal meditative practices, thus WP engagement, that probe the innermost dimensions of consciousness in silence. In addition to the artistic, pedagogical, and transformative benefits of this engagement, it renders jazz an agent to bridge further divides that hinder the progress of humanity. Central is the rift between science and spirituality/religion, extremist forms of both of which perpetuate an unsustainable fissure that poses grave consequences for the world. Even the most compelling inroads into understanding and manipulating the exterior world without deep grounding in the innermost recesses of human consciousness, which is the source of compassion, love, and interconnectedness among human beings and the environment, risk dissociating into any number of crises. By the same token, interiority, or attempts thereat, disconnected from coherent reasoning and exterior application readily invites fundamentalist misinterpretation that all too often results in violence. A jazz-inspired revolution in creativity and consciousness has the capacity to help heal these divides by illuminating how disciplines and cultures, when realized as self-transcending tributaries to unified foundations, both enhance their respective integrities and also co-evolve in contemporary interaction with one another. While preliminary glimpses of jazz-driven creative transformation may be seen in what has been called "New Jazz Studies," the grounding of creativity in consciousness opens up entirely new vistas of transformation.[1]

Chapter 5, "A Jazz-Based Integral Perspective on Consciousness," launches the investigation, which lays groundwork for a fuller understanding of improvisation, as explored in chapter 6, "A Consciousness-Based Integral Perspective on Improvisation." Chapter 7, "Jazz and the Integral Revolution," explores how a jazz-based integral paradigm of music studies has the capacity to catalyze a transformative impact that extends across the academy and societal landscape.

Chapter Five

A Jazz-Based Integral Perspective on Consciousness

What is consciousness?

No question is more fundamental to understanding the nature of the human being and human potential—and thus poses greater ramifications for how humanity navigates this extraordinary juncture in the history of the world—than that of consciousness. Nor does any question remain more distanced, and even subject to suspicion on those occasions when it is broached, in our educational systems, which will naturally need to play a central role in this transformation. Indeed, when it comes to day-to-day thinking and practice, much of education continues to be dominated by the specialized concerns of particular disciplines, even with increasing recognition of the need for an expanded vision. The prevailing guiding question—What does it mean to be educated in a given field?—needs to open up to an essential successor—What does it mean to be an educated human being?—if there is reason for optimism about the future. And from this question, one that is yet more expansive can then assume center stage: What is the nature of the human being who is being educated?[1] Which, of course, bringing the conversation full circle, is synonymous with the question, What is consciousness?

This chapter responds to the question from a jazz-inspired, integral perspective, significant aspects of which I have already introduced. Prominent are the inextricable, nondual link between individual human consciousness and cosmic wholeness that lies at the heart of the integral worldview, and what I call the strong nonduality thesis, which is predicated on the improvisatory foundations of creativity on human and cosmic scales. I lay groundwork for further inquiry in this direction with a brief overview of three central philosophies of mind—dualism, materialism, and nondualism. Materialism is the prevailing worldview in the sciences and thus the academic world, even if there are signs of a retreat from that position. An overarching Matrix of Materialism[2] nonetheless shapes much of what transpires, including corresponding approaches to teaching and learning, where education tends to be reduced to information, and—more germane to the topic at hand—music is reduced to repertory created by others at the expense of the creative process. Dualism, predicated on the separation of objective and subjective realities, and thus science and spirituality/religion, is the prevailing worldview in society. Integralism unites objective and subjective dimensions, with jazz's whole/whole-to-parts scope a vehicle for directly experiencing the first-second-third-person/spirituality-art-science dimensions of the integral vision.

I then probe self-awareness as a connecting thread between creativity and consciousness, and how it manifests in core form in the pure consciousness of meditation, which in turn promotes integration into active life through a series of higher developmental stages that are associated with consciousness evolution.[3] I illustrate how these represent progressively more differentiated levels of development that promote grounding personal experience, and by extension the emergent music studies and overall educational framework, in the interior circuitry optimally conducive to integration of creativity and consciousness from the soul level. This is followed by a host of criteria that help diagnose and dismantle the materialist matrix, and consideration of broader transformative ramifications for the world.

Some commentary is in order in regard to my significant appropriation of ideas and terminology from the Vedantic tradition, even as I also draw from other spiritual lineages. The point is not to privilege Vedanta, but rather to identify this lineage as a particularly rich source of principles that can be enlivened in other spiritual traditions in the quest for an overarching spiritual wholeness.[4] Moreover, as Hua Hsu points out, "For black artists, especially, pursuing other systems of belief became a way of rethinking one's relationship with America. Though they had both grown up in strict Christian households, John and Alice Coltrane in the sixties began immersing themselves in other faiths,"[5] though not, I would add, driven by aspirations to abandon their original religious roots, but in a quest for a more universal spirituality that transcended, yet included denominational boundaries. I believe the dynamic interplay between the nondual worldview of Vedanta and its powerful meditative practices that could yield direct experience of the divine was an important factor in their gravitating in this direction. Whether or not one shares my idea that connections between the Vedantic notion of cosmic, improvisatory play and the improvisatory roots of jazz also factored into this trajectory, at the very least the direct connection between epistemology and worldview cannot be ignored. From this standpoint, it may also be instructive to observe a parallel in the Judeo-Christian strands of the Abrahamic trinity as it has taken hold in the West and the European classical tradition: in both realms, epistemological roots have been compromised, while in recent decades showing signs of restoration, albeit to different degrees. The growing interest, for example, in contemplative forms of Judaic and Christian practice indicates the resurrection of core modes of spiritual experience and insight. While a parallel resurgence of interest in improvisation in European classical music may be less robust, it is at least discernible.[6]

Jazz, as the site of the return of the Contemporary Improviser Composer Performer that prevailed in earlier times in music of the West, and that is key to contemporary musical navigation, might be therefore considered a site where both improvisatory and spiritual epistemic streams unite. I therefore consider Vedanta as a kind of parallel source in terms of embodying core epistemological and ontological principles that may be enlivened across denominations. The point, then, is not that everyone become a Vedantist, but that the jazz-Vedanta nexus can illuminate powerful features of creativity and consciousness development that can be harnessed through the lenses of all artistic and spiritual traditions.

MODELS OF MIND

Views of consciousness may be most readily grasped when placed among one of three general categories or variations thereof: *dualism*, *nondualism*, and *materialism*.[7] Central to *dualism* is that consciousness, or subjectivity, and the material world, or objectivity, represent fundamentally separate realms of experience and reality. In other words, as commonly associated with the work of the French philosopher Rene Descartes, the universe can be understood in terms of two coexisting, yet distinct realms, one of matter, the other of mind. Stephen Jay Gould's more recent depiction of science and religion as "nonoverlapping magisteria" exemplifies the dualist worldview and the need for lines between the respective epistemologies to not be blurred: the purview of science is matter; that of religion is spirit.[8]

Nondualism, as defined from an integral vantage point and that of traditions such as *advaita* Vedanta, views consciousness as primary in the cosmos. Not only is the entirety of human experience and creative achievement a manifestation of an overarching, infinite, and eternal dimension of consciousness, but so also is the entire physical creation—from quarks and electrons to mountain ranges and rain forests to solar systems and galaxies. "Consciousness," states Sri Aurobindo, "is the inherent self-awareness in existence. [It] is the fundamental thing in existence—it is the energy, the motion, the movement of consciousness that creates the universe and all that is in it—not only the macrocosm, but the microcosm is nothing but consciousness arranging itself."[9]

Max Planck, the father of quantum physics, arrives at the same perspective through the lens of scientific inquiry: "I regard consciousness as fundamental. I regard matter as derivative from consciousness. We cannot get behind consciousness. Everything that we talk about, everything that we regard as existing, postulates consciousness."[10] To dispel a common misunderstanding that is encountered in response to this viewpoint: the assertion that consciousness is primary is not that some aspect of objective reality does not exist unless some human being is conscious of it—in other words, that the reality of a stone or a tree depends on an individual being conscious of such. Rather, it is that an eternal realm of spirit, or consciousness, is the source of all Being—meaning physical and nonphysical creation. At which point, correlations between the nondual integral view of consciousness and most of the world's spiritual/religious traditions become apparent.

Moreover, what is called *idealism* in Western philosophy is also a form of nondualism in its positioning of mind—again, providing mind is construed as the cosmic subject—as ontologically central in the broader scheme of creation. *Panpsychism*[11] is another closely related view of consciousness that is sometimes distinguished from nondual, idealist thought on its view that neither matter nor mind are ontologically foundational to one another, and that all of creation, from the most minuscule subatomic particles to the infinitely massive astronomical phenomena, are imbued with some quality of intelligence or awareness. Though distinctions between panpsychism and nondualism may be thus considered largely semantic in nature, the former has a rich history and is attracting increasing attention in philosophy-of-mind circles.[12] Of the various accounts of consciousness, panpsychism and nondualism—regardless of whether or not one distinguishes between the two—are the most compatible with the integral worldview.

Materialism, in stark contrast with nondualism and its subsets, views matter as primary in the universe, and thus tends to be averse to spirituality as anything more than a comforting illusion about the nature of reality.[13] Two kinds of materialist positions yield two very different conceptions of consciousness, even if these differ fundamentally from dualist and nondualist accounts. *Reductionism*, the most extreme form of materialism, holds that consciousness is "nothing but" electrochemical activity of the brain. Thus, not only is the idea illusory of an ocean of consciousness—and with it all of humanity's spiritual convictions, including the idea of soul or physically transcendent dimensions of consciousness—but also even the wave is suspect as an ontologically veridical entity. Conscious experience is reducible, as it were, to the drops—the water molecules and their physical attributes. *Epiphenomenalism* is a more moderate materialist position that denies the reducibility of consciousness to neurons or any constituent parts; rather, consciousness is emergent or epiphenomenal to these components. As John Searle puts it, "consciousness is an emergent property of the brain" that, even as it arises from "lower level neural processes," is irreducible to the physical level.[14] Because consciousness is still regarded as a by-product of a physical substrate, however, epiphenomenalism falls clearly within the materialist end of the spectrum. Notions of intrinsic meaning and purpose to human and cosmic existence that lie at the heart of the world's wisdom traditions are thus rejected as lingering artifacts of religious superstition. "The more the universe seems comprehensible," states Stephen Weinberg from a staunch materialist position, "the more it seems pointless." The human being? "A farcical outcome of a chain of accidents reaching back to the first three minutes" (following the Big Bang).[15]

To be sure, it is difficult to imagine more contrasting perspectives on the nature of consciousness, as well as the relationship of the human being to the cosmic wholeness. As I discuss below, this is significant in that overarching worldview serves as a conceptual backdrop for one's vision of possibilities for oneself and the world, and thus directly informs day-to-day investment of time and energy. While this may seem insignificant for many individuals given the vicissitudes of life and unique circumstances everyone faces, worldview is a key source of meaning and purpose. For change agents/activists, referring to those who overtly engage in transforming existing systems, radically different strategies come into view when this work is grounded in materialist, dualist, or nondualist worldviews. While not everyone will share my contention that philosophical materialism and dualism are as unsustainable for humanity as musical materialism (the neo-Eurocentric paradigm) and dualism (neo-Eurocentric-plus/multiculturalism) are for musical practice, I believe that most change agents will agree that this kind of inquiry is immensely significant to the future of the world. At the end of chapter 7, I introduce a framework called Deep Inquiry that systematically expands conventional educational conversations to the biggest questions of human nature, existence, and purpose—the realm of Ultimate Reality and Meaning, or URAM for short, to invoke the name of an organization founded on this purpose.[16]

Among the compelling features of the nondual, integral worldview that jazz brings into focus is the inextricable link between practice and idea. Just as improvisation and musical understanding were seen in chapter 1 to be inextricably intertwined (the first is the basis for the second), the integral view of consciousness, particularly if it is to yield transformative impact, cannot be understood adequately apart from direct engagement in its core epistemology: meditation.

MEDITATION, SELF-REFERENCE, AND PURE CONSCIOUSNESS

Were consciousness to be defined in a single sentence, one need look no further than Webster's for a deceptively concise yet fertile example: Consciousness is "the state of being conscious."[17] Inherent in this definition, moreover, is not only the self-referral core of consciousness, but also the interplay of first-, second-, and third-person dimensions. "Consciousness," the first-person subjective facet, is the "state," which is third-person objectivity, of "being conscious," which is second-person process reality. Teilhard de Chardin offers a particularly powerful description of both the self-referral basis of human experience and its fruits: "Beings endowed with self-awareness become, precisely in virtue of that bending back upon themselves, immediately capable of rising into a new sphere of existence," wrote the twentieth-century Christian mystic. "Abstract thought, logic, reasoned choice and invention, mathematics, art, the exact computation of space and time, the dreams and anxieties of love, are simply the bubbling up of the newly formed life centre as it explodes upon itself."[18]

The question thus becomes, How can this self-referral power be harnessed for optimal creativity and consciousness development?

If improvisation represents the most primordial form of self-referral awareness in activity, reflecting the parts-to-whole epistemic core of jazz, meditation provides access to an even more fundamental form of such awareness in the form of pure consciousness, thus underpinning the complementary whole-to-parts development trajectory.

Meditation as Pure Consciousness in Silence

Meditation is a process whereby one steps back from ordinary mental, physical, sensory, and emotional engagement and allows the mind to experience deeper dimensions of itself. The procedure is often explained using a wave-ocean metaphor. Whereas much of day-to-day life involves being caught up in surface turbulence, hence the level of the wave, meditation involves contact with the ocean's silent depths. Over time, with regular practice, the quiescent clarity of the transcendent depths of the ocean infuses itself into everyday activity; wave and ocean coexist, resulting in ever-expanding creativity and consciousness. Or put another way, the personal self—which correlates with the wave—realizes itself as but an aspect of a transcendent and unbounded Self, which then promotes self-Self union, synonymous with yoga, or religion, in all facets of life. Transcendence in meditation is thus a self-referral condition of consciousness, in contrast to an object-referral orientation—where the self is overshadowed by objects of perception or active engagement, thus losing sight of its transcendent moorings—that prevails for many individuals in much of life. While meditation offers a respite from the turbulence of everyday life, its fuller purpose is to promote the capacity to engage with that turbulence from the standpoint of transcendent grounding.

Many forms of meditation exist. In addition to silent, sitting practice—perhaps the most commonly acknowledged modality—are contemplative approaches to movement, centering prayer, martial arts, tai chi, nature communion, writing, creative expression, reading, and interpersonal interaction. In all of these approaches, the intention is to render the activity a vehicle for some kind of deeper experience. Key features of such experience are heightened mental clarity, mind-body integration, self-awareness, experience of oneness with others and environment, compassion, and intuition. Inasmuch as any given individual will only be able to engage on a regular basis in a relatively small portion of the practices that might be deemed part of the meditative continuum, questions arise as to how to arrive at a personalized program that is meaningful, manageable, and productive.[19] While the range of possibilities will naturally vary considerably from one individual to another, I believe a strong case may be made for the inclusion of some period of silent, sitting meditation as a kind of anchor for whatever broader spectrum one arrives at. A look at the phenomenon of pure consciousness sheds light on this point.

Pure Consciousness as Contemplative Anchor

Pure consciousness is perhaps best understood as the coexistence of two realms of experience that, at first glance, may seem incompatible. On one hand is the experience of profound mental-physical stillness; on the other is an unmatched degree of radiant wakefulness. Both of these are difficult to imagine from the standpoint of ordinary consciousness. At first glance, the idea of infinitely silent, contentless consciousness may bear some similarity to sleep. However, nothing could be further from the case in that pure consciousness, which can be described as awareness of nothing but awareness itself, is also characterized by extraordinary degrees of alertness and clarity.[20] It is this coexistence of apparently extreme opposites—pristine silence and extraordinary wakefulness—that renders pure consciousness so foundational in the broader spectrum of contemplative engagement. With regular meditation practice over time, this core experience of self-Self integration has the capacity to inform and enhance depth of experience in more active contemplative modalities, and thus day-to-day activity—which is the ultimate purpose of meditation practice. Key benefits include heightened mental clarity, mind-body integration, well-being, self-awareness, oneness, intuition, personal relations, and creativity. Just as the systematic improvisation development continuum encompasses a broad range of increasingly differentiated modalities of musical engagement that extend from—yet coevolve with—the improvisatory source, what can be considered a parallel "systematic meditative development continuum" can be identified—as articulated above—in which a range of more differentiated modalities can similarly coevolve with the silent pure consciousness experience to promote transcendent integration over time. In the Upanishads, at the heart of the Vedantic literature, the experience of transcendent, self-Self union is called "turiya," which translates as the "fourth," meaning a state of consciousness beyond waking, dreaming, and sleeping. Alice Coltrane's adopted Sanskrit name—*turiyasangitananda*—reflects her grounding in the pure awareness that is the gateway to the broader spectrum of consciousness evolution.

At which point, the discussion shifts from temporary episodes of heightened consciousness, whether invoked in meditation or spontaneously occurring in one form of activity or another, as in peak experiences or flow,[21] to enduring transcendence—where self-Self integration is established as a permanent aspect of the totality of one's day-to-day experience, including waking, sleeping, and dreaming. When fleeting states become enduring stages, or the wave (self) realizes itself as permanent facet of the ocean (Self), this is called realization, or enlightenment. A growing body of literature on this evolutionary capacity, even if realized by a relatively small portion of the population in any era, underscores not only its universality, but also the fact that it tends to unfold in discrete evolutionary stages.[22]

HIGHER DEVELOPMENTAL STAGES

Turiyatita Chetena

The first of three higher, and thus enduring, stages is *turiyatita chetena*—which translates as transcendent integration of consciousness all the time, not just in isolated episodes.[23] With the onset of *turiyatita*, the personal self permanently experiences itself as a facet of the transcendent, eternal Self, which means liberation from objects of perception. Activity is thus endowed with the features noted above—profound fluidity, mind-body integration, extraordinary clarity, and well-being—and is accompanied by a witnessing quality, as if one is a silent observer to even the most intensive turbulence of everyday life.

In terms of conventional models or theories of consciousness, *turiyatita chetena* correlates with a very high form of dualism, a point that will become more apparent with consideration of two further higher stages that are progressively nondual in nature. Even though the personal self is no longer shrouded from its true nature as an aspect of the transcendent Self, subjective and objective reality are still experienced as fundamentally separate. I thus characterize this as "high" dualism in order to distinguish its perceptual criteria from conventional notions of dualism, which is what most individuals experience in ordinary consciousness. Whereas ordinary dualism is a facet of bondage to relativistic attachments, which masquerade as ontologically primary, the high dualism of *turiyatita,* a primary facet of which is liberation from such attachments, represents a radically new level of creativity and consciousness experience and functioning, including extraordinary levels of subject-object interconnectedness. Nonetheless, because objective reality is still perceived, albeit on a subtle scale, as distinct from subjective reality, some fact of dualism—which is perhaps thought of as a lingering remnant of the prior fragmentation—constrains awareness.

In terms of musical manifestations, improvisatory performance from this stage of consciousness development is characterized by heightened freedom, execution of ideas, and exceptional spontaneity. The conditions for evolution of the personal creative voice take a quantum stride forward, as liberation from conditioning allows a wider array of influences to inform that voice over time.[24] Although it is possible for nonimprovising musicians to glimpse and even gain enduring grounding in *turiyatita,* the sheer force of the improvisatory impulse that is inherent in consciousness on individual and cosmic scales will strongly seek openings in the daily practice of any such musicians. I have witnessed a number of instances where improvisation would gradually become part of the identity of fine interpretive performance specialists who took up meditation.

In terms of social justice ramifications, the very liberation from objects of perception and conditioned impressions that is central to enhanced fluidity of expression and individuation also aids in the identification, critical interrogation, and rectification of inherited ethnocentric/racialized, sexist, and other limiting patterns in thought, speech, and action. However, recalling my comments on critical thinking in chapter 4, in no way does this mean that these forms of liberation occur spontaneously, and that individuals operating from this level of creativity and consciousness development need not commit to the intensive work required for this kind of healing in the majority of the population. Rather, individuals established in *turiyatita* have a deep internal basis from which extraordinary progress may unfold, and possibly quite swiftly along any given pathological line.[25] In other words, an abiding love for humanity endemic to enduring self-Self union does not immediately presuppose a love that flows freely within all cultural, gender, and other channels, even if the waves of this love seek to overflow whatever obstacles stand in the way; individuals must attend to these obstacles through domain-specific modalities.

Bhagavat Chetena

A second higher stage is *bhagavat chetana.*[26] Here, in addition to the enduring self-Self integration characteristic of *turatita* and all the corresponding transformative aspects of experience, two key developments blossom with profound ramifications for creativity, consciousness, and social activism. One is that perception becomes more refined, opening up to subtle dimensions of relativistic creation that were not as accessible in the previous stage. Second is a powerful heart opening with both strong devotional qualities and also the enlivenment of subtle dimensions of feeling and intuition that are key to subtle perception. This perception can manifest in the apprehension of deities, or discarnate entities, as in the ancestors of African and other religious lineages, or nature spirits. It is sometimes described as celestial perception, and accompanied by an intense luminosity in all aspects of one's surroundings. This level of perception correlates with the archetypal realm, that primordial junction point at which the first sproutings of differentiation from eternal, undifferentiated wholeness become manifest. An integral perspective illuminates parallels between Jung's conception of the archetypal domain and other readings from sources East and West.[27] Contrary to common, object-mediated misunderstandings of his conception, Jung was explicit on the nature of the archetype not as a discrete, fixed form—perhaps some sort of ethereal, metaphysical entity that might be mirrored in its exterior manifestation—but as a dynamic impulse that originates at the most subtle scales of cosmic differentiation. Archetypes "are very varied structures which all point back to one essentially unrepresentable basic form. The archetype belongs to the invisible, ultraviolet end of the psychic spectrum"[28]—which correlates with the subtlest stirring of the transcendent, cosmic Self as it reverberates within itself.

Particularly important is the role of heart and expanded capacities for feeling as key to apprehending this level of creation. Sometimes the onset of *bhagavat chetena* is described in terms of a level of devotion for, and appreciation of, the creation of such force that the Creator is inspired to reveal its most profound treasures and secrets to the individual possessed of such love and feeling. In the limited commentary one encounters about Alice Coltrane's life and work, a deeply heartfelt dissolution of personal ego in service to the divine is clearly evident in her spiritual vision, experience, and music. *Om Rama*, *Journey to Satchidananda*, and *Rama Katha* are among the many examples. Indeed, one need not look far for further examples of devotional music in jazz—Mary Lou Williams's *Mass*, Duke Ellington's *Sacred Concerts*, John Coltrane's *A Love Supreme*—let alone other musical traditions. The character of devotion that defines *bhagavat chetena* represents a particularly deep and sustained opening of the heart that is accompanied by expansion of perception of the subtlest realms of objective reality.

Therefore, whereas the prior stage of *turiyatita* involves a radical expansion of experience characterized by liberation from the bondage of objects of perception and thus awareness of the grounding of personal self in the transcendent Self, *bhagavat* opens up to the subtlest interstices at which self, and objective perception, differentiates from the eternal subject, the Self. Accordingly, while *bhagavat* might, as with its predecessor, still be seen as a high form of dualism, the boundaries between objective and subjective reality begin to significantly dissolve in this developmental stage. It is thus more aptly correlated with the panpsychism view of consciousness (see above commentary) due to the direct perception of all facets of objective reality—

even the most seemingly inanimate phenomena of the physical world—as teeming with life.[29] Just as *turiyatita* is a more differentiated, self-referral level of experience than ordinary, object-referral consciousness, *bhagavat* is a more differentiated level of experience along the higher stage, self-referral continuum.

In terms of musical ramifications, improvisation that is grounded in *bhagavat* will therefore not only exemplify all the qualities of *turiyatita*, but also be capable of even deeper levels of expressivity and interaction due to further heart opening and refinement of perception. Improvisers at this level will also evolve a nuanced understanding of musical reality that is significantly informed by the primordial, archetypal dimensions just discussed. For example, a strong case may be made that Black Atlantic Rhythm—the term Pressing used to describe globally resonant rhythmic languages with African and African American origins—is archetypally rich and will thus likely be central to the creativity, pedagogy, and inquiry among improvisers operating from the *bhagavat* level. An aesthetics of improvised music that transcends (yet includes) cultural boundaries, rooted in a primordial improvisatory archetypal awareness, will begin to crystallize in awareness. Moreover, the heart-opening characteristic of *bhagavat*, combined with its expanded cognitive capacities, provide an entirely new basis for the embrace of diverse cultures. When perception penetrates to the transcendent dimensions of a culture, mere tolerance—to cite a common buzzword used to advocate greater openness to other cultures than one's own—opens up to celebratory and loving embrace, in recognition of the fact that engagement with other cultures deepens one's own creative and spiritual development.[30] Here, too, is where the dynamic interplay between transcultural/exploratory and culture-specific grounding comes vividly into view; whereas artists grounded in *turiyatita* may still be prone to subordination of culture specific due to a robust exploratory thrust, in *bhagavat*, recognition of the beauty and power of the best of both worlds gains firm interior grounding.

At this stage, the improvisatory thrust in musical identity becomes even stronger than in *turiyatita*. It is far less likely that musicians established in *bhagavat* who come up through Interpretive Performance Specialist backgrounds will confine their work to interpretive performance. The sheer force of primordial creativity is too strong to impede the cosmic impulse to improvise. However, as discussed in earlier chapters, this is not to suggest one would therefore abandon interpretive performance even if it likely—despite being greatly enhanced by the expanded creative, cognitive, and transpersonal capacities—occupies a less prominent place in the broader musicianship palette.

I think of *bhagavat chetena* as the first stage of opening to the "primordial junction point" that is among the three key landmarks in the emergent, integral understanding of consciousness that jazz brings into view.

Brahmi Chetena

The third higher stage is *brahmi chetena*, some version of which appears as the culminating nondual stage across traditions.[31] Here a paradigmatic stride in consciousness occurs that is arguably as foundational as that which distinguishes the transformation from ordinary consciousness to *turiyatita*, and from *turiyatita* to *bhavagat*. This involves the direct experience of the totality of creation as a manifestation of the self, or Self—distinctions between which thus disappear. Or put another way, the personal self is so fully grounded in the eternal, universal Self that it not only is freed from object-referral attachments, but also has taken the next evolutionary stride of permanently experiencing all of creation—"all levels of mind and objective reality," notes Charles Alexander—"in terms of the Self."[32] Maharishi Mahesh Yogi explains that at this stage "the experiencer and the object of experience have both been brought to the same level of infinite value, and this encompasses the entire phenomenon of perception and action. The gulf between the knower and the object of knowing has been bridged."[33] An advanced follower of his reports the prevailing experience that "I am the entire universe. When I look at anything, I see consciousness. . . . I see subjectivity which has taken a form, which has adopted an appearance of matter."[34]

Therefore, whereas in *turiyatita*, even with its liberation from objects of perception and self-Self union, and *bhagavat*, with its unveiling of new dimensions of objective perception, experience is still dominated by some sense of an interior subjective world as distinct from an exterior, objective world, in *brahmi chetena*, subject-object boundaries disappear. All phenomena—from the tiniest particles of the quantum world to the most enormous dimensions spanned by the galaxies—are experienced as the divine spirit that is at the core of one's own being. *Aham Bramsmi*—"The individual is cosmic."[35] Articulation of this stage of consciousness evolution abounds across cultures: "If you draw aside the veils of the stars and the spheres," stated the ancient Iranian mystic Attar of Nishapur, "you see that all is one with the Essence of your own pure soul."[36] Thomas Traherne similarly recounted experiencing "the earth, the sea, the sky (as) the substance of my mind."[37]

As with the prior higher stages, a number of musical and activist ramifications extend from the *brahmi* stage of consciousness evolution. At the heart of the entire transformative continuum, however, is a particularly rich account of cosmic creation called *lila,* which translates as "play," from the Vedantic tradition that uniquely comes into view with this developmental level. With the onset of *brahmi chetena*, not only does *lila* become more than a concept—a directly experienced reality—but so does the idea of human improvising as a direct manifestation of the improvisatory foundations of the cosmos. No more powerful foundations exist for new paradigms of transformative musical artistry and activism.

Lila

The story begins with Brahman, the eternal cosmic source of all Being that exists at once as an infinite field of undifferentiated silence, yet also, being self-aware, as an unbounded reservoir of creative potentiality. In the activity of self-awareness, or the curving back of eternal consciousness onto itself, primordial ripples are generated in the ocean of pure, undifferentiated Brahmanic Being.[38] These constitute the core vibrations, or frequencies that are thought to be the building blocks of all creation. Note that inherent in this scenario is the interplay of first-second-third-person impulses—the integral trinity—on a primordial scale. Brahman as undifferentiated spirit or consciousness is first-person, subjective reality; the "folding back" of consciousness onto itself is second-person, process; and the primordial vibrations are the first stirrings of third-person, objective reality.[39]

Note too that the first sproutings of objective reality take hold as frequency, or sound, as a result of the self-reflexive movement of consciousness. Inherent in the "capacity for self-referral," or the capacity for consciousness to "double back on itself," according to the ancient sage Abhinavagupta, "there always arises a spontaneous sound"[40]—or "*spanda*"—that is the "essence of all." In more recent times, Maharishi Mahesh Yogi has elucidated a "mechanics of transformation of self-referral intelligence into the ever-expanding material universe," in which "all the material and nonmaterial expressions of creation have specific frequencies." In his *Apaurusheya Bhashya*, or commentary on Rig Veda, Maharishi elaborates at length on how not only the most primordial dimensions of material creation, but also music, originate in the self-referral play of creation that sustains the cosmos. "Gandharva music," as he expounds on the traditional Vedantic account, "is the music of the universe, the music of the basic intelligence, the melody in which the fundamental intelligence of Nature moves and administers and governs all the infinite diversity in the universe in the most orderly way."[41] His identification of the same self-referral dynamics of consciousness as the eternal essence of atma, or soul, further underscores the music-consciousness-cosmos relationship.[42]

"The concept of the harmony of the spheres," as the physicist Hans Kayser reminds us, is not unique to Indian philosophy, and "is as old as the first awakening of mankind to consciousness."[43] Corresponding correlations have been between musical pitch systems and intervals and phenomena as wide-ranging as planetary orbits, the orbits of electrons around the atomic nucleus, and the periodic table of the elements.[44] However, whereas these relationships have often been fathomed from a structural perspective, the notion of *lila* brings into view both structural and process dimensions of this correlation that are important to the emergent, transformation-based understanding of improvised musical art. For example, the Time Theory of Indian music, paralleling ideas from Plato and Pythagoras about the effect of modes on human behavior, can be thought of as structural in its correlations between the intervallic structure of the raga with the particular frequencies that prevail during different periods of the daily cycle. Performance of a morning raga is thereby thought to enliven dominant frequencies of that time period and generate a harmonizing and transformative effect on performer and environment. The relationship between interval structure and frequency of time of day is structural; the implicit requisite that the actual performance must be rooted in a deep level of consciousness that is receptive to these subtle dimensions of creation clearly reflects a process aspect.[45]

The process dimension becomes particularly vivid in the *lila* account, and particularly in the idea inferred from that account of an improvisatory core to human and cosmic creation. The roots of the process dimension lie in the activity of cosmic self-reference itself, which can be thought of as spontaneous invention on a primordial scale. The common notion of self-awareness may provide a fertile lens through which to grasp this idea. While self-awareness may be seen as a static conception of the essential nature of consciousness, Maharishi's notion of consciousness as a self-referral phenomenon invites a more dynamic, process-based understanding. His frequent reference to the self-referral nature of atma, or soul, is a primary example. Now conception of this innermost dimension of human nature as some form of object becomes grounded in understanding of soul as the movement or, more aptly put, reverberation of consciousness within itself on the eternal scale where individual and cosmic intelligence unite. Moreover, because the self-referral principle, as discussed, underlies creativity, it is but a small step to understand this in terms of spontaneous, self-interactive, invention—hence improvisation—on a most fundamental scale.

Further light is shed on this idea by the view of *lila,* as it is commonly portrayed, as a capricious, almost whimsical venture on the part of an eternal cosmic intelligence, inherent in which, as a field of all possibilities, is the choice to either create or not create. Ananda Coomaraswamy, for example, summarizing various traditional accounts, describes lila as "a kind of game and dalliance"[46] on the part of the eternal, unmanifested source of all Being that, as if confronted with the option of having a manifest creation or not, opts—perhaps out of a sense of loneliness—for the former. Rabindranath Tagore muses that "there is something in common between the lila of childhood and the works of God . . . (inherent in) their shared self-willed joy."[47] William Sax's characterization of *lila* as "mere sport" or "amusement"[48] is further consistent with the idea that the primordial impulse to differentiate constitutes a form of improvisatory play.

The notion of free will provides another connecting thread that is coherent with the human-cosmos improvisatory relationship. If Brahman—or God, Tao, Ushai, Great Spirit—can decide whether or not to create a universe due to its self-referral nature, human beings can opt to create on a day-to-day, moment-to-moment basis based in that same fundamental aspect of consciousness. Free will is at its core an improvisatory capacity rooted in the self-referral improvisatory foundations of cosmic existence. Interesting light is shed from this vantage point on the fact that denial of free will is perhaps the one area, even if from radically different vantage points, in which the extreme religious fundamentalist and scientific materialist/fundamentalist unite. Whereas the first worships a distant God that directs all facets of life in a deterministic, supernatural universe, the second worships matter as the basis of all experience and action in an equally deterministic, and equally supernatural, universe.[49] Both extremes are the result of notably weak improvising when it comes to the nature of consciousness and reality, and thus the denial of the improvisatory essence of that reality is perhaps not surprising.

To be sure, there is no denying the speculative nature of the human-cosmos improvisatory connection, and it goes without saying that readers will come to their own conclusions on this account. While, as intimated in chapter 1, my primary interest lies not in making a case for this point, but rather in harnessing practical applications from principles that might be inferred from this possibility, I believe it is worth considering how coherence between inferred premises and applications and the broader thesis may nonetheless uphold both ontological and practical functions. In chapter 6, for example, I distinguish between degrees of improvisatory expertise according to the degree of self-referral vitality that drives the creative process, by which I contrast heightened improvisatory functioning with diminished, object-referral improvising that is constrained by attachments to conditioned patterns. If one subscribes to the "general nonduality thesis," by which human consciousness is inextricably linked to divine universal consciousness, a precept that again is compatible with spiritual/religious wisdom traditions across the globe, then it is but a relatively small step to embrace the "strong nonduality thesis" and its positioning improvisation as a human-cosmic connecting thread according to shared self-referral dynamics.

The fact, moreover, that improvisation in one form or another is central to most of the world's music might thus be seen as a direct manifestation of, and further supporting consideration for, this precept. Also of note is that, returning to the Time Theory of Indian music, performance of the raga is almost completely improvised, suggesting that this particular kind of epistemological channel is required for primordial impulses to be enlivened and flow from the transcendent, atma/soul level and exert their transformative impact on individual and environment. Which, in turn, poses important ramifications for jazz as the primary improvisatory channel in the West.

MUSICAL AND TRANSFORMATIVE ACTIVIST RAMIFICATIONS

First involves the systematic improvisatory development continuum becoming most fully grounded in musical identity. If individual self-awareness is experienced as cosmic self-awareness, then individual improvisatory identity is rooted in the cosmic improvisatory thrust. Moreover, because higher stages are more differentiated than their predecessors, then musical identity in *brahmi chetena* is optimally differentiated—thus encompassing not only the expanded scope of the systematic improvisatory continuum, but also its rich diversity and integration within that scope. *Brahmi* is where the vertical positioning of this improvisatory continuum both gains deepest grounding and is also capable of maximal horizontal expanse. For musicians grounded in *brahmi*, an improvisation-based identity is not only at the heart of their artistic and personal being, but also rooted in direct apprehension of the improvisatory-core of cosmic Being. The individual-cosmic connection also renders improvisation-driven musical development as uniquely rigorous and self-organizing, not to mention critically and self-critically robust. Such musicians will also likely sustain self-cultural grounding along with some form of engagement with traditions (if different from self-cultural) in which connections between musical languages and cosmic order are robust.

Second is that musicians operating from the level of *brahmi*, because they are most fully capable of navigating the subtle intersection between undifferentiated, eternal consciousness and the most primordial, archetypal strata of differentiation, are most capable of evolving deep connections with the cultural diversity of the musical world. The transcultural paradigm may thus blossom most fully in musical understanding. Diverse ethnicities, cultures, genders, and disciplines are experienced not only in their manifest form, but also as subtle reverberations in the deepest dimensions of spiritual Being. The principle that black, white, yellow, red, and all the color-coded ethnicities that comprise the world's human rainbow are inherent in the consciousness in every single individual is thus more than an inspiring concept; it is a directly experienced reality. As the task of the human being is to realize this rainbow by embracing the contributions of all constituencies in all creative endeavors, the archetypal topographies discussed in the context of *bhagavat chetena*—Black Atlantic Rhythm, improvisation as divine feminine—become even more vivid. In chapter 6, consideration of improvisation and the Afrological wave in the musical ocean as manifestations of divine feminine archetypal energy, and composition—and the Eurological—as masculine—are rooted in a nondual, *brahmi chetena* perspective.[50]

Third are correlations between large improvising ensembles and collective meditation, both of which harness the transformative power of intersubjective consciousness.[51] Amid the growing body of research, to be considered more fully shortly, that points toward a nonmaterialist, integral understanding of consciousness is a class of findings that support the idea of a collective dimension of consciousness. Of particular interest among these findings, moreover, are those that suggest large meditation groups may generate a harmonizing influence on surroundings. The basic idea extends from the premise that the experience of pure consciousness in individual meditation practice, in which the self-referral condition of consciousness is optimal, enlivens the self-referral mechanics of cosmic intelligence. In groups, this enlivenment is intensified, resulting in—according to some studies—reduced accident, crime, and hospitalization rates.[52] While far more research is needed in this area, I believe these preliminary findings at the very least warrant serious consideration given the potential implications for addressing terrorism, war, and even environmental crises.

The principle of intersubjective consciousness, moreover, suggests direct application to the idea of jazz as catalyst for an arts-driven revolution in creativity and consciousness. The emergence of the large stylistically open improvising ensemble, a development that extends organically from jazz, is the correlate to the large meditation group. Here is where the idea of complementary parts-to-whole/whole-to-parts epistemologies inherent in the jazz tradition spawn a new level of manifestation: whereas the large meditation group is a whole-to-parts social transformative modality, the large improvising ensemble is a parts-to-whole arts transformative modality. Were a music studies paradigm predicated on preparing musicians to function in such improvising ensembles, which would invite, and require, the totality of the systematic improvisatory development continuum, this would promote receptivity to engagement in large meditation groups, where intersubjective consciousness is enlivened from the standpoint of collective silence. And of course, participation in such groups would feed back to inspire engagement—for practicing musicians and listeners alike—with large improvisatory ensemble music making. The point, moreover, is not that large-group improvising would replace small group playing, nor that collective meditation would replace individual meditation, but that the expanded spectrum would open up broader aesthetic and societal transformative possibilities.

The principle of collective consciousness in turn spawns a fourth musical/activist ramification, involving the transcendence of language-bound categories, with "science" and "spirituality" as primary examples. Now competing domains, the division between which poses serious ramifications for the future of the world, may be optimally seen as complementary self-transcending gateways to wholeness. Important to the science-spirituality union is the diagnosis of lingering and pervasive materialist tendencies, for which jazz-inspired insights may be invaluable.

THE COLLAPSE OF MATERIALISM: EMPIRICAL, THEORETICAL, AND ACTIVIST CONSIDERATIONS IN SUPPORT OF THE INTEGRAL VIEW OF CONSCIOUSNESS

Anomaly Centering and Psi

Perhaps the most powerful contribution that jazz has to make is in its capacities to transcend language-bound categories and promote thinking and dialogue that extend beyond conventional horizons. The kind of robust creative exploration, rigorous attention to detail and craft, and deep penetration to the innermost regions of consciousness—which bring into play the most far-reaching questions about Ultimate Reality and Meaning—that extend organically from an integral view of jazz represent a scope of inquiry few fields can match. Among the ramifications of this scope are capacities for what I call "anomaly centering," where ideas and practical possibilities that extend far beyond the horizons of conventional, materialist thought are placed front and center, where they can be critically examined in terms of their validity and future application and development. No more vivid example is to be found than that of "psi" phenomena, involving extended capacities of consciousness, that have been the subject of thousands of scientific experiments and that—even if a tiny fraction of the findings are valid—issue fatal challenges to materialism.

Psi research has been conducted at laboratories at top educational institutions, medical centers, private laboratories, and the U.S. military. Key examples include *remote cognition*, the ability to gain information at a distance without the aid of ordinary sensory perception. *Telepathy* involves transmission of information from one mind to another. *Discarnate consciousness* (consciousness without a physical substrate) has been studied in three forms: out-of-body experiences, communication with discarnate entities, and reincarnation studies. *Intersubjective consciousness*, or collective mind, as discussed above involves a field aspect of consciousness, much akin to C. G. Jung's notion of collective unconscious, to which all of human experience is connected. *Psychokinesis* involves mind-matter interactions.[53] It might also be noted that psi capacities correlate with advanced yogic practices, as in the siddhis of Patanjali's yoga sutras, claims and testimonies for which abound in spiritual traditions from time immemorial. Psi research may provide the beginnings of empirical support for these capacities.

Edgar Mitchell founded the Institute for Noetic Sciences to study these phenomena, with organizations such as Society for Scientific Exploration, World Institute for Scientific Exploration, Scientific and Medical Network and the Society for Consciousness Studies, the Global Consciousness Project, and the University of Virginia Medical School's Division of Perceptual Studies also committed to this work. By now, the sheer volume of scientific research in support of these capacities, and in turn of a view of consciousness as physically transcendent, nonlocal, and intersubjective—all of which shatter the materialist paradigm—is nothing short of overwhelming.[54]

Nonetheless, in light of Kuhn's analysis of paradigmatic change in the sciences, one can only imagine the resistance to these ideas, let alone findings, that is inherent in the materialist-bound scientific community. Consistent with much of the literature on the topic, psychologist Imants Baruss and neuroscientist Julia Mossbridge not only underscore the compelling scope and nature of the evidence and support it with theoretical rationale, but also do not mince words about the sociopolitical dynamics of prevailing—even if eroding—materialist ideology that either refuses to acknowledge this body of work, or overtly seeks to refute it without an informed basis. In revealing "materialism as dogma," as opposed to critically robust theory, the authors identify a range of prevailing objections to anomalous phenomena that "distort science so that it no longer functions properly but devolves into scientism, with materialism as its central tenet." These kneejerk reactions to psi findings and their fatal challenges to materialism include "false insistence that there is no evidence," uninformed explanation of findings from carefully constructed scientific studies as "hallucination, delusion, or wishful thinking," categorical "rejection of papers from scientific journals simply due to their content," and derogatory characterization of this research as "fraudulent."[55]

Materialism succumbs to a further lapse in critical integrity when research that correlates subjective experience with measurable neurobiological activity is cited as evidence for its (materialist) platform and against alternatives, if not in many materialists' minds, incontrovertible proof of the physical basis of consciousness. But this violates a basic tenet of scientific method: correlation does not equal causation. In other words, just because objective correlates may be identified does not mean the subjective realm is caused by, or is even a by-product of, the objective. The same findings that show subjective experience has objective correlates could be interpreted to support nonphysicalist accounts of consciousness such as the integral, nondual view.[56] As Baruss and Mossbridge note, inviting parallels to neo-Eurocentric and neo-Eurocentric-plus/multicultural paradigms in music studies: "In the course of their training, scientists are seldom led through a process of self-development whereby they can identify and neutralize the various distorting mechanisms."[57] These observations are consistent with leading psi researcher Dean Radin's pioneering contributions to both the research and assessment of the sociopolitical dynamics that prevail in the conventional science community, as reflected in the title of a chapter called "A Field Guide to Skepticism" from an early book of his.[58] In short, what commonly masquerades as critical integrity is revealed, upon closer inspection, to be rigid and exclusionary bias that is driven by fear, misinformation, and arguably even misconduct. Or as it might be framed from an integral jazz perspective, extremely weak improvising in the mainstream science community that rivals that of the mainstream music studies community. While, as noted, there are clear signs that the foundations of the materialist empire have begun to tremble, the integral change activist is wise to be abreast of the lingering inertia of this worldview.[59]

Conceptual Conundrums:
Two Hard Problems of Consciousness

While materialism so far has been able to evade direct confrontation with the growing body of consciousness research that would likely be its undoing, it has also—from a position of loftier intention—raised important questions that are equally critical to an understanding of consciousness. Among these questions is the "hard problem" of consciousness, based on the epiphenomalist assumption that consciousness emerges from a physical substrate. The easy problem of consciousness is the understanding that mind and brain are linked, which as noted above, is typically viewed in terms of neurobiological and other physiological correlates with (but not causes of) subjective experience. The hard problem is predicated on brain as foundational to mind, and thus the question of how the first gives rises to the second.[60]

From an integral perspective, the foundational premise of matter or biology as foundational to consciousness is skewed. "How does the self-aware entity emerge from deeper and more elementary physical processes?" asks the physicist Fred Alan Wolff in his challenge to the very assumptions underlying the hard problem. "The answer is, it doesn't, and this is very difficult to deal with in today's materialist science." Pointing instead toward a nondual vision, he asserts that "one eternal consciousness"[61] is the ontological ground of reality, an idea that is compatible with what mystics from the world's wisdom traditions have been asserting for millennia. David Chalmers, whose work has been seminal in framing the hard problem in the first place, while long reticent to embrace the nondual primacy of consciousness, initially deferred to dualism as, at least, a more palatable alternative to the materialist position. More recently, he has entertained the possibility of a view of consciousness that leans in an integral, nondual direction. As he quips, "One starts as a materialist, then turns into a dualist, then a panpsychist, then an idealist."[62] This is largely due to conceptual conundrums inherent in the spectrum short of the integral, nondual (synonymous with idealism) viewpoint, without taking anomalous empirical findings such as psi into account.[63]

What's a materialist to do? As I have put it, colleagues that harbor materialist inclinations find themselves caught between a "reductionist rock and an epiphenomenalist hard place."[64] In other words, if on one hand the idea that consciousness is nothing but the brain defies all experience, intuition, and reasoning, and on the other hand, the idea that consciousness emerges from a physical substrate is becoming increasingly difficult to explain, adherents of the conventional physicalist paradigm confront a scarcity of options.

In my view, integral nonduality only adds to the challenges by bringing in both new levels of critical vitality to the inquiry itself as well as further possibilities that point in the direction of an integral understanding of consciousness. For example, I have proposed a "second-tier hard problem" of consciousness that is based in the possibility of intersubjective consciousness discussed above.[65] Returning to this idea from a different angle, at first glance, intersubjective or collective consciousness would appear to be an emergent feature of individual consciousness. In other words, the personal consciousness of every individual from this vantage point would inform an overarching field of consciousness that is epiphenomenal to the localized awareness of each individual. At which point, a parallel question to that of the basic hard problem comes into view: *How* does intersubjectivity emerge from subjectivity? From an integral standpoint, so does a parallel reply: it doesn't; intersubjectivity is primary to subjectivity. In other words, individual consciousness is epiphenomenal to collective, or intersubjective, consciousness, not the other way around. Or put another way: intersubjectivity—consistent with de Chardin's notion of "noosphere"—is primordial to individuality. This, however, is not to rule out a two-way interaction, where individuality also informs collectivity. But in terms of ontological origins, the intersubjective is primordial in that it is none other than the eternal field of consciousness from which the infinitely diverse creation emerges. As such, enlivenment of collective consciousness through collective meditation practices, group improvisatory creativity, and other collective endeavors has great transformative potential.[66]

Taken alone, the conceptual coherence that the integral, nondual worldview exhibits across a wide range of application that, in my view, dwarfs that which is found in materialist discourse, which in fact is incoherent within a narrow range of applications. When, as noted, this is combined with empirical support, as in psi research, the integral argument only gains strength. Nonetheless, the materialist backdrop—what above I call the Matrix of Materialism—continues to exert its influence far and wide, even infiltrating spiritual discourse that one might presume to be immune to materialist influence.

Inertia of Anatta: Pseudo-Buddhist Materialist Dogma

Connections are sometimes drawn between materialism and the Buddhist doctrine of *anatta*, or *anatman*, which translates as "no self," in attempts to highlight, if not privilege, the unique contributions of Buddhism in the overall spiritual landscape. However, the *anatta* concept is properly understood as the transitory and conditioned nature of the personal self, not—as it is commonly misunderstood—the ontological absence of transcendent Self, or soul. As Owen Flannagan nevertheless proclaims to the contrary, Buddhism—precisely due to its *anatman* underpinnings—stands out among the world's spiritual traditions in its alignment with "how science says we ought to see the world," a view in which there "are no souls, no disembodied spirits" nor other metaphysical constructs such as reincarnation that purportedly undermine the credibility of other spiritual traditions.[67] Just as materialism denies the soul, as a dimension of consciousness that transcends the physical, so—the thinking erroneously goes—does Buddhism.

It is difficult to imagine a more striking irony, nor glaring misrepresentation, in this position: Flannagan, who is quick to mention his direct contact with the Dalai Lama, fails to acknowledge that these same dimensions of human consciousness he claims are anomalous to Buddhist cosmology are, in fact, central to that of the very Buddhist lineage in which His Holiness is a leading exponent. As Nan Huaijin admonishes in response to this kind of misconception: "When this [doctrine of no self] flowed into the world of learning, especially when it was disseminated in the West, some people thought that the Buddhist idea of no self was nihilism and that it denied the soul, and they maintained that Buddhism is atheistic. This is really a joke."[68] Even a brief look at the Tibetan view of consciousness, with its principle of *alaya-vijnana*, or universal mind, and the various strata of *bardos*, or stations through which disembodied spirits progress in between incarnations, reveals the integral foundations of authentic Buddhism and the skewed nature of the emergent, Westernized interpretation of these tenets and this tradition. Regardless of how one views the viability of these integral precepts, or my argument that they are consistent with both ancient accounts of consciousness and cutting-edge consciousness research, to ignore them amidst claims for a Buddhism-science confluence is to sell both Buddhism and science short in terms of the deeper understanding of both realms that is possible and needed in today's world. Yet another example of scientific materialist inertia.[69]

As I have argued, this conception of Buddhism has constrained the burgeoning contemplative studies movement that has taken hold in higher education over the past two decades. Although this movement lays claim to a commitment to diverse approaches, the prevalence of mindfulness practice, the origins of which are most directly traced to Buddhism, has promoted a kind of de facto quasi-Buddhist conceptual backdrop in contemplative studies circles. Because, as just noted, Western Buddhism—even when adherents do not identify as materialists—is constrained by materialist inclinations, ambivalence to spiritual or metaphysical considerations pervades the culture of the emergent field. To be fair, concerns about religious incursion in the academy have never been higher given today's highly charged, theopolitical climate, thereby fueling a backdrop of suspicion against which contemplative education advocates—already with their hands full in advancing an entirely new epistemological paradigm—must operate. Still, I do not believe it is unreasonable to identify interior, self-induced obstacles that work in tandem with those inherited externally. As I argue elsewhere, the time has come to not retreat further into the trenches of church-state boundaries, but in fact to revisit that divide and penetrate more fully into the self-transcending nondual foundations of human consciousness, thereby reinventing, at once, the very notions of religion and education, and their inextricable relationship. I believe the contemplative studies movement, providing it examines its own materialist inertia, can play a key role in this transformation.[70]

Connections might also be noted with the "spiritual-but-not-religious" (SBNR) movement that has gained momentum since the latter half of the twentieth century. While little commentary is required as to why one might seek a spiritual identity outside of organized religion, it is also important to acknowledge the prospects by which one sort of dogma might replace the other. Whereas conventional religious denominations succumb to a conception of God as some external, judgmental entity that rules the world, SBNR thinking can take the other extreme and succumb to vague conceptions of wholeness that lack the dynamic, coevolutionary, nondual creative connections that may be read in the world's wisdom traditions. Moreover, religious lineages are steeped in rituals that, even if not often fully understood, may enliven subtle, primordial impulses that resonate with individuals of a given culture. The primary task of twenty-first-century spiritual leadership is not to inspire ambivalence, let alone aversion, to religious traditions but to inspire deeper fathoming of the transcendent underpinnings of these traditions and reclaiming of the yogic, unitive practices that integrate self and Self. It may be that adopting a spiritual but not religious identity serves a purpose during the journey, and that for some this constitutes a viable pathway in itself. However, I believe it is imperative that a fuller account of possibilities and pathologies—including the SBNR identity as a potential kind of dissociation in itself—is placed front and center if individuals are to make the most informed choices. From this standpoint, SBNR identification may at times succumb, much like multiculturalism, to being more of a reaction to an oppressive worldview than the embrace of a worldview unto itself.[71]

Important social justice transgressions also come into view as a result of materialist inertia.

Social Justice Considerations

Several angles may be identified. The first involves the epistemology-ethnology relationship: the privileging of third-person, object-mediated modes of inquiry—which are the central locus of the scientific method—represents a culturally mediated privileging, that of the dissociated lens of the past few centuries of Western culture. Moreover, this disadvantages individuals who come from underprivileged backgrounds and for whom the disconnection of spirituality/religion from scientific inquiry (whether in science per se or overall academic practice, thus including humanities) is far more egregious in its impact than for individuals of privileged backgrounds. In other words, the obstacles inherent in day-to-day survival that are part and parcel of underserved communities render connection with spiritual/religious foundations more meaningful and relevant—if not necessary—in all areas of inquiry. This is not a statement about deficient intelligence or coping mechanisms that need to be developed, but in fact a recognition of circumstances by which oppressed constituencies, already denied overlying resources for conventional educational success, are also denied access—due to the materialist educational paradigm—to the integrative and transcendent foundations of knowledge that could be important to self-identity, fulfillment, meaning, purpose, and well-being. The point is not that students of privileged backgrounds do not also need this kind of grounding. Rather, it is that they typically do not need to worry in nearly the same way as students from underprivileged communities about threats of violence on their way to school, or where their next meal might come from (or when), nor do they need to overcome race-based challenges to self-esteem, baseline happiness, sense of belonging, and hopefulness—for all of which scientific research is consistent with my assessment[72]—that pose undue hurdles to learning. Therefore, students from privileged backgrounds can at least function in the culture of competition, fragmentation, and epistemic dearth that increasingly characterizes the educational system and rise through its ranks far more readily. The playing field is anything but level when it comes to the conditions that determine who succeeds in this important stratum of society and who does not.

Therefore, to the phenomenon of white privilege, and what I proposed as white musical privilege (which is rooted in a creativity crisis), I suggest the addition of a more general pattern of "white epistemic privilege," which is rooted in the overwhelming foregrounding of dominant-culture, object-mediated pedagogy at the expense of interior experience and development. While this outmoded and unsustainable educational paradigm spawns casualties throughout the societal spectrum, it places the black child at far greater risk as a result of its limited foundations. Moreover, inasmuch as the educational paradigm is a direct manifestation of an overarching, yet scarcely examined, materialist notion of the human being, it is not an unreasonable stretch to characterize the prevailing scientific materialist worldview as racist—not in its explicit horizons of understanding, but in terms of the knowledge and constituencies it excludes as a result of its overarching impact. Given that there are many in the science community, perhaps even a majority, who are intensely committed to social justice in general, and the alleviation of racism in particular, there is no denying the deeply problematic, if not outrageous nature of my assessment. I would level a parallel assessment when it comes to the environment; many of the very adherents of the scientific materialist paradigm are also deeply concerned about climate change and staunch advocates of ecological activism of various kinds, even as the materialist worldview contributes to the crises and may preclude important consciousness-based interventions.

Both instances are further examples of the worldview/workplace paradox that I examined in the previous chapter in respect to music. Whereas participants in the neo-Eurocentric framework are challenged to reconcile progressive societal inclinations with inherent ethnocentric/racialized underpinnings of their musical grounding, participants in the conventional science field are similarly challenged to reconcile overarching progressivism with the overarching ideology in their workplace. This kind of analysis exemplifies the power of the jazz-inspired integral perspective to move fluidly across, and to critically interrogate, boundaries and assumptions that otherwise go unnoticed—when it comes to paradigmatic change. In chapter 7, I discuss the important contributions that an "Integral Improvisatory Hermeneutics" has to offer in identifying and addressing these patterns.

CLOSING THOUGHTS: CONSCIOUSNESS EXPLAINED BEST

Daniel Dennett's *Consciousness Explained*[73] has been hailed by some as a landmark in materialist philosophy and may be as radical in its questioning of the very existence of consciousness as the integral nondual account is in ascribing consciousness to cosmic origins. Allan Combs's delightfully titled *Consciousness Explained Better*,[74] while not engaging Dennett head-on, clearly serves as a rejoinder in powerfully steering the conversation in an integral direction. I believe the jazz-inspired account I advance above is among the most complete in the integral literature on consciousness due to the range of criteria it brings together in a composite ontological lens. These include the centering of the creativity-consciousness relationship and its self-referral foundations on human and cosmic scales, particularly as illuminated through improvisatory creativity; broad continua of meditative and improvisatory practices that reveal, respectively, rich contemplative and creative topographies; developmental stages and extended capacities of consciousness (psi), particularly involving intersubjective consciousness; new perspectives on prevailing conundrums (hard problem of consciousness, plus my notion of second-tier hard problems); and potential societal transformation applications. Whereas materialist literature, as I have noted, is remarkably narrow in terms of its parameters of inquiry, I believe the jazz-inspired inquiry ventured herein introduces fundamentally new perspectives and thus expands the spectrum of nonmaterialist approaches as well. Furthermore, although the social justice ramifications (ethnocentric/racialized biases in materialist ideology) that I draw may not uphold an ontological function, meaning contributing to the *what* of consciousness, I believe they add to the overall coherence of the vision I put forth. If materialism is revealed to be on shaky ground in response to any one or two of these angles, it collapses dramatically under the weight of the totality. While it goes without saying that readers will come to their own conclusions about the nature of consciousness, I hope if nothing else those still disposed toward materialism in one form or another will not settle for the narrow horizons within which materialism—which again I attribute to a form of white epistemic privilege—is typically framed. Not only are the boundaries between cultural provincialism (ethnology) and intellectual provincialism (epistemology) thin, but also the integral worldview reveals them to be nonexistent.

I also hope that colleagues will situate the inquiry within the context of the ramifications of the worldview to which they subscribe for the future of our planet. In other words, what kind of worldview is optimally equipped to address the challenges—ecological, economic, epidemiological, social justice, cultural, ideological, theological—of our times?

A materialist worldview that depicts the human being as an accidental outgrowth in a physical universe devoid of meaning and purpose, denies the existence of soul or transcendent, interior dimensions of consciousness, and regards spirituality/religion as outmoded superstition?

A dualist worldview that subscribes to the notion of a distant deity and spiritual reality that occupy a fundamentally separate plane of existence from human life?

Or an integral worldview that, celebrating the most profound wisdom of the world's spiritual/religious traditions as well as contemporary developments and understanding, views human consciousness—and thus soul—as inextricably linked to the eternal, cosmic intelligence that is the source of all Being and Creation, and positions the human being as co-evolutionary participant in the cosmic improvisatory unfolding?

Perhaps the most important criterion upon which to reply is, What is the most exciting worldview, in terms of personal resonance, and vision of possibilities for the world? For me, materialism not only is internally incoherent but also provides the least sense of hope, optimism, and excitement for the future of humanity. The ideas, on the other hand, inherent in the nondual, integral view of consciousness that the mechanics by which the cosmos creates its infinite diversity exists right in our own consciousness—and that we can not only tap into these mechanics individually but also come together in collective improvisatory and meditative formats and enliven these principles to heal the world and catapult humanity to a new evolutionary plateau—are, to me, brimming with hope and excitement.

In chapter 7, I reflect further on consciousness as the next major frontier in human exploration and future visioning, and propose that within this frontier, the principles as discussed in this chapter of pure consciousness, intersubjective or collective consciousness, and the primordial junction point are key landmarks that jazz helps bring into view. First, however, a more complete probing of the improvisatory foundations of jazz, which the above account of consciousness uniquely makes possible, is in order.

Chapter Six

A Consciousness-Based Integral Perspective on Improvisation

Defining *improvisation* may seem much less daunting than defining *consciousness*. For one thing, competing viewpoints on the first topic are much more difficult to find than on the second. Whereas, as discussed in the previous chapter, a wide range of possibilities—including dualism, reductionism, epiphenomenalism, panpsychism, and integralism—might be considered in respect to the nature of consciousness, improvisation boasts no such spectrum of interpretations. The everyday notion of improvisation as "spontaneous creativity with little or nothing planned in advance" seems to suffice, and in fact yields a perfectly viable platform for integral elaboration.

However, a more problematic subset of this definition also prevails in music circles that directly contradicts integral principles yet goes largely unquestioned. This is the view of improvisation as spontaneous, real-time composition.[1] In other words, the idea that the improviser in a single, continuous creative episode—which often involves collective formats—engages in the same kind of moment-to-moment decision-making processes as does the composer, who works alone over a discontinuous series of creative episodes. Why is this problematic? Because, among a number of factors, understanding improvisation as a subspecies of composition perpetuates lingering stereotypes of improvisation, and thus a significantly improvisatory artform such as jazz, as a less-sophisticated, undisciplined endeavor.[2] I also consider how this misconception overlooks foundational cognitive and cultural distinctions between the processes, thus limiting awareness of the different roles they uphold in navigating and understanding the musical world around us. I show how the two creative modalities, when understood as contrasting, yet complementary, creative modalities within a given skill set, such as that of the

CICP, provide a basis for an entirely new paradigm of music studies and practice.[3]

In my view, therefore, the lack of competing viewpoints on the nature of improvisation is more indicative of a conversation that, unlike that regarding the nature of consciousness, has scarcely begun to take hold, rather than being reflective of critical consensus that has been achieved following extensive deliberations on the topic. The improvisation-as-real-time-composition assumption, even if widely harbored, is thus most aptly viewed as a received precept inherited from a paradigm-blind compositioncentric culture. I build on prior efforts to, at the very least, elevate critical discourse by extricating improvisation from the prevailing classification and viewing each process on its own terms. Although I argue that contemporary manifestations of improvising and composing have differentiated from a common improvisatory ancestor, an understanding of them as fundamentally distinct expressive streams underscores the richness of possibilities in the CICP paradigm and contemporary creative practice. As Steve Lacy has wisely reflected, "There is a music which music be composed, there is another that can only be improvised."[4]

However, I do not suggest that the two creative processes share no points of intersection, as in musical terrain, in which the lines between them are blurred. Indeed, as I comment later, one of the features of an integral aesthetic paradigm, signs of which are increasingly evident, is the emergence of creative expression in which improvisation and composition merge in new ways. Nonetheless, not only does a vast amount of music exist in which the lines are clear, but this will also continue in the future, with, in fact, the emergence of stylistically open large improvisation ensembles that comprise the basis for an integral improvised music aesthetics. Accordingly, extrication of improvisation from erroneous classification as an accelerated form of composition is essential to fathoming much current practice, as well as shedding light on new evolutionary strides.

I frame my account through a model called Nonlinear Time Dynamics, central to which is the relationship between time and consciousness. Composers invoke transcendent states of consciousness through an expanding, linear conception of time; improvisers invoke transcendence via an innerdirected, nonlinear conception of time.[5] The first is conducive to the kind of large-scale formal architectures typically associated with composed, notated repertory. The second, while exhibiting its own kind of structural richness, is conducive to the spontaneous inventive and interactive creativity that is at the heart of an improvisation-based aesthetic. The point is not to privilege one process or aesthetic paradigm over the other, but to illuminate them as contrasting epistemologies with very different cultural and transpersonal roots in order to underscore the richly differentiated creative scope inherent in the jazz-based Contemporary Improviser Composer Performer template.[6]

I begin with an overview of five parameters of distinctions between improvisation and composition. I then delve into the inner mechanics of the two processes as contrasting pathways to transcendence. Looking at improvisation through the lens of collective, free improvisation from the outset, the chapter then takes up improvisation in preordained creative frameworks, using the harmonic-rhythmic structures of jazz as an example. Connections between improvisation, composition, and culture are then considered, followed by investigation of archetypal correlations that might be drawn with the respective creative modalities. The chapter closes with a look at pedagogical and societal ramifications to be drawn from the distinctions. Tendencies to define improvisation as a subset of composition may be correlated with materialist conceptions of consciousness as reducible, or epiphenomenal to, a physical substrate—in both instances, a prevailing third-person backdrop imposes its objective imprint on all that it sees. Just as understanding consciousness through a materialist lens radically diminishes the vision of human potential, the quest to understand improvisation as a composition subcategory sells both processes short and radically diminishes our understanding of the musical world around us.

OVERVIEW OF FIVE DISTINGUISHING PARAMETERS

To begin with an overview of five parameters of distinctions between improvisation and composition, first involves the contrasting conditions of the two processes, which will help clarify my conception of the terms: composition typically occurs through a series of discontinuous creative episodes, while improvisation happens in a single continuous creative stream. Composers can alter ideas during the creative process; improvisers have no such provision.[7] Compositions are typically created at times and places that differ from rehearsal, which differs from those of performance. Improvisation entails simultaneous creation and performance. Composition involves a single creating individual working in isolation, while improvisation—which certainly can happen in an unaccompanied format—often is collective. Later I show how the nonlinear temporality that is intrinsic to collective improvising informs unaccompanied improvising and enables distinctions between that and what might seem to be the identical practice of extemporaneous composition, with the only differences being semantic.

From these contrasting conditions stems a second key parameter of difference—involving contrasting modes of temporal experience. In other words, time is experienced differently in the two creative modalities. Composers experience time in a linear way, in which temporal relationships between present moments and past predecessors and future successors may be conceived, altered, and developed. The discontinuous and unaccompanied nature of the compositional process is conducive to this kind of attention to temporal relationships, which is key to the construction of large-scale formal architectures.[8]

Improvisers experience time in a nonlinear way, in which the conception of the localized present is heightened, and relationships to past and future are subordinate. Because the future is unknown in improvisation, awareness is directed toward the moment. An important factor for this in collective improvisation formats is what I call "interfering implications,"[9] where the need to continually negotiate the interplay of ideas of improvising partners drives awareness to the point in time about which one can be most sure—again, the present. While this inner-directed, nonlinear conception is not conducive to the construction of large-scale architectures, at least as they are possible in composition, it is conducive to powerful and transformative interactive engagement, key to an improvised music aesthetics.

Third, the contrasting temporalities of the two operations serve as contrasting channels to transcendent experience. Compositional transcendence is driven by the expansion of ordinary consciousness boundaries of the present in the expanding, linear flow. Improvisatory transcendence is driven by the collapse of ordinary consciousness-present boundaries within the inner-directed, nonlinear flow of time. Object-referral patterns in composition manifest themselves in "weak spans," in composition in the form of "inflated points."[10]

These differences are consistent with composers' and improvisers' accounts of transcendent experience. Composers describe peak experiences in terms of conceptions of large-scale forms in a given instant; improvisers recount episodes of heightened interaction and creative flow. Cultural distinctions are examined through the lens of connections between the nonlinear temporality of improvisation and related temporal orientations seen in various non-Western language systems.

Finally, improvisation and composition correlate with feminine and masculine archetypal streams, meaning that they are direct manifestations of primordial impulses that originate in the most subtle, transcendent regions of the cosmic wholeness.[11]

What emerges are two contrasting yet complementary paradigms of creative expression with ramifications not only for music studies but also for the broader creativity and consciousness revolution. The idea that improvisation is primordial to, while also enjoying co-evolutionary relationship with, composition gains strength. This fortifies the Afro-Euro-global nexus that is key to the jazz-based transcultural vision. It is coherent with the sequential unfolding of differentiated strata of creation from the self-referral mechanics central to individual and cosmic creativity. In chapter 7, I draw correlations between global improvisatory problem solving—including issues such as social justice, environment, and peace—and the transformation of linear to nonlinear temporal projections that govern the most miniscule musical improvisatory moments.

TIME, CONSCIOUSNESS, AND MUSIC

The idea that improvisation and composition represent contrasting pathways to transcendence lies at the heart of the Nonlinear Time Dynamics framework. An important starting point is the relationship between time and consciousness: time is experienced differently in ordinary and heightened states of consciousness. In ordinary consciousness, temporal experience is confined to past-present-future sequential relationships. In heightened consciousness, time cognition spans both the past-present-future dimension and an eternal presence that is transcendent of overlying temporal relationships. To probe these further, recall that ordinary consciousness involves the perceptual dissociation of the personal self from its grounding in the transcendent Self; heightened consciousness is the perceptual unity of the two aspects, hence self-Self, or self-referral union. The personal self is the realm of past-present-future relationships, the transcendent Self that of the eternal present. Just as in heightened consciousness, where individuals are able to immerse themselves in the most turbulent activity with grounding in inner, transcendent silence, the same holds for experience of time: engagement in past-present-future relationships coexists with transcendence of that stratum of time, representing a richly differentiated experience.[12] Whereas the experience of pure consciousness in the silence of meditation embodies consciousness in its most fundamental, self-referral form, the experience of heightened consciousness in peak improvisatory creativity exemplifies self-referral consciousness in activity.

This point is underscored by a look at the antithesis of self-reference, which as examined previously is the object-referral awareness that is characteristic of ordinary consciousness. Because music manifests in time, so do conditioned, object-referral attachments. In improvisatory creativity/ordinary consciousness, object-referral attachments take the form of conditioned patterns that impose past-present-future relationships on the inner-directed flow of time and impede spontaneity and interactivity. I call these "inflated points," which are riddled by dissociation. Why? Because the relativistic self—in being overshadowed by perceived objects, in the form of musical ideas, loses sight of the transcendent Self. Whereas in improvisatory creativity/heightened consciousness, object-referral tendencies are neutralized due to self-Self grounding, in which perception of, and heightened engagement with objects occurs against a backdrop of self-referral unity. The experience of "robust points" prevails. This represents a more differentiated level of improvisatory creativity because in any given unit of time as measured by the clock, more self-referral moments are possible, whereas in the same unit of time, fewer self-referral moments transpire.[13]

Compositional creativity/ordinary consciousness is driven by an expanding, linear time conception, which is predicated on development of past-present-future relationships. Now a very different scenario prevails, where object-referral patterns impede expansion; these are "weak spans." In other words, whereas conditioned attachments in improvisation inhibit the interior collapse of the boundaries of the present, conditioned attachments in composition inhibit the exterior collapse of those same boundaries. In compositional creativity/heightened consciousness, these patterns are neutralized and composers are able to ride the waves of expanding conception that lies at the heart of the process; weak spans become robust spans.[14]

Further light is shed on these principles through probing improvisatory and compositional moments at their core.

Inner Mechanics A

I begin by looking at the point at which improvising and composing intersect. Both improvisers and composers sustain creative decision-making in temporal sequence within which a given idea is articulated or played, and from which one or more possible successors—implications—are generated. In other words, an idea at moment A projects some sense of what might come next, in the form of moments/ideas B, C, D, and so on. A next idea is chosen, or realized, and then becomes part of the new present moment from which further implications, and realizations, take form.

Where the processes differ pertains to the relationships between present moments, possible successors, and the past. Composers, due to the discontinuous nature of the process, are able to conceive of an idea at moment A, ruminate at length (minutes, hours, or more) about what might follow, prior to the realization of a subsequent moment B. Implied or possible futures, from C on, are generated from cumulative structure AB. The same holds as cumulative structures ABC, ABCD, ABCDE, and so on, take shape. Compositional, linear time conception is not only cumulative but also reversible, in that composers can enter the "timescape" of the ever-evolving work, proceed directly to some later moment, and upon defining what takes place there, can return to and modify some prior moment in the piece.[15]

Improvisers have no such options. While this may appear to be a creative liability from a compositioncentric standpoint, it represents a creative attribute from a broader, improvisation-based aesthetic. In other words, the lack of provisions to attend to large-scale formal relationships is "counterbalanced" in improvisation by capacities to transform perceptions of present ideas, and in so doing unearth new inventive and interactive possibilities. Here a counterpart to the cumulative ABCDE, etc., of composed structure emerges in the AB BC CD DE structuralization of improvisatory form. In other words, the improviser—like the composer—at moment A generates one or more possible successors, which gives rise to idea AB. But now, due to improvisatory temporal conception, moment A is subordinated in the inner-directed, nonlinear flow and B assumes greater cognitive strength in generating new possibilities. This results in idea BC, at which point B begins to fade from central status and C becomes the present temporal locus. The same thing happens with the realization of ideas CD, DE, EF, FG, and so on in the improvisatory creative flow. Note that each moment is conceived as past byproduct of what precedes it, yet present generator of new possible successors. Shortly I will examine this in terms of the breaking down of time frames and unearthing of more deeply grounded inventive possibilities, and the interactive capacities that, as noted, are key to an improvised music aesthetic paradigm.

In sum, if improvisation, from a compositioncentric viewpoint, can be seen as deficient due to its continuous creativity, nonlinear temporality, and corresponding capacities to achieve the architectural results of composition; then composition, from an improvisationcentric perspective, can be seen as limited by its parallel discontinuity, linear temporality, and incapacities to promote the interactive unity possible when creation and performance happen simultaneously. An integral vantage point enables us to step beyond these competing, centrist perspectives and appreciate both processes on their own terms, and thus harvest the fruits of a process scope—for which the jazz CICP is an unmatched exemplar—that includes both. An important first step, however, in arriving at this dual appreciation is to diagnose prevailing compositioncentric assumptions that obscure these distinctions.[16]

Some clarifications are in order prior to further commentary. First, while I fully realize my highly generalized characterization of composition encompasses but a portion of the broad continuum of compositional strategies, some of which may more closely broach improvisatory approaches than others, I believe important distinctions nonetheless hold when the processes are juxtaposed through the temporality/consciousness lens. Furthermore, the account does not rule out provisions for improvisers to invoke compositional strategies whereby they attend to relationships between the present and past, or to project awareness to future possibilities. What I call retensive and retensive-protensive awareness is indeed possible in improvisatory creativity. Here improvisers consciously strive to fulfill some kind of overarching formal trajectory; attention to future possibilities is protensive, and recollection and reiteration/development of past events is retensive. The degree to which these capacities are possible, however, is directly dependent upon the degree of heightened, inner-directed conception that is invoked. Nor does the model deny the possibility of composers creating with a kind of improvisatory intention, in which subsequent decisions are made with minimal consideration for the cumulative past. However, compositional approaches to improvisation and improvisatory approaches to composition will never match the respective formal (composition) and spontaneous (improvisation) achievements that are possible in the two processes due to the contrasting modes of temporal conception involved.[17]

Inner Mechanics B: Cognitive Event Cycle Frequency

This leads to the concept of event cycle frequency, which is central to the inner workings of improvised music. A cognitive event cycle consists of a localized present moment, a slate of one or more implications or possible successors, and the realization from that slate of a new present moment. The greater the event cycle frequency in improvised performance, the more robust the creative possibilities, meaning inventiveness and interaction in a given moment, and the evolution of the individual voice over time.

Suppose an event A sounds, followed by some scheme of possible successors—some sense of what might come next. Suppose, moreover, that, due to ordinary/object-referral consciousness, the improviser succumbs to a conditioned attachment to a future idea that is triggered by event A. The idea occupies some corresponding time frame—let's call it A-D. This inflated point, the status of which is determined by the conditioned perception of D as an inevitable successor to A, need not be thought of in terms of a specific, fully formed line; it could manifest itself simply in terms of a kind of a general melodic shape, or schema, that is conceived at moment A yet inheres temporal commitment to future point D. Therefore, the actual length of time frame A-D, which may be relatively short as measured by the clock, even if characterized as an inflated point, is not important when it comes to degree of nonlinear perception; what matters is that the conditioned attachment impedes the inner directed movement of temporal perception that, in breaking down an ordinary consciousness time frame into constituent creative moments, is key to the improvisatory creative paradigm.

A look at what happens when the conditioned, object-referral attachment that binds A-D is neutralized illuminates how inflated points impede, and robust points enhance, creative expression and interaction. Suppose now that the improviser generates the same kind of idea or event A, which generates a similar scheme of potential successors, but now from a more heightened state of consciousness. Suppose even that idea A-D assumes, as it did in the above scenario, significant cognitive strength within this decision-making framework due to the background of the improviser and perhaps the current environment. But now, imagine the improviser, more able to liberate from conditioning, breaking down that attachment to A-D, and realizing some constituent possibilities—this might happen in response to spontaneously emergent ideas generated by an improvising partner, or just something new or perhaps more compelling that was unearthed in one's own creative flow. So now what would have been time frame A-D is broken down into constituent time frames AB BC CD (or some such representation). Event cycle frequency is heightened, rendering what was a less differentiated event A-D a more differentiated, more improvisatory sequence.[18]

Why is this significant? Because it indicates a larger number of creative decision-making moments within any given time frame as measured by the clock. Improvising becomes more spontaneous, more in the moment, more rooted in the nonlinear thrust that is central to the nature, and expressive power, of improvised music. Even if the difference between ordinary and heightened event cycle frequency, as measured by the clock, is only a fraction of a second, this represents a foundational shift in awareness. It is comparable to a tiny switch in railroad tracks that enables a train heading east from Chicago to head toward Montreal instead of Miami.

Here, too, it must be stressed that event cycle frequency has nothing to do with speed of note activity, and everything to do with interior experience. Imagine a note of relatively long duration, lasting perhaps five or more seconds. Played from the state of ordinary consciousness, the choice to play that note might be made at the moment (A) in which it is conceived, with no subsequent awareness, and thus potential decisions—during the course of holding the note—of alternative possibilities or the initial plan of a long note occupying time frame A-D. Now imagine a different scenario unfolding from the same moment (A), where the decision to play the long note that is to occupy time frame A-D is followed by interim decisions, perhaps in response to spontaneously arising developments in the improvisatory environment in which the initial plan might be abandoned and some new material is generated. However, the improviser nonetheless elects to stay with the initial plan, or some semblance thereof. The result is the same overarching idea AD, but now realized through a more richly differentiated, and thus more improvisatory, temporal flow consisting of some series of interim moments as, say, AB, BC, and CD (or even A1, A2, A3, B1, B2, B3, etc., C1, C2, C3, etc.). This is an example of heightened event cycle frequency, which again is an interior endeavor, even amid very slow surface note activity.[19]

The same holds for more rapid passages. A lengthy, high-density musical idea can be conceived and realized in a low event cycle frequency context, in which the idea that is initiated at moment A is realized to span time frame A-D, thereby reflecting minimal potential constituent interactive and inventive moments. Or the same idea could be realized from a high event cycle frequency vantage point, in which, following the initial impulse to begin the line, constituent moments within A-D were entertained in which other pathways might have been chosen, but the improviser ends up playing the line initially conceived, now from a more robust improvisatory awareness.

Among the most dramatic examples of heightened event cycle frequency as an interior phenomenon involves the use of silence in free, unaccompanied improvising. I have devised a series of exercises called "silence studies" to cultivate the capacity to sustain high event cycle frequency even when no sounds are being made. Here the improviser sets up the space of silence, which when prepared effectively may last ten seconds or more, and engages fully in that powerful musical fabric not from a static standpoint, but through a dynamic series of creative decisions to continue the silence as opposed to not continuing it, prior to the decision to interrupt the silence by playing a sound. One of my graduate students was particularly facile with this idea and the result was consistently palpable; one could feel, as I put it, that she continues "improvising throughout the silence."[20]

How does this relate to transcendence in improvisatory performance? The answer could not be more direct: high event cycle frequency embodies the curving back of the self onto the Self, or the self-awareness that is key to optimal creativity and consciousness. The higher the event cycle frequency, the more that any moment of time as measured by the clock is more differentiated.

In this regard, it is important to keep in mind that heightened consciousness is most realistically understood not as an expansion of ordinary consciousness; rather, heightened consciousness is the underlying reality, from which ordinary consciousness is a dissociated deviation. Therefore, liberation from object-referral attachments may be more aptly thought of as the removal of a dam, which was artificially imposed, that allows two separated bodies of water to spontaneously reconnect and reclaim their original and natural unity, as compared to the construction of a canal between two lakes. Even the slightest freeing up from conditioning, then, can catalyze this unity. This also sheds light on questions that sometimes arise regarding the length of the present moment—how short is the shortest conception of the present? While various attempts have been made at this sort of measurement, in the Nonlinear Time Dynamics Model, the question is moot: what matters is the movement from ordinary present conception to higher event cycle, heightened consciousness conception, not the quantification of the length of either ordinary or heightened present moments. Because object-referral obstacles to transcendent unity are structured in time, even the slightest breaking down of time frames can elevate the inner-directedness of time conception enough to catalyze transcendence in addition to heightened inventiveness and interaction.[21]

Among the important ramifications of this account is that it illuminates exterior dimensions of human improvisation—such as spontaneous adaptation and spontaneous invention—as rooted in an interior self-referral mechanics that differentiates it from improvisation among other species. Think of a squirrel crossing a busy street, and how it quickly reaches the halfway point, stops, darts one way, and then another, and then another, as it assesses its prospects for clear passage based on spontaneously emerging perceptions. This is a form of high-level event cycle frequency. However, the dynamic self-referral foundations of human consciousness enable vertical openings, by which improvisers have the capacity to transform the perception of a given moment as exclusively bound to a sole place in a linear temporal chain into constituent moments to one where more events that were previously only conceived as causal results of what preceded them could be perceived as generators for new possibilities. Again, note the difference between an ordinary consciousness chain that might be represented as ABC CDE EFG and a heightened consciousness AB BC CD DE EF chain. Expanded overlying and thus horizontal possibilities are made possible by deeper vertical penetration, revealing the improvisatory moment—exemplified in the robust point—as exemplary of the overarching principle discussed in chapters 1 and 2, whereby the key to broader, horizontal navigation whether in terms of cultural or disciplinary horizons—is vertical penetration into the roots of creativity. From this standpoint, the enlivened point conception in heightened event cycle frequency can be thought of as a kind of "cognitive fractal,"[22] to appropriate a principle of complex systems thought, and more particularly its chaos theory branch, where the condition of a system depends on "sensitive dependence on initial conditions"[23]—in this case, the degree to which improvisers transform linear attachments into constituent nonlinear instants. This capacity to invoke transformations within improvisatory perception and uncover new possibilities within any given moment is the basis for uniquely human capacities to not only develop improvisatory capacities but also formulate theories of improvisation, and recognize spiritual dimensions of the process.

One can readily envision applications of these principles to improvising across fields, as in the patient-physician relationship, classroom teaching, athletics, emergency response, social and environmental activism, and peace and conflict resolution on local and even national scales. I go into this more in the next chapter.

Transcendence in Composition

Returning to the generation of ideas over time—which is the connecting thread between improvisatory and compositional creativity—composers and improvisers in a moment (A) generate possible successors (B) and so on to yield an event AB. As soon as the composer stops, steps outside the timescape of the piece, and reflects on cumulative structure AB, he or she enters an entirely different creative universe. Time moves from inner-directed and nonlinear to expanding and linear. Even if the moment of discontinuity spans a few seconds where the composer pauses to notate an idea, this is enough to shift the temporal locus from the primordial, improvisatory to the more differentiated compositional pathway. Imagine, then, the extent of departure from the improvisatory when the composer stops to have a cup of tea, or walk the dog, all the while reflecting on even far greater cumulative structures than event AB. With each moment of reflection, the forces that promote expanding, linear conception are strengthened. The very temporal discontinuity that preempts the interactive, expressive, and transformative power of the improvised music paradigm is key to the architectural designs that uphold the power and richness of the composed music paradigm.

Transcendent experience in composition—and again, I base my analysis on a generalized account of composition that I propose to encompass much, but not all composing—may be therefore understood as the expansion of ordinary consciousness temporal relationships between moments and their predecessors and successors to broader past-present-future relationships. As the boundaries that define ordinary experience of the localized present collapse, the logic patterns that bind consciousness to its ordinary, object-referral status dissolve and allow the floodgates to open up to the underlying realm of transcendent consciousness. The situation is somewhat comparable to the impact of a Zen koan, where the shattering of ordinary logic patterns opens up spontaneously to heightened consciousness. Whereas in improvisatory creativity, inflated points—which again impede inner-directed flow—are broken down to become robust points, in compositional creativity, weak spans—which impede expanding flow—are broadened to become robust spans.

In sum, improvisers invoke transcendent experience by riding the waves of inner-directed temporal flow and, in peak performance, breaking down inflated points that preempt inner-directedness. Put another way, improvisers transcend by collapsing the innermost boundaries of localized present experience, uncovering constituent moments within overarching moments. Composers, by contrast, transcend by collapsing the outermost boundaries of localized present experience. As noted, these distinctions do not preclude composers from creating with an improvisatory intention, nor improvisers from creating with a compositional intention. However, they do underscore limitations in both of those scenarios. Most important is that the distinctions highlight how the processes, particularly when the respective temporal dynamics are fully enlivened, can work together within the regular practice of Contemporary Improvisers Composers Performers.

COMPARING IMPROVISERS' AND COMPOSERS' ACCOUNTS OF PEAK EXPERIENCES

Paul Hindemith distinguished great composers from good composers along the following criterion—that great composers conceive of large passages in a single instant, and good composers tend to chisel away at piecing ideas together. This is coherent with reports from composers such as Mozart, Brahms, and Wagner, in which the experience of a fully finished work, in all its detail, would appear to them in a flash.[24]

At first glance, these experiences might also suggest peak improvisatory moments given the spontaneity of the event. However, any such experience would run counter to the requirements of optimal collective improvisation—where participants respond to each other's ideas on a moment-to-moment basis; thus instead of realizing a preordained future vision, they create and re-create possible and real futures on an ongoing basis. Indeed, improvisers' descriptions of peak experiences differ fundamentally from those of the above composers. Here the primary indicators are heightened interactions between participants, the melding of players, listeners, and environment into a unified whole. As Melba Liston describes it, "we breathe together, we swell together," as if all participants comprise a single organism, the beauty and integrity of which is dependent on moment-to-moment interplay, not a preordained structure.[25] Nowhere in the literature on improvisation, real or imagined, would an improviser—particularly in a collective setting—declare that he or she conceived of an entire solo at the outset and then realized that solo. As discussed above, even the idea of conceiving of single ideas—say two bars in length—at a given moment and then realizing them intact amid input from one's cohorts raises questions about improvisatory integrity.

These contrasting descriptions of peak creative moments are consistent with, and thus further underscore, the above theoretical differentiations between improvisation and composition processes.

Ramifications for Creativity Research

Important ramifications extend from the above analysis for creativity research, the primary domain for which is typically the field of psychology. While it is not uncommon for creativity researchers to look at jazz improvisation for insights into creativity at large, I believe several fallacies have cropped up in the literature that reflect limited assumptions about creativity that are dispelled in the above commentary.

The first involves what I call the "novelty fallacy"—that peak creativity must always result in something new. In fact, the concept of cognitive event cycle frequency, which shifts the locus for creative vitality from exterior ideas to interior experience, makes it possible for improvisers to play material that is quite normative, meaning conventional, in nature, yet which comes from deep, transcendent awareness and in heightened response to the precise developments of a given moment, with powerful transformative impact. By the same token, an idea that is comprised of radically new materials may be expressed from ordinary consciousness, perhaps shaped more according to the dictates of fashion (e.g., by improvisers who work in experimental circles) than depth.

Closely related is what I call the "creativity as object" fallacy. Here, creativity is assessed in terms of the products that result, a notion prominent in Mihaly Csikszentmihalyi's systems view of creativity, which in turn has influenced discourse on music creativity.[26] The view of improvisatory creativity that stems from Nonlinear Time Dynamics reveals that the locus for creativity resides in the process. Similarly, the "either or" fallacy—the idea that an expression is creative or not—is dispelled by the view that everything is creative, which shifts the guiding question from distinguishing between what is, and what is not, creative to one that I believe is far more productive: How can creativity be developed? This enables a framework whereby one can celebrate the creative expressions of children as readily as those of accomplished professionals and attend to the evolution of this core human capacity.[27]

A fourth fallacy carries with it social justice ramifications. This is what is sometimes called the "motive explanation"[28]—the idea that jazz improvisers, as it were, stockpile material that is regurgitated at strategic moments. What, in other words, appear to be magical strokes of spontaneous genius, the thinking goes, are revealed to be the result of preprogrammed content. The integral perspective responds to this dismissive account by placing it within a broader context. For one thing, all of human behavior consists of the interplay of conditioned patterns and spontaneous adaptations, the balance between which will always depend on individual circumstances and dispositions. How do we know some music that we have never heard is by Beethoven, or Ravel, or Ellington, or Monk? Because master artists internalize style elements that define their personal voice. Why, then, the motive explanation would be applied with particular scrutiny to jazz raises interesting questions about potential hidden ethnocentric/racialized biases within the investigative community. However, a second and most important point bears emphasis—that jazz improvisation also involves an exquisitely robust spontaneous creative element that transcends crude notions about the regurgitation of ingrained material.

I think of this in terms of a "syntactic threshold." In other words, improvisers when playing over challenging harmonic structures at fast tempos will be more prone to relying on internalized material than when playing at medium or slower tempos, and on less challenging (not to be conflated with less sophisticated) harmonic forms. When coming up against the syntactic threshold, improvisatory decision making will be more bound by the technical demands of the syntactic constraints and less mediated by spontaneous interactive and inventive strategies. Inasmuch as most jazz—I would venture at least 70 percent on any performance or recording—is at medium or slow tempos, the prospects for highly dynamic spontaneous creativity are high, and I believe the history of the music bears this out. In no way is this to suggest that interaction and invention is absent in fast and/or harmonically dense music; it is simply to view these capacities within a relativistic scale and reply to the misleading concerns derived from motive theory in a more informed manner.

An expanded perspective emerges for examining jazz improvisation, in which syntactic parameters of harmony and rhythm are ordained from the outset, and its origins in blues.

Jazz Improvisation

Two important principles might be cited at the outset. One is that Nonlinear Time Dynamics still holds, the only difference being that the generation of ideas and implications will be strongly shaped by the underlying harmonic-rhythmic format, or what Pressing called the "referent."[29] In other words, when the jazz improviser plays an idea over a C7 chord, it is with the knowledge and internal hearing of the upcoming Fmin7 chord. Nonetheless, conditioned, object-referral attachments are still possible, as is liberation therefrom. Indeed, syntactically rich improvising backdrops elicit strong reliance on conditioned patterns, and top improvisers are able to transcend this conditioning to create magical statements on these progressions.

This leads to a second point related to improvisation in jazz and related frameworks. This involves the impact of cyclical iterations of the underlying improvisatory backdrop. In short—the cyclical effect contributes to the inner-directed nature of time conception. Even if the referent undergoes significant transformation with subsequent repetitions, the cognitive impact is one of undermining large-scale temporal relationships and heightened sense of the localized present. Moment-to-moment breaking down of time frames, heightened event cycle frequency, can thus be thought of as a kind of microcosm of this broader temporal thrust.[30]

UNACCOMPANIED IMPROVISATION AND EXTEMPORANEOUS COMPOSITION

Improvising and composing perhaps most closely unite when improvising happens in solo, unaccompanied rather than collective formats, and composition happens not in a discontinuous series of creative episodes but in a single, real-time endeavor. In the first capacity, an important criterion that directs time conception toward a nonlinear thrust is the removal of interfering implications from co-improvisers. In other words, whereas in collective improvisation, each musician must continually contend with a stream of ideas from improvising colleagues that heightened perception of the localized present, no such constraints exist in unaccompanied formats. In regard to the second, compositional format, one hears legendary reports of Bach and Mozart creating entire works in a single uninterrupted creative flow. Are either of these scenarios to be classified as improvisations or compositions? Might such instances represent a point of intersection where distinctions between improvising and composing are more semantic than ontological in nature?

While one can only concede the possibility that here is where distinctions become moot, two points might be made. One involves the prior observation that tremendous amounts of music are made in collective improvisatory and discontinuous compositional frameworks that support the generalized distinctions while granting exceptions. Here, the much more rare phenomenon of real-time composing compared to unaccompanied improvising further underscores the place for differentiating between improvisatory and compositional modes of creative expression. A second point is that nonlinear temporal perception may still be invoked, even without the constraint of interfering implications, in unaccompanied improvisation. In other words, the breaking down of time frames, whereby within any given moment and its implied future new constituent moments and creative possibilities may be spontaneously inferred, is just as possible in solo performance as in collective formats. Moreover, inasmuch as many if not most improvisers engage in both collective and unaccompanied improvisation, I do not believe it is unreasonable to surmise that the expressive strategies unique to the first might carry over to the second.[31]

CULTURAL CONNECTIONS: TIME AND LANGUAGE AS FURTHER DISTINGUISHING PARAMETERS

Theoretical and subjective distinctions also correlate with cultural distinctions. Though improvisation was central in earlier eras of the European classical tradition, the destiny of that great lineage was to incubate and evolve a compositional process, the likes of which had never been seen, and contribute this to the world. The central creative contribution of American musical culture, enabled by the African American experience, which is an important aspect of American culture, is to deliver a transcultural improvisatory wave—the black roots of which extend to innumerable hybrid forms that defy categorization—to the global musical ocean that had yet to be seen. While there is no dearth of commentary on compositional structure in the European-dominated culture of musical academe, there is very little on improvisatory invention and interaction, underscoring the need for expanding the cultural horizons of music studies. Nonlinear Time Dynamics, which lies at the heart of Integral Musicology, is important in addressing this lack, and aligning the culture of music studies with the epistemic roots of American culture.

Within these overarching cultural predispositions, the topic of language may offer particularly important support. A number of investigators have noted nonlinear aspects inherent in non-Western and indigenous language systems that correspond to the improvisatory nonlinearity that I posit, which differ from linear language features in Western systems. Dorothy Lee, for example, points to what she calls the "nonlineal" language structures of the Trobriand Islanders. "There are no tenses, no linguistic distinction between past or present. There is no arrangement of activities or events into means and ends, no causal or teleologic relationships." In contrast to the goal-directed aspects of Western temporality, which may be correlated to the architectural forms of Western classical music, there "is no lineal development, no climax."[32] Judith Becker conveys similar thoughts in regard to Balinese and Javanese languages, which are "tenseless," where the "sense of linear, progressive time" is subordinate, as does John Broomfield with the language of the Hopi.[33]

Underlying the cultural level is the primordial archetypal level, which further extends the parameters along which improvisation-composition distinctions may be made.

ARCHETYPAL CORRELATIONS

The key principle here is that human improvisation is the manifestation of the feminine archetype. Recall the idea of archetypal impulses that originate in deep dimensions of consciousness and manifest themselves in various realms of human activity and creative expression. Direct correlations may be drawn with the theme increasingly prominent in contemporary spirituality, involving the ascendance of a divine feminine archetypal wave in collective consciousness. Composition could thus be thought of as the manifestation of the archetypal masculine principle.

On what grounds might these correlations be drawn? Central is the spontaneous and interactive nature of improvisatory creativity, as opposed to the individual creativity of composers working alone. Heide Göttner-Abendroth's distinctions between what she calls a "matriarchal aesthetic" and "patriarchal" modes of expression exhibit strong coherence with this point. Informed by mythological and archeological evidence, she surmises that ancient women-centered rituals lent themselves to ample latitude for freedom of expression, spontaneity, and improvisation. Matriarchal art "is not a thing but a process," whereas movement in societies in a patriarchal direction would see "the ingenious fabric woven of social politics, psychology, science, and aesthetics . . . unravel into its individual threads, which became the individual formal categories of reason that replaced the ecstatic unity."[34] Therefore, the impulse toward freedom of expression and gesture, collective interaction, and dissolution of boundaries between participants and between ritualistic expression and life at large—all embodied in improvisation—that equate with the feminine differ fundamentally from the masculine compositional paradigm. Undertaken alone and within a discontinuous series of creative episodes, the creative event is dominated by the voice of a single individual. In no way is this to dismiss the artistic products that uniquely stem from this compositional framework but simply to distinguish it from its improvisatory partner, and ancestor.

The integral nondual framework allows an even deeper investigation into these correlations (improvisation as archetypally feminine, composition as masculine). Recounting the story of *lila*, the creation account from advaita Vedanta, where the first-second-third person/spirituality-art-science interplay is seen to occur on a primordial scale: The pure consciousness of silent meditation is the most direct manifestation of Brahman in its most foundational undifferentiated state. Improvisation is the most direct manifestation of Brahman curving back on itself and generating the first, faint stirrings of differentiation in the eternal silent field of infinite potentiality. A sequential reordering thus comes into view by which whatever vestiges of improvisation as a subspecies of composition might linger in spite of the previous account are likely toppled. Within this scheme, improvisation can be seen as a process-mediated, second-person primary creative process, with this primordial dimension as the basis for the corresponding feminine archetypal energy that, depending on the receptivity in individual and collective human consciousness, permeates all of creation. Composition, next in the sequence, is an object-mediated, second-person primary process that has differentiated from its primordial, improvisatory ancestor. From this differentiated basis, masculine archetypal energy extends that objective composition-mediated thrust and, left unbalanced by improvisatory creativity, can also permeate all of creation. Interpretive performance represents an even further node toward the masculine end of the integral creative process continuum as it sequentially differentiates. In comparison with improvisation and composition, interpretive performance is characterized as an object-mediated, second-person (because it falls within the arts) secondary creative process.

Here, too, it is important to emphasize that, even though the conventional neo-Eurocentric framework that prevails in music studies can be described as a composed music paradigm, this refers to the objects of composition, not the process. Therefore, the fact that the vast majority of participants in this model do not compose underscores its object-mediated, masculine orientation. Put another way to illuminate the ramifications of the distinction: were the field of music studies to be populated largely by composers—and thus CCPs instead of CICPs—this would represent paradigmatic change; even if short of that CICP-driven, that would require foundational overhaul. Jazz, however, would continue to be marginalized in the CCP model, even if not quite as dramatically as in neo-Eurocentric and neo-Eurocentric-plus frameworks. Because improvisation is not a subspecies of composition, music studies can only be transformed atop improvisatory foundations if composition and the broader spectrum of music studies is to blossom on unprecedented scales. Jazz embodies this epistemic relationship in restoring improvisation to its proper foundational place.

Blues as Archetypally Rich, Improvisatory Incubator

Imagine blowing bubbles as a child, and every so often seeing one maintain its integrity even as it is swept far away on a breezy day prior to popping. Archetypally rich expressions are bubbles in the flow of consciousness that retain their primordial integrity, without ever popping, even amid the most turbulent and highly differentiated strata of existence. As such, they guide awareness, to reinvoke Jung, to the "wellsprings of life."

Blues is a powerful example of what must be considered among the most archetypally rich musical expressions of the past century of Western music. This comes into view when one seeks to define blues in conventional, analytical prose. Indeed, the question "What is blues?" makes efforts to define *consciousness* (chapter 5) and *improvisation* in this chapter look like ontological walks in the park. Is blues primarily a pitch structure? Rhythmic? Improvisatory? A feeling? A manifestation of words/music nexus? The fact that blues defies identification of any of these features as primary, yet is all of these components and more operating synergistically, lends support for the argument that blues retains its primordial essence at manifest scales in ways that defy language-bound analysis.

Two points, moreover, are noteworthy in this light. The first, from a structural vantage point, entails pitch language: elsewhere I concur with, and elaborate upon, Joachim Berendt's assessment that blues is fundamentally modal in nature, even if much blues since the early part of the twentieth century, particularly in jazz, exhibits tonal features. This analysis is consistent with the principle that modality is primordial to tonality. Therefore, tonal harmonic relationships could be built atop modal foundations that even at times render the particular piece tonal, even if blues originated in a modal archetypal thrust.

A second point involves emotion. While it goes without saying that music as a vehicle for expression of feeling is almost universally recognized, when it comes to blues the association is particularly vivid. If a look at most blues lyrics clearly conveys this point, a broader look at the origins of the blues in the African American experience of oppression only provides further support. However, and here is where the emotional/feeling line opens up to the primordial, I believe Martin Luther King Jr.'s characterization of blues as, ultimately, "triumphant music"[35] paints a more accurate picture. To be sure, while blues may be seen as the result of untold suffering, it is also an expression for the deeply spiritual level of healing that is driven by the divine or cosmic nature of human creativity. The negative circumstances in which blues originated, and which took hold in musical structures, can be seen as surface (not superficial) conditions that open up to transcendent realms that are the source of hope. Here we are reminded that the primordial stratum of creation from which music emerges is fathomed through subtle feeling, as discussed in the context of *bhagavat chetena*, the penultimate higher stage of consciousness development. Recall, too, that here is where the opening of the heart opens up to subtle realms of perceptual phenomena that remain hidden from view in not only ordinary consciousness but also even a prior stage of realization—*turiyatita chetena*. Blues is a powerful source of emotion because of its capacity to retain aspects of primordial feeling at manifest scales.

I therefore view blues as an archetypally rich process-structure matrix that has deep African roots and that has retained its essential "Africanisms,"[36] as LeRoi Jones terms it, even amid the "unthinkably cruel" circumstances by which African music has been transported to the West. Eurological influences were assimilated in jazz and other blues-based manifestations of African American music atop Afrological archetypal foundations. One could argue for this from any number of standpoints: improvisation, far more an Afrological contribution to world culture than Eurological (even if improvisation was prevalent in early times in European practice), is central to blues and through blues made its significant infusion in Western music. While it is important to recognize the significance of Eurological composition to jazz composition, improvisation is primordial to composition in the broader epistemological spectrum, thus supporting the vertical argument of jazz's Afrological foundations as the basis for Eurological infusion. The same holds for the jazz pitchscape, which while having blossomed rich tonal practices, is—having evolved from blues and its Afrological roots—fundamentally modal in nature. Modality is primordial to tonality; tonality took hold atop jazz Afrological modal foundations. When it comes to rhythm, the case for jazz's Afrological roots and thus the vertical argument is overwhelming as the influence of Eurological rhythmic practice on jazz is, generally speaking, minimal if not scarcely perceptible.

An archetypal reading of the blues also provides a means to respond to an interesting and important question—Would there be jazz if there had not been slavery?—when it comes to broader transformative ramifications of jazz. From a second-person, postmodern perspective, where knowledge and creativity are culturally mediated, the answer is, pessimistically, no. In other words, jazz is a music borne of oppression, and thus the powerful freedom impetus, manifesting itself in a strong improvisatory component as well as quest to evolve an individual voice, is a compensatory reaction to that oppression. From a first-person standpoint, which does not categorically reject second-person criteria, but simply situates them within a broader context, jazz is understood as the result of primordial forces that transcend sociocultural developments. Jazz from this standpoint is the manifestation of an archetypal improvisatory, freedom-driven, divine feminine, and global syncretic thrust that would find corresponding surface outlets regardless of circumstances. The advent of improvisation and African-based rhythm as a basis for infusion of Western and subsequently broader global influences, did not require slavery. All it would need is the advent of technology for travel and cultural exchange, sufficient degrees of which were already in place centuries before the advent of jazz, or even slavery in America. While the resultant music would have likely been named differently, something quite like jazz, and the planetary syncretism that it initiated and has just begun to blossom, would have nonetheless emerged. The nondual view of consciousness also opens up the possibility that inherent in the African psyche are deeply rooted creative and spiritual forces that are also inherent in the collective psyche of humanity, but that for much of the world lay dormant, and that require the empowerment of the African and African American expressivity to enliven in global culture.

If consideration of blues represents a look at the archetypally rich origins of jazz, the idea of the emergence of large stylistically open improvisatory ensembles, precursors for which are a small yet important part of the jazz tradition, represents a probing of future horizons of the music that are also grounded in a powerful archetypal thrust.

LARGE ENSEMBLE IMPROVISATION REVISITED

As suggested earlier, an important outgrowth of the improvisation-based cultural and archetypal aesthetic will be the emergence of large, stylistically open improvisation ensembles. The significance of this development comes into view through the parts-to-whole and whole-to-parts epistemological axes of the jazz-inspired view of consciousness and its intersubjective dimensions. The large improvising ensemble provides a PW forum for enlivening collective consciousness via the creative process. It also symbolizes the unified musical ocean into which infinitely diverse culture-specific and person-specific tributaries may flow, and enrich the resultant unity. Three kinds of skill domains—the second and third of which extend the horizons of conventional jazz study and its multicultural horizons—highlight both the pedagogical and aesthetic horizons of the large ensemble improvisatory phenomenon. First is that participants will require strong grounding as individual improvisers that includes tradition-specific foundations in jazz. Second are strong transcultural navigational skills that are predicated on syncretism from diverse sources. Third involves foundations in large ensemble improvising, which means entirely new levels of listening, interactive, and inventive skills compared to even the formidable levels required of small ensemble improvising. In my extensive experience working with groups of this nature consisting of over twenty musicians, I have found that ensembles of more than eight members or so—regardless of degree of individual competence among the members—call for an entirely new kind of preparation. Once this threshold is passed, and particularly when the group approaches or surpasses twenty players, the bar is raised considerably in terms of the third dimension of preparation. I describe this kind of playing as "high risk, high yield," meaning that there is often little or no middle ground—either the results are magical and powerfully transformative, as if some exterior force (which of course is interior, collective consciousness) overtakes the music and its coherent unfolding, or the situation collapses into utter cacophony. Here meditation practice is invaluable in heightening listening skills and engendering capacities to lay out for long stretches of times while others take the lead, or play soft or transparent background roles, or pounce explosively into the forefront as situations may arise.

The combination of large ensemble improvisation and meditation set the stage for whole-to-parts principles to come into play. First of all, just as individual improvisers glimpsing heightened consciousness in their creative excursions may exhibit interest in formal meditation practice, participants in large improvising ensembles may similarly invoke experiences of peak collective transcendence that elicit interest in collective meditation practice. Here is where an emergent aesthetic principle in contemporary arts practice unites with an emergent principle in contemporary social transformation practice. Moreover, whereas the large improvising ensemble is the localized manifestation of the overarching musical ocean in which all cultures unite, the large meditating group—which may consist of hundreds if not thousands of participants—is the manifestation of the ocean of consciousness within which all humanity unites. Additionally, to return to the principle that emerged in the previous chapter, the large meditating group represents the forum in which individuals come together, penetrate deep into their own self-referral consciousness—the level of soul, or atma—and enliven the very mechanics by which the cosmos creates. Yet again, the axiom stated early on comes back into focus: no substantive inquiry into the nature of consciousness can transpire without broaching creativity, and conversely, no substantive inquiry into the nature of creativity—as seen here through the lens of improvisation—can transpire without broaching consciousness.

At which point, the question arises—How might these principles be operationalized in the music studies reform conversation and corresponding emergent models? A framework for practice and inquiry called Integral Musicology, in which Nonlinear Time Dynamics and its distinctions between improvisatory and compositional creativity play a central role, unites much of the commentary and analysis of parts I and II of the book in response to this question. Integral Musicology not only redefines the scope of musical inquiry, but in positioning improvisation and composition as core means for musical understanding, also redefines the profile of *who* conducts the investigation, and *how* it is conducted.

INTEGRAL MUSICOLOGY AS NEW PARADIGM FOR MUSIC PRACTICE AND INQUIRY

Musicology is typically viewed in terms of three primary branches—historical musicology, ethnomusicology, and systematic musicology. Historical musicology concerns itself primarily with European classical music, ethnomusicology with music of other cultures, and systematic musicology is a broad and less-defined area that has come to encompass cognitive processes and other concerns.[37] Consistent with neo-Eurocentric and neo-Eurocentric-plus frameworks, and general academic protocol, scholarly inquiry in the areas tends to be separate from practice. Colleagues in the various realms of musicology are appointed and gain tenure according to their scholarly research and publications, not their music-making activity. Integral Musicology turns this paradigm upside down by establishing not only improvising and composing, but also meditation and consciousness-based inquiry, as the basis for musical understanding. The integral musicologist will thus be a CICP-plus practitioner.

Figures 6.1 and 6.2 illustrate the basic premise, which I call Nested Synergies, that underlies the Integral Musicology paradigm. The term *synergy* refers to the co-evolutionary relationship between any two components of musical engagement and the whole. *Nested* refers to the sequential positioning of progressively more differentiated strata of relationships atop less-differentiated, primordial foundations.

Improvisation, represented at the base of figure 6.1, is the most primordial mode of musical expression and inquiry, which when established as central to artistic identity has the capacity to spawn and integrate an unprecedented spectrum of skills and understanding. Recalling the systematic improvisatory development framework from chapter 1, note how each strata of differentiation from the improvisatory core unfolds sequentially in a series of synergistic relationships. Improvisation gives rise to improvisation-composition synergy, followed by improvisation-composition-performance, and so on to generate an exceptionally broad range of further relationships. Note, too, how improvisation not only undergirds the entire model, but also appears at every overlying tier. This represents both horizontal and vertical synergistic relationships that promote the exquisite circuitry through which creativity and consciousness may flow from the level of soul, or atma, and inform the entire system. The point is, therefore, not to suggest a pedagogical sequence, where one begins with improvisation and then adds the more differentiated components, but to depict the alignment in musical identity that is optimally conducive to the organic integration of all components as they blossom from an interior, vertical source. Every synergistic relationship can be thought of as a kind of localized synapse whereby a more differentiated relationship rests, or nests, atop a less-differentiated, primordial predecessor.

Figure 6.2 takes the thinking a step further by introducing meditation, which now occupies an even more fundamental stratum than improvisation. As noted previously, the pure consciousness of silent meditation represents the most primordial manifestation of self-referral awareness. Improvisation is the most self-referral condition of consciousness in the midst of activity. The subsequent meditation-improvisation synergistic relationship at the second stratum is particularly powerful in encompassing the whole-to-parts/parts-to-whole interplay. The prior (from figure 6.1) improvisation-composition synergy now gains added strength when situated within a meditation-improvisation-composition synergistic interaction. The same holds for all overlying strata of synergistic relationships, again underscoring how maximal horizontal expanse—and integration within that expanse, rigor, excel-

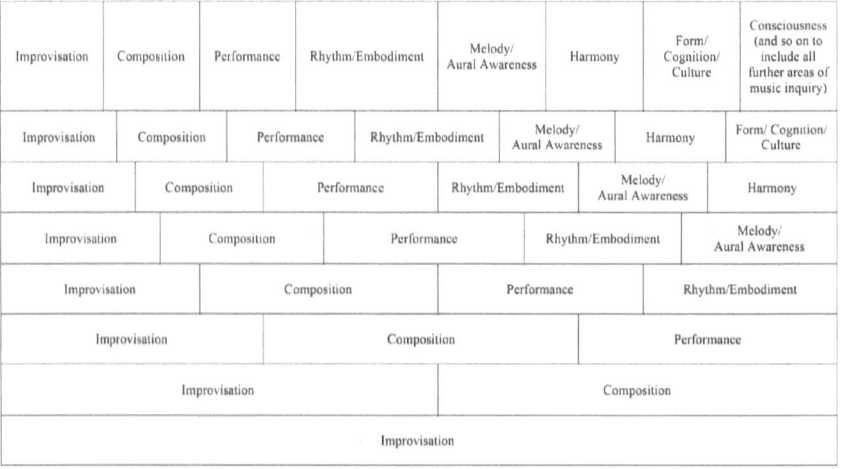

Figure 6.1. Nested Synergies: Improvisation Anchored

A Consciousness-Based Integral Perspective on Improvisation 155

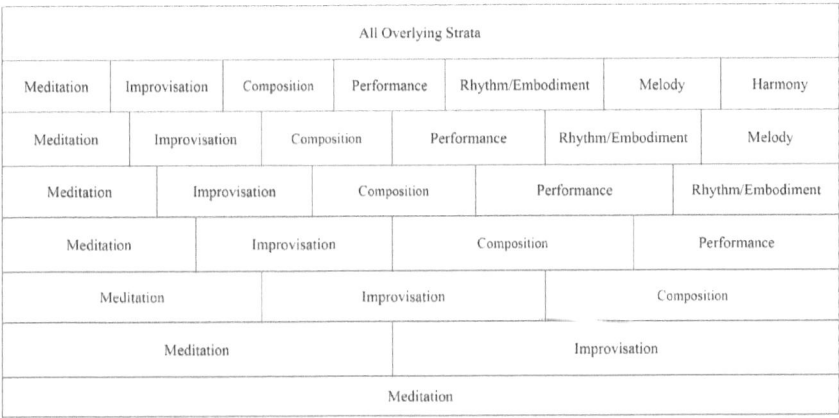

Figure 6.2. Nested Synergies: Meditation Anchored

lence, and self-organizing thrust—can be achieved through a music studies framework built on deep creativity/consciousness foundations. Meditation grounds the model in the undifferentiated eternal intelligence, or spirit, from which the cosmos unfolds, improvisation grounds the model in the primordial curving back of cosmic intelligence onto itself that is the essence of art, and composition picks up with object-mediated creativity that is the basis for a scientific thrust, all of which blossom in the broader spectrum of experiences.

Note also that when it comes to operationalizing the framework, correlations are evident with the five pillars of an integral music studies program discussed in chapter 3. Music and consciousness represents the fundamental tier, music creation the next three tiers (improvisation, composition, and performance), with music inquiry and craft, music pedagogy, and music and society the overlying tiers.

Although not easily indicated in the schematic, it is important to recognize within the meditation realm vertical topographies that might unfold from silent, sitting meditation practice as an anchor to the broader contemplative continuum. Recall the principle that the experience of pure consciousness in silence establishes a self-referral core that can then flow upward into contemplative approaches to embodiment (tai chi, martial arts), nature communion, writing, reading, and creative expression among a broader spectrum of contemplative modalities. Indeed, an entire diagram might be made even within the contemplative continuum that illustrates the nested, synergistic relationships within that realm. One can thus readily imagine even more differentiated, sequential unfolding of synergistic relationships through which creativity and consciousness may flow.

The same, of course, holds for the improvisatory realm. Here, for example, free improvisation and style-specific improvising can be seen to embody a robust exploratory-emulative relationship, in which the first is primordial to, and then coevolves with, the more differentiated second. This is yet another instance of a more differentiated tapestry that invites vertical connection and flow from the soul level that cascades throughout the system. Moreover, even within the realm of style-specific improvisation, particularly in a genre with such porous boundaries as jazz, one could locate an exploratory-emulative, and thus primordial-differentiated, sequential unfolding. Think, for example, of the unbounded creative excursions, and thus exploratory vitality, that might stem from modal jazz or even adventurous interpretations of jazz standards in which emulative engagement serves as a point of departure.[38]

Of paramount importance is the bridging of the divide between direct musical and spiritual engagement and understanding, and thus research. The integral musicologist is a CICP-plus practitioner who probes deeply his/her creative and transpersonal explorations and unearths and articulates insights that not only inform his/her artistic and spiritual growth but also can serve as a guide for others. Contact with basic musical and extramusical elements in fluid and malleable form; direct experience of how these interact with one another to inform the individual voice; realization of how overarching musical disciplines and genre categories are collective manifestations of personal individuation; distinctions between primary (improvisatory and compositional) and secondary (performative) creativity, and between improvisatory and compositional creativity within the primary realm; and recognition of human improvisatory creativity as grounded in the same self-referral mechanics as cosmic creativity are but aspects of an emergent model of inquiry and understanding that is key to twenty-first-century musical practice and arts-driven leadership.

The emergence of heightened critical interrogation faculties that are inherent in this model is also noteworthy. Distinctions between the prevailing neo-Eurocentric framework, the creativity-based European classical tradition prior to the division of labor, and neo-Eurocentric-plus/multicultural as opposed to integral/transcultural efforts to rectify the prevailing model are key to the transformation of music studies. The recognition, moreover, of the inextricable link between epistemology and ethnology is a particularly important precept to the transformation, as this illuminates prevailing multicultural discourse to be not only ethnologically impaired, but epistemically deficient as well.

CLOSING THOUGHTS

Just as the symphony orchestra might be viewed as among the culminating developments in the composed-notated music wave and its rich architectural possibilities, the large, stylistically open improvising ensemble may be viewed as a counterpart within the improvised music wave and its aesthetic of spontaneous, transcultural invention and interaction. The extrication of improvisation from erroneous classification as a subspecies of composition is key to understanding the significance of these two waves in the twenty-first-century musical ocean and navigating between them as discrete yet also fluid regions. The cultivation of the skills and understanding necessary for this kind of creative excursion must be recognized as the primary aim of twenty-first-century music studies, and key to fulfillment of entirely new levels of conventional expertise within a vastly expanded spectrum of achievement. In disentangling improvisation and composition, and then situating the first at the heart of the model, the point is not to dethrone composition from its prevailing central status in the academy. Rather, it is to resituate this foundational creative process within the sequentially unfolding creative modalities from an improvisatory source, where all aspects can coevolve in synergistic interaction. As the first stratum of differentiation within the systematic improvisatory development continuum, which it must always be kept in mind encompasses all aspects of musical engagement that are currently in place and imagined, the improvisation-composition relationship is particularly important to the organic integration of the broader strata of experience. When, moreover, this systematic improvisatory development spectrum is situated atop systematic meditative development foundations, not only do the roots of the system extend more deeply into the innermost recesses of the soul, or *atma*, but also that creativity and consciousness can then flow more profusely from that level and permeate the expanded dimensions of the system. Improvisation can now be understood as not only a powerful means of music expression, but also a transformative experience and—perhaps most elusive from a conventional standpoint—a core means for musical understanding.

The ramifications of the model are particularly vivid when viewed through the closely related, but often separated, lenses of epistemology and ethnology. Most foundational to the epistemic lens is that improvisation exemplifies the self-referral condition of consciousness, which is the heart of human self-awareness, in the realm of activity, and that meditation exemplifies self-referral condition of consciousness in silence. When the pure, self-referral consciousness of meditation underlies the dynamic self-referral consciousness of improvisation—which in turn underlies the more differentiated self-referral consciousness of composition—then the host of further strata of differentiation are aligned with the primordial improvisatory thrust not only in the human psyche but also in the cosmic psyche. Large group improvisatory musical creativity enlivens the mechanics of cosmic creativity through the gateways of sound, sensory perception, and time. Large group meditation practice enlivens the mechanics of cosmic creativity through transcendence of sound, sensory perception, and time.

From an ethnological standpoint, with epistemic considerations never far from view, differentiation and subsequent sequential alignment of improvisation and composition underlies the Afro-Euro-global nexus that is key to the Integral Musicology framework and emergent music studies paradigm in America, and perhaps elsewhere. Europe delivered the notated-compositional framework to the world, Africa the improvisatory to the West, which would then take hold in America and in turn invite unlimited further global infusion en route to the transcultural improvised music wave. The misguided view of improvisation as subspecies of composition represents a foundational instance of Eurocentric colonialism; the extrication of improvisation from such represents a foundational instance of liberation therefrom. The fact that multiculturalism has been only vaguely receptive to the idea of contrasting improvised and composed music paradigms, analytical accounts for which in any case are scarce, and has failed to advance pedagogical models or even conceptual frameworks that harness the improvisation-composition interaction (regardless of which is deemed foundational) as key to evolving a culturally diverse awareness, further confirms my assessment of limited multicultural contributions to evolving that awareness. When it comes to the black music advocacy for which multiculturalism has been suspiciously ambivalent, yet which arguably warrants a central place in contemporary diversity conversations in America, the absence of improvisation-composition distinctions is particularly conspicuous. For these distinctions deepen the understanding of not only the denigration of jazz but also where it—in uniquely, among all ethnological streams, uniting the two epistemologies—has the potential to shine.

Epistemic/ethnological analysis also sheds light on distinctions between conventional musicology and what I propose as Integral Musicology. The separation of historical musicology and ethnomusicology, which is ethnologically driven (or more aptly, ethnocentrically/racially driven), within the first is a primary example. From social justice lapse extends epistemic lapse that sustains the overarching division and its pathological impact. Integral Musicology, however, reveals epistemology as key to diagnosis and healing of the system. Were the improvisatory foundations of earlier eras of European classical music and most music across the globe to be recognized not only as shared practices but also as foundational means of understanding, whereby musicologists would necessarily be improvising musicians, this core epistemic thread would likely yield something along the lines of the integral model, and thus circumvent prevailing ethnocentric/racialized divisions.

Nonlinear Time Dynamics and its emancipation of improvisation from misconstrued compositional step-child is where the system may be rectified.

The separation of popular music, as it increasingly makes advances in the academy, from its African American roots, with—as considered—the exclusion of jazz as a powerful source of tools for popular musicians, represents another set of epistemological/ethnological complications extending from the prevailing musicological orientation and its historical-ethno split. Here it might be noted that popular music advocacy is seen among both ethnomusicologists and, perhaps ironically and to a lesser extent, historical musicologists who have managed to expand their monocultural roots in a multicultural direction. The popular music–black music divide clearly reflects a multicultural perspective. Because the separation occurs within the overarching ethnological region of black music, it might appear to be largely epistemic— meaning that one form of black musical practice is seen as fundamentally distinct from another form of black musical practice. However, the fact that the majority of colleagues teaching, researching, and advocating the area are white raises important ethnological questions—as in my earlier assessment (in chapter 2) that the separation of popular music from its black roots represents yet another example of key contributions of African Americans being rendered invisible. The fact that the primary casualty of this invisibility is the conspicuously scarce place of jazz, despite the powerful tools the idiom offers popular musicians, in the emergent visioning and curricular models might be assessed as both an epistemological lapse with serious ethnological consequences, and an ethnological lapse with serious epistemic consequences.

Nonlinear Time Dynamics, and the overarching Integral Musicology paradigm of which it is a subset, not only radically expand the vision of what might comprise musicianship and music studies in the twenty-first century, but also raise the bar in terms of activism. In terms of curricular activism, whatever purpose distinctions between historical musicology and ethnomusicology might have heretofore served, the time has come to not only remove those boundaries but also fundamentally reconceive of the entire musicological enterprise. If this risks erring in the direction of wholesale elimination of the disciplines in the core curriculum, which is essentially what I propose in chapter 3, I believe this is a risk worth taking, particularly when weighed against that of incurring even the most residual traces, let alone substantive remnants, of the respective monocultural and multicultural platforms. At which point, curricular activism aligns itself with the all-important social activism for which music studies is in desperate need.

The above considerations further underscore commentary in part I regarding the need for change agents to commit to significant critical introspection to liberate from both neo-Eurocentric and neo-Eurocentric-plus indoctrination, or what might be considered part and parcel of inner activism. Moreover, yet a further type of activism, one that is oriented both internally and externally, may be inferred in the Nonlinear Time Dynamics model. Here the improvisatory core of musical creativity, and its foundations in consciousness, open up new possibilities for fundamentally reconceiving the horizons of education and social practice at a juncture in human history for which expert individual, community, national, and planetary improvising may have never been more urgent.

Chapter Seven

Jazz and the Integral Revolution

> To be a jazz freedom fighter is to attempt to galvanize and energize world-weary people into forms of organization with accountable leadership that promote critical exchange and broad reflection. —Cornell West[1]

From my earliest days as assistant professor, educational reform was as important to my personal and professional identity as furthering my career as creative artist, pedagogue, and scholar. I viewed the creativity and diversity crises in music studies as localized manifestations of overarching educational patterns, and was driven by the possibility that inroads in my own field could catalyze broader change. Bringing consciousness studies to the academy was also high on my agenda, which was the basis for one of my most important change initiatives—the design of a bachelor of fine arts in jazz and contemplative studies degree.[2] Inspired by the newly launched contemplative studies movement, this curriculum would be the first degree program at a public college or university with a significant component involving meditation and related studies in consciousness.[3] Although, consistent with prevailing reactions to even moderate kinds of change in the academic world, I anticipated the idea would meet with some degree of resistance, I was unprepared for the kind of opposition this particular proposal would elicit.

One colleague objected that the curriculum would, harkening back to educational "experiments" of the 1960s, "set the school back 50 years"—an interesting remark given that this person's area of focus was music of three centuries ago. Another viewed meditation as little more than a means for stress reduction, comparing it to a kind of antidepressant: "You can accomplish the same thing with Prozac. But you don't see me proposing a degree in music and Prozac studies!" Yet another line of resistance reflected at least some modicum of understanding of the place of meditation in overall consciousness development. This was expressed in the argument that, if the purpose of meditation is to cultivate enlightenment, "there is no provision in the proposal to addressing the scenario whereby a student failed to achieve enlightenment over the course of the four years." In other words, all other curricula, in the school, and throughout the university clearly delineated parameters by which it could be determined whether or not a student passed or failed. With the jazz and contemplative studies degree, however, "a student could fail and still obtain the degree. This is an unacceptable risk when it comes to academic integrity."[4]

Despite these arguments, following protracted debate in which opposition was particularly animated, and with many late nights spent replying to objections, the proposal passed by close to a two-thirds majority. Not only was I thrilled at what this degree program would offer the students enrolled in it, but I was also proud to have successfully advanced a framework that is among the rare occasions in which the educational enterprise circumvents the interior-exterior divide that has long beset the academic world. My hope was that the BFA in jazz and contemplative studies would serve as a kind of prototype for the broader revolution in creativity and consciousness that is central to my vision.

I was also gratified to have single-handedly catalyzed a kind of conversation and reflection about the educational mission that essentially stopped a top-ranked school of the performing arts in its tracks. The more I reflect back on that moment, the more I realize that of equal importance to the substance of any new idea is the kind of critical discourse that change agents are able to sustain in its advocacy. If the common slogan in education reform circles—that it is "easier to move a cemetery than change a curriculum"[5]—holds in terms of modifying curricular models already in place, the obstacles are all the more formidable when it comes to new curricular design. Therefore, as entertaining as it may be to recount aspects of the above exchange long after the dust has settled, it is also sobering and highly instructive to have seen these patterns play out firsthand, even if I was fortunate that my initiative would see the light of day. On that account, it is important to regard my particular inroad, even if an inspiring glimpse of things to come, as a notable exception against the overarching backdrop of educational stasis.

Without losing sight, moreover, of the discriminatory obstacles that have hindered the advancement of jazz in the academy, and it would be naïve to not think this informed some of the above resistance, I have come to view the systemic aversion to change in the academic world as a crisis in imagination. Indeed, if the above curricular deliberations are any guide, one might reasonably conclude that some of the most imaginative thinking among faculty is exhibited in reaction against innovative efforts by others![6] Whereas one might expect higher education to be a hotbed of new and innovative ideas, boundary crossing, risk taking, and embrace of paradigmatically new horizons, all of which come to fruition through ongoing curricular renovation and design, the opposite is more the norm.[7] As I have argued, education is the key site in society where prevailing conceptions of the human being and human potential can either be perpetuated or open up to a new and expanded vision. Unfortunately, educational leadership of the latter kind has yet to emerge on any significant scale. While conversation about educational reform is nothing new, rarely does it penetrate to the level of curricular policy—or more aptly, curricular politics—that impede the kind of change that is urgently needed in our time. The patterns that define lower order discourse in music studies, let alone the prevailing neo-Eurocentric paradigm, are a subset of the overarching visioning malaise.

Nonetheless, I remain optimistic that the imaginative capacities inherent in human nature and potential may be enlivened, even in an educational world that appears predicated on the eradication of such, and that our colleges and universities will usher in a new paradigm of what it means to be an educated human being in a world fraught with peril, yet brimming with evolutionary potential. While the importance of reform at the K–12 level is not to be overlooked, higher education is where public school teachers and administrators gain their training. If, as I argue, jazz is to serve as a central change catalyst, no field more dramatically exemplifies the need for transformed teacher training than tertiary-level music studies, where jazz remains on the curricular and cultural periphery. In this culminating chapter, I reflect on the ramifications of jazz-driven integral reform in music studies for broader educational and societal change.

AN IMPROVISING PLANET IN AN IMPROVISATORY COSMOS

At first glance, the idea that principles from jazz might inform how humanity approaches issues such as environment, social justice, economy, and international conflict may seem farfetched. But think about it: Does not collective policy come down to individuals making decisions on a moment-to-moment basis? Moreover, do not individuals have to contend with the inertia of conditioned ways of thinking and acting, and do they not at times rise above the norm to break free from these patterns? If this liberation from ordinary conception to heightened conception can happen in a music improvising ensemble, why not in a community, or nation? Why not on a planetary scale?

When viewed from the standpoint of the jazz-inspired parts-to-whole/whole-to-parts interplay, the ramifications of these connections become even more pronounced. Parts-to-whole entails heightened moment-to-moment improvisatory intention, by which conditioned tendencies of ordinary consciousness and its confinement to linear temporal dimensions may begin to open up to transcendent experience and its more fluid and expansive nonlinear capacities. Whole-to-parts engagement, grounded in the pure consciousness of meditation, brings into play three key WP transformative principles discussed throughout the book: The first is that pure consciousness provides an overarching backdrop of nonlinear presence that enhances PW capacities for heightened event cycle frequency and moment-to-moment, linear-to-nonlinear transformations. The second is that the pure consciousness of individual meditation, which exemplifies self-referral awareness in silence, provides a basis for collective practice, and thus intensified enlivenment of the self-referral mechanics of cosmic, improvisatory unfolding that give rise to entirely new dimensions of transformation and healing. The harmonizing effect of large-group meditation on society is a primary example. This directly informs a third principle, which involves heightened capacities to navigate the primordial junction point between undifferentiated, eternal Being, or Spirit, and the subtlest strata of manifest, differentiated creation. Here is where further potential new interventions in response to social justice, ecological, and other crises come into view.

A look at particularly pressing issues in the world at large—beginning with social justice and environmental justice—sheds light on these principles.

IMPROVISATION, ENVIRONMENTAL JUSTICE, AND SOCIAL JUSTICE

Approaching environmental and social justice as closely intertwined not only yields new kinds of understanding and solutions for each area but also highlights principles that apply to a broader range of applications. As I explain below in the context of transdisciplinary education, academic knowledge disciplines and contemporary real-world challenges can be seen as differentiated developmental lines that unfold from undifferentiated wholeness, and can thus be rendered transformative pathways through creativity/consciousness-based, integral approaches. Improvisation provides a particularly useful lens into the interconnectedness of the transdisciplinary matrix.

Parts-to-Whole Analysis

From a parts-to-whole perspective, the basis for one's relationship with both physical and social surroundings is moment-to-moment thinking, feeling, and action and the level of consciousness that underlies that improvisatory flow. When improvisatory engagement is limited, decisions tend to be mediated by conditioned patterns. In the realm of environmental relationship, decisions about food, resource and energy consumption and waste, as well as the general health of the natural world, are thus driven by the inertia of exterior perception and habit that is disconnected from interior awareness. The realm of human relationship may be dominated by ingrained stereotypes about, or even fear of, other individuals. Improvisatory engagement can thus be analyzed as confined to third-person, objective/exterior reality.

More robust improvising brings to the mix a second-person thrust that begins to ground environmental and social relationships in more integrated interior awareness. As individuals break down linear conception and invoke more moment-to-moment functioning, they are more able to identify and liberate from ingrained habit and unearth new creative possibilities. In the environmental realm, what I call "improvisatory ecologies" begin to blossom in awareness. Just as improvisers are able to render the most minute detail a catalyst for new ideas and pathways, individuals in all modes of activity can similarly uncover new worlds of perception in the most localized and mundane environmental detail. The same holds for all moments of human relationship, with jazz a powerful example in terms of spontaneously transforming even the subtlest interpersonal gesture, let alone more overt expressive statements, into innovative gateways. As considered in chapters 1 and 2 in the context of the evolution of the individual voice, improvisation-based intimacy with the range of influences that inform this voice is the basis for entirely new kinds of relationship with the world that cross ethnic, racial, gender, and other boundaries.

When second-person improvisatory engagement opens up to transcendent experience, hence first-person experience, environmental and social relationships begin to be seen as spiritual pathways.

Whole-to-Parts Analysis

Systematic meditation-based, and thus whole-to-parts engagement further enhances physical and human ecologies by grounding improvisatory engagement in regular, and increasingly enduring, experience of pure consciousness. A range of ramifications may be identified that can be seen as elaborations on the three WP premises cited above—pure consciousness, collective consciousness, and navigation of the primordial junction point.

First, the experience of pure consciousness invoked apart from ordinary physical, emotional, sensory, interpersonal engagement most fully transcends environmental, societal, and other kinds of conditioning. This is not to suggest that the experience in itself constitutes enduring liberation from conditioning, but that it provides the most complete glimpse thereof. Moreover, because heightened moment-to-moment perception is now invoked against a backdrop of eternal presence, nonlinear parts-to-whole intention becomes grounded in an even deeper stratum of nonlinear wholeness that, through WP engagement, enhances the realization of that intention.

Second, and perhaps among the most powerful ramifications of the whole-to-parts trajectory, is the principle of intersubjective consciousness and related new ways of environmental and human understanding and relationship. Key is the nondual relationship between individual consciousness and cosmic intelligence, and the idea that collective creative and spiritual practice may enliven the mechanics of cosmic creativity.[8] If, as posited, the experience of pure, self-referral consciousness invoked in individual meditation aligns awareness with the self-referral mechanics of cosmic creativity, collective practice may intensify this alignment, and also enlivenment of the mechanics of cosmic unfolding for both localized and global transformative and healing impact. The idea discussed in chapter 5 that collective meditation may generate harmonizing influence that results in reduced crime, accidents, and illness is a direct application of this principle. It has also been surmised that this harmonizing influence may also be an antidote to terrorism and war—all of which can be seen as manifestations of object-referral pathology along the human relationship/social justice line.[9]

Third is that enlivened intersubjective consciousness may enhance navigation of the primordial junction point between undifferentiated, eternal wholeness and the subtlest strata of differentiation, and harnessing of yet further interventions. Here is where mind-matter interaction at subtle scales, and thus conceivably at more manifest scales, may yield particularly powerful ramifications for addressing ecological crises. Notions such as Dean Radin's teams of "intention experts"[10] that have been trained to direct their awareness to the primordial junction point to address draught-stricken regions may not be that far off in terms of research and development; little commentary is needed on the timeliness of this kind of investigation. Here it is noteworthy to distinguish between collective meditation practice and this latter kind of intervention: the first is not predicated on participants focusing attention on a given issue, but simply allowing awareness to dissolve into the innermost, transcendent dimensions of Being, thereby intensifying cosmic processes. Meditators in this circumstance do not intend for a specific result, even if this might involve some environmental effect. The second intervention, however, involves actual attention to specific situations, which may call for particular kinds of meditation practice to ground intention. The jazz-inspired integral vision recognizes and celebrates both approaches and how they may work together.[11]

Important social justice ramifications also extend from enhanced capacities, made possible by the PW/WP interplay, to navigate the primordial junction point. For this primordial stratum is where ethno-cultural-gender streams differentiate from the unmanifest, transcendent source of creation and connections to which may be thus established at deep levels of feeling and perception. Recall from commentary on the *bhagavat chetena* stage of consciousness development the opening of the heart as key to this grounding. Here is where direct perception of the primordial, archetypal roots of all cultures, ethnicities, and genders as facets of one's own consciousness is accompanied, if not driven by, a "supreme love," to paraphrase the title of

John Coltrane's iconic recording *A Love Supreme*, for the creator and all of creation. As discussed previously, the social justice imperative to welcome individuals from all backgrounds, as well as their unique ways of knowing and creative expression, in all educational and societal settings gains even deeper grounding in the innermost recesses of the heart and soul; immersion with, and thus celebration of, a wide a diversity of people and perspectives becomes the driving force for one's very Being. Yet again, horizontal multiculturalism gives way to transcultural vertical roots that entirely transform the diversity vision.

An important parallel might be cited in the realm of environmental justice. Without WP grounding, concern about the health of rivers, lakes, wetlands, and forests might be confined to recreational considerations, thus another example of horizontal relationship. Enlivened primordial connection represents a deeper, vertical relationship that is ultimately key to addressing the crises and rendering them gateways to ecological flourishing. Here wisdom from indigenous traditions across the globe, and from time immemorial, offers powerful guidance in terms of the spiritual dimensions of nature communion. The natural world is not separate; it is part of us, and needs to be engaged with sacred intention and coevolutionary commitment.

Maharishi Mahesh Yogi was emphatic decades ago that "nature knows how to organize better than man"—meaning that enlivenment of the mechanics by which the cosmos creates through collective creativity and consciousness modalities has the capacity to activate self-organizing, nonlinear healing processes on a global scale that are far greater in transformative impact than the sum of any amount of linear strategies imaginable. I believe this wisdom is particularly relevant in light of sobering assessments about the prospects for circumventing environmental destruction prior to reaching a point of no return, which some claim has already been reached. It is not that there is no place for linear, parts-to-whole, domain-specific strategies, but that they need to be grounded in a nonlinear whole-to-parts evolutionary thrust.

This principle holds as well when it comes to the prospects for global peace.

Improvisation and Peace

The basis for peace is the union of personal self and transcendent Self that is the most fundamental level at which individuals can connect with themselves, their surroundings, and other human beings. As analyzed above, heightened moment-to-moment improvisatory access to transcendent experience provides a parts-to-whole opening to this core experience. Whole-to-parts engagement promotes more enduring grounding, which feeds back to inform parts-to-whole thinking and action that promotes peace on individual and collective scales. Critical inquiry faculties are heightened that help identify, diagnose, and heal ingrained tendencies that escalate conflict. Individuals become more alert to how patterns in day-to-day human interactions, between family, friends, and coworkers, may be localized manifestations of those that result in conflict on national scales.

However, I believe one of the most promising and exciting principles that extends from the jazz-inspired integral vision involves collective consciousness, as discussed above, as a backdrop that promotes heightened improvisatory thinking and behavior in relationships among individuals, communities, and nations. If the backdrop is incoherent, meaning fraught with tension, then this will be reflected in moment-to-moment decision-making.[12] Here it is important to keep in mind that violent action, whether between individuals, or on larger scales as in terrorist acts, and in national military conflicts, always involves moment-to-moment improvisatory decisions among individual actors. If the collective field is harmonious, individuals or groups with violent tendencies will be less inclined to act on these tendencies. Moreover, because harmonious consciousness fields are more differentiated (and more differentiated consciousness fields more harmonious), this promotes higher frequency event cycles within any time frame that transpires between the intention to commit violence and enactment of that violence. This means more decision-making moments whereby individuals prone to such activity may, instead of carrying out the initial impulse, reconsider.

The enlivenment of more differentiated, coherent field consciousness also raises the prospects that one or more among the multitude of factors that need to fall into place for a violent plan to be carried out as intended may be thwarted. For example, an acquaintance of the perpetrator might spontaneously decide to alert authorities, or some vital piece of information might be unearthed that was previously overlooked in law enforcement or intelligence circles, as more differentiated flow of consciousness permeates the awareness and improvisatory behavior of all who are involved. Furthermore, when one factors in the possibility that mind-matter interactions that take hold at subtle strata of creation impact macroscale material phenomena, it is even conceivable that the malfunction of a weapon, transport vehicle, line of communication, or any of the many mechanical aspects necessary to execution of a violent event may be influenced by heightened collective consciousness. If, in other words, individual consciousness is a manifestation of cosmic intelligence, and heightened collective consciousness enlivens the mechanics of cosmic creativity, overlying material conditions that are necessary to destructive action may be neutralized due to greater coherence at underlying strata where subjective and objective worlds begin to differentiate. Again, these principles are as applicable to healing interactions between two individuals, rendering our schools and public spaces safe from the senseless slaughter that is increasingly on the rise, equally heinous terrorist activity that is promoted by organizations, and military conflict between nations. The advent of increasingly devastating weaponry on all levels, with signs of re-escalating cold war tensions between not only the world's superpowers but also other nations makes it all the more urgent for paradigmatically new approaches to understanding and addressing these challenges. I believe the jazz-inspired, integral approach, with its expanded conception of improvisation and its relationship with consciousness, warrants serious consideration in this regard.

Yet again, collective creative and spiritual practice looms large as a new frontier within the emergent creativity-consciousness revolution. While from a conventional, materialist science perspective, and even the perspective of conventional environmental and social activism, consideration of these kinds of possibilities clearly stretches the boundaries of prevailing thinking, and may even elicit incredulity. However, when one steps back from conventional thinking, a strong case may be made that these and other consciousness-based anomalous potentialities are, at the very least, (a) far more coherent with cutting-edge research into consciousness that takes place, albeit in small and isolated pockets, in the academy, than materialist findings or ideas that preclude these possibilities, and (b) resonant with ideas that date back millennia in indigenous and other spiritual traditions, but that—particularly when it comes to epistemological engagement—remain at the academic fringes.

As I have suggested in chapter 4 in regard to the issue of critical integrity, the ability to shift the lens to epistemology is a key to raising the critical bar and thus capability of invoking paradigmatic and thus vertical change, as opposed to ornamental or horizontal change. On this account, readers who may be startled by the above notions are invited to reflect on the viability of two very different epistemic frameworks: one is confined to third-person, conventional scientific inquiry that excludes consciousness and spiritual dimensions; another unites spiritual, artistic, and scientific perspectives in a synergistic interplay.

I believe that most individuals, when given the choice, will opt for the second, more expanded epistemological framework. Why, in other words, remain confined to a narrow materialist lens when a wide-angle integral lens—which could situate any insights into physical reality gleaned from materialist-based inquiry—is readily available? I believe the latter not only brings into view fundamentally new modes of understanding and application to real-world challenges, but is also far more conducive to critical interrogation of its own assumptions and those that underlie contrasting models.[13] Unfortunately, conventional education does not provide students, or even faculty, with this kind of choice, thereby limiting the contemporary imagination at a time when its cultivation has never been more urgently needed.

At which point the conversation broaches the realm of ideological extremism through an improvisatory lens.

IMPROVISATION AND IDEOLOGICAL EXTREMISM

To begin, I am not only talking about commonly acknowledged manifestations of extremism such as religious fundamentalism, ethnosupremacy, and ultranationalist identity. I am also talking about fundamentalism as it manifests in less-recognized realms such as science and the arts. By juxtaposing religious, scientific, and artistic fundamentalism and examining them from an improvisatory angle, important principles come into view that are key to addressing the overarching problem. As I consider, common to all forms of extremism is object-referral attachment to some idea or conviction that privileges one's domain and denigrates other perspectives, and impedes capacities to critically examine one's ideological platform. Moreover, language plays a key role in reifying these attachments.

Language and Extremism: Tales of Three Fundamentalisms

Recall my statement from chapter 2 that the paradigmatic distance between multicultural and transcultural conceptions of the term *jazz* is greater than that which separates multicultural conceptions of European classical music and jazz. As I observed, ethnomusicologists are keen to the idea of contrasting musical paradigms, and might even cite Eurological and Afrological models as particularly dramatic examples. However, when it comes to what I call "paradigms within paradigms," one example of which involves applying the principle of foundationally distinct models within the African American roots of our own American musical culture, multicultural ethnomusicology falls dramatically short. *Jazz* means jazz, a name that designates one among an infinitude of other self-confining locations along vast multicultural horizons, regardless of the unmatched self-transcending tools for traversing (meaning infusing influences and collaborating with musicians from, and fostering deep connections to) those horizons. If multiculturalism, which is predicated on cultural diversity, is prone to this kind of interpretive lapse and corresponding hegemonic tendencies, one can only imagine the extent to which these principles apply to monocultural, neo-Eurocentric thinking.

Similarly, the terms *science* and *religion* can also be seen as susceptible to radically different interpretations from conventional and integral standpoints. As discussed, an integral science paradigm opens up to religion, albeit often viewed as its nemesis, and the reverse also holds. Conceptions of science and religion as self-confining destinations, which thus fall short of self-transcending status, are not only vastly incomplete but also susceptible to misguided assumptions about the nature of reality. Musical fundamentalism, embodied by (but not limited to) the neo-Eurocentric paradigm as discussed in prior chapters, succumbs to self-confining tendencies in its rejection of the improvisatory foundations of the European classical tradition as well as the contemporary musical world.

Religious, scientific, and musical fundamentalism may be analyzed in terms of third-person, objective attachment to their respective kinds of scriptural interpretation that overshadows broader inner-outer engagement and understanding. Just as religious fundamentalists take at face value interpretations of scriptural narrative—such as the Earth being created ten thousand years ago and humans living alongside dinosaurs, against all contrasting evidence, scientific "scriptural dogma" takes hold in superficial interpretation of empirical findings as the complete picture of physical reality, when inquiry into the underpinnings of matter from science itself points to consciousness as, at the very least, a leading contender for foundational status in this quest. Though Max Planck's assertion that "consciousness is primary" has not yet become the central position among physicists, he is far from alone in terms of past and present practitioners in the field who at least seriously entertain this possibility. While consciousness might provide a bridge between science and spirituality/religion, materialist ideology categorically rejects a domain that might represent the fulfillment of the scientific mission.

The locus for "scriptural dogma" in music is the body of masterworks from the European classical tradition, performance and study of which has become central activity in music schools. However, just as the problem underlying religious fundamentalism is not scripture itself but its interpretation, nor for scientific fundamentalism physical creation but interpretation of corresponding findings, the root problem in musical fundamentalism is not composed-notated repertory—the greatness of which is beyond dispute—but the fact that interpretation has precluded creation—the result of which is the rejection of other musical paradigms.

How does improvisation impact identification and rectification of the three fundamentalisms?

Key is the role of improvisation as a second-person modality that unites first-person and third-person realms, and in so doing expands the critical gaze that reveals conditioned attachment to language-bound, limiting assumptions. First-person experience in scientific practice may take hold in the sense of awe at the sheer richness, beauty, and complexity of the physical world that accompanies, or evolves over time from, peak or transcendent experience. Improvisatory intention expands both the epistemological and ethnological spectrum through which that experience may be critically examined to impact interpretation of physical reality and can be seen as the correlate to the establishment of a creativity/consciousness-based CICP identity in music. Weak improvisatory intention and engagement may leave practitioners prone to overarching materialist conclusions that are sustained by unexamined ethnological and epistemological assumptions. Materialism, for example, is a distinctively Western ideology that, particularly in terms of its present stranglehold, is a relatively recent development even in the West.[14] Even with quantum conundrums bringing epistemology and thus subjectivity—which had been kept safely at a distance in conventional scientific method—into the forefront, the inertia of materialism remains formidable. Strong improvisatory engagement could stimulate critical inquiry into epistemological and ethnological assumptions, and at the very least, elicit open consideration of the origins of matter in consciousness, and thus a transcendent realm of spirit. However, without this second-person grounding, even the most vivid first-person experience is inadequate to dislodge scientific materialism from its third-person moorings. From an integral standpoint, moreover—which stipulates that domain-specific engagement is optimal when the domain is realized as a self-transcending gateway to first-second-third person synthesis—even that third-person orientation is limited.

In terms of religious fundamentalism, first-person experience is invoked within the context of third-person conceptual convictions. Strong improvisatory intention, which expands the epistemic scope, could enliven critical examination of ethnological considerations, whereby parallels across culturally diverse religious lineages, and intersections with science, might be fathomed with deeper reading of the same scriptural passages. Without this grounding, tendencies toward rejection of wisdom from other cultures and disciplines prevail. Religious fundamentalism may be thus analyzed as a first-person orientation, albeit one that may masquerade as deeply rooted, that fails to penetrate to the transcendent core of religion that unites all cultures and disciplines, while also celebrating tradition-specific, denominational richness.

Arts fundamentalism, particularly as it manifests in the neo-Eurocentric music studies paradigm, presents an interesting case given the improvisatory foundations of much artistic creativity, which were particularly prominent in earlier times in that particular tradition. This epistemic expansion would help practitioners penetrate to the inner workings of music; recognize how influences from many areas of life, including across cultures, shape the evolution of the individual voice; and comprise the basis for deep connections with other musical cultures. Improvisation would also provide a means for first-person transcendent experience that coexists with that experience as it is invoked in interpretive performance. Without the second-person improvisatory domain, interpretive-based peak experience occurs against a third-person conceptual backdrop of inherent musical superiority. In other words, some degree of the notion that the European masterwork is the closest to the divine among all humanity's musical achievement pervades the curricular, cultural, and organizational structure of music schools. It is inevitable that the transcendent experience invoked by the interpretive performer, even those who are inclined toward some degree of cultural diversity, reifies this deeply rooted assumption. The point is in no way to denigrate this transcendent experience, but simply to recognize its ramifications when invoked outside a first-second-third-person framework, and when situated within the quest for a culturally diverse music studies paradigm. Not only is this form of fundamentalism ethnocentric, but it can also be seen as theocentric. Even strong grounding in meditation practice, which while to be celebrated in terms of enhancing interpretive experience, is inadequate to rectify the problem.

The fact that restoration of the Contemporary Improviser Composer Performer identity that was once central in the European tradition is key to transforming the self-confining orientation to self-transcending status underscores principles that are common to the three fundamentalisms: Just as the solution to musical fundamentalism in European classical music is not a retreat from the tradition but a deeper engagement in its epistemic foundations, the solutions to fundamentalist religion and science are similarly not a retreat from those realms but a deeper engagement in their respective epistemological foundations.

Indeed, one need not look far for reminders of the urgency of the science-religion-art unity. On one hand is the violence, including terrorism, that results from religious fundamentalism. On the other, scientific side, are risks inherent in artificial intelligence and probing of the genetic realm and potential modifications thereof—whether in the form of designing new life-forms or genetic modification of the food supply. Penetration to these fundamental strata of physical and biological creation separate from grounding in transcendent dimensions of consciousness, particularly from a nondual standpoint that might highlight both rational and ethical ramifications of this work from deep levels of feeling and perception, could yield catastrophic consequences for the world.[15]

Emergence of Arts-Driven Science and Spirituality Paradigms

If the science-religion divide is a primary example of weak improvising among extremists of both sides, healing this divide may be seen as a primary example of the transformation of a moment that is perceived as bound to linear relationships to a generator of new possibilities, via heightened nonlinear conception. I view the emergence of arts-driven science and spirituality paradigms through which science and religion take their next evolutionary strides as an important result of this healing.

Jazz, among the arts, is uniquely equipped to catalyze this movement due to its improvisatory roots that, as I have shown, are core to the creativity-consciousness relationship across fields. An important reason for this is that the arts, even if typically occupying the curricular fringes for students not majoring in the arts, in general at least occupy a prominent place in the cultural life of most college and university campuses. I am regularly impressed, moreover, at the sophisticated awareness of the arts exhibited by colleagues in sciences and humanities. In many instances, I encounter not only conversance with diverse musical cultures but also a kind fluency with basic transcultural principles that exceeds what I typically encounter among music colleagues. The arts, therefore, have one foot in the academic door and are an ideologically neutral site in which a consciousness inquiry might take hold that, at once, celebrates conventional scientific contributions—as in, for example, mind-brain connections as related to the creative process—and also broaches spiritual dimensions. While there is no denying that the latter connections will be more problematic, with the establishment of a robust environment of critical inquiry, and emphasis on the principle that an integral understanding of consciousness promotes both scientific integrity and spiritual vitality, significant inroads may be established. As the academic environment becomes more critically astute to the need for penetrating beyond conventional interpretation of common language and terminology, receptivity to the idea of a consciousness studies paradigm that invites insights from spiritual/religious lineages as well as the arts and sciences will evolve apace.

Education is the key site where this revolution will need to take hold if it is to come about in society at large.

IMPROVISATION AND EDUCATION

Following are several angles of inquiry into the jazz-driven emergence of an integral educational paradigm that has the capacity to catalyze the broader creativity/consciousness integral revolution. The first involves examination of the term *education* and its different meanings through the lens of the two Latin words *educare* and *educere*. *Educare* translates as "to train," or "to mold," and arguably corresponds with conventional, exterior-oriented educational practice, while *educere* means "to draw out," the interior unfolding that is inherent in the integral paradigm and its precursors. When Alfred North Whitehead in 1929 declared that "a stage of precision is barren without a prior stage of romance,"[16] he was talking about the need to open up the prevailing focus on *educare* to also include *educere*, as was, decades later, Abraham Maslow when he emphasized the need to "develop a new kind of human being who is comfortable with change, who is able to improvise,"[17] and bell hooks when she later wrote about experiences of joy and ecstasy in the context of "teaching to transgress."[18]

Jazz exemplifies the educare-educere synergy in its interplay of exploratory and emulative engagement that lies at the heart of the systematic improvisatory development continuum, with its parts-to-whole/whole-to-parts trajectories providing strong interior grounding for the whole enterprise. More recent movements in higher education with more overt intentions of interiority may also be noted in support of progress in an integral direction. Here I am talking of the parallel, emergent streams of contemplative studies and consciousness studies.[19]

Contemplative Studies and Consciousness Studies

Particularly instructive is to consider contrasting ways in which each contributes, yet also falls short of—and thus, if rectified, could promote—important integral inroads. To start with a general observation: consciousness studies is fairly robust when it comes to worldview delineation (meaning vigorous debates among materialists, dualists, and nondual integralists), yet generally ambivalent when it comes to epistemology. Contemplative studies, on the other hand, is predicated on direct epistemic engagement of varying kinds, but tends to be worldview ambivalent. To be more precise, it is not that consciousness researchers, particularly those who are disposed toward non-materialist perspectives, do not engage with meditation and related practices, but that these are not generally regarded by the field as reliable ontological lenses when it comes to the nature of mind and reality. Nor is it that contemplative educators, whose work is driven by incorporation of meditation and related practices in college coursework, do not harbor worldview dispositions. However, this latter kind of inquiry remains distanced in contemplative studies discourse. The fact, moreover, that if anything, a default reliance on a received, quasi-Buddhist perspective, as considered in chapter 5, surfaces when worldview questions occasionally arise reflects compromised improvisatory integrity and lingering influence of materialist, exterior predilections even amid seemingly progressive efforts. Recall discussion of the misinterpretation of *anatta* as the absence of a nonphysical, eternal dimension of consciousness—soul or otherwise—that in turn confines notions of the human being, human potential and corresponding worldview inquiry within limited parameters. From this standpoint, statements such as Owen Flanagan's that Buddhism, due to its rejection of the notion of soul, discarnate entities, or other mystical phenomena, is uniquely aligned with "how science says we should see the world"[20] in a single stroke sells both Buddhism and science radically short. Recall, too, social justice transgressions that stem from this misconception for constituencies for whom soul is endemic to their experience and worldview. Exploration of practical and pedagogical applications of the nondual relationship between individual consciousness and cosmic wholeness requires corresponding conceptual foundations, or at least imagining.

I believe that as the jazz-driven creativity and consciousness revolution takes hold in education, the integral nondual worldview will help transform these kinds of perspectives into more expansive and inclusive accounts of human nature and evolutionary potential. While I anticipate the recognition of Vedanta as an important source for the emergent vision, the point—as I have stressed previously—is not that everyone become a Vedantist, but that this source is recognized as a catalyst for rediscovery of integral nondual principles across traditions, including Buddhism. Just as jazz restores the Contemporary Improviser Composer Performer identity to transcultural musical practice in the transformation of music studies, Vedanta may uphold a similar function in the creativity/consciousness revolution of education at large. As also discussed previously, the fact that John Coltrane's and Alice Coltrane's trajectories as artists and spiritual visionaries straddled both realms—jazz and Vedanta—may be more than coincidence, but in fact may reflect deep penetration to musical and spiritual streams with uniquely unifying impact. The fact that a significant lineage of physicists, in large part due to conundrums about the relationship of consciousness and physical reality raised by quantum explorations, seriously investigated Vedanta as a source of unifying principles is also noteworthy.[21]

Tales of Two Epistemologies (aka Academic Amnesia)

The jazz-Vedanta relationship was the inspiration for the jazz and contemplative studies (JCS) curriculum mentioned at the outset of the chapter. Further insights come into view regarding the complicated dynamics of educational reform, and particularly the crisis in imagination, that were encountered when that curriculum was proposed. The JCS curriculum challenged the academy along two epistemic lines (improvisation and meditation) and an ethnological line (African American culture). Of particular relevance to the present discussion is resistance to the two epistemologies, which might be seen as forms of "academic amnesia." In other words, both improvisatory and contemplative epistemologies were once central in their respective knowledge systems yet encounter resistance when it comes to what may be reasonably seen as their reentry in the conventional education world.

The centrality of improvisation in earlier eras of European classical music is a more commonly recognized historical reality. Nonetheless, long-standing resistance to improvisation in the curriculum, let alone to the process occupying central status, eludes critical interrogation as a glaring epistemic contradiction among contemporary adherents of that tradition. Less commonly known, to cite a parallel and overarching contradiction, is that contemplative engagement was central to the systems of logic and rational thinking that evolved in ancient Greek and Roman cultures and are viewed as the bedrock of the conventional academy. Pierre Hadot has been a leading voice on this account, showing that "a profound difference exists between the representations which the ancients made of *philosophia* and the representation which is usually made of philosophy today." While there is "no denying the extraordinary ability of the ancient philosophers to develop theoretical reflection on the most subtle problems of the theory of knowledge, logic, or physics," it is also important to recognize the dietary, discursive, meditative, and contemplative practices among the ancients that were "intended to effect a modification and transformation in the subject who practiced them."[22] From the standpoint of paradigmatic change, the fact that resistance to efforts to advance these practices in the academy, much like that elicited by advocacy for improvisation, goes far beyond the endemic aversion to new developments that has long pervaded the academic world cannot be overstated in its significance. The fact that this resistance entails rejection of the very epistemological foundations from which conventional music studies and overall academic models evolved eludes critical interrogation, and that the original foundations are rejected as "foreign intruders" to be rejected at all costs, indicates an entirely new spectrum of self-annihilating educational pathology that boggles the imagination (or what is left of it).

Still, the jazz-based integral visionary has reason to remain optimistic about paradigmatic overhaul, at which point the question arises: Are the above epistemic lapses to be rectified through modifications to existing models, as in multicultural, neo-Eurocentric-plus approaches to music studies reform, or through foundational overhaul, as in the transcultural music vision, the correlate to which is a transdenominational model of contemporary spirituality?

The time has come for the latter if the jazz-driven integral revolution is to take hold. Which brings with it complications due to the church-state boundaries that are firmly etched in conventional as well as progressive educational ideology.

Church-State Boundaries

Few pedagogical approaches are more problematic in the academy than those even remotely resembling religious engagement. However, elsewhere I have advanced an argument that, as firmly entrenched as church-state boundaries are in the conventional academic identity, the issue has not yet been placed front and center and critically examined with any sort of heightened improvisatory presence.[23] In other words, church-state boundaries are typically considered in linear reaction to some sort of incident, such as a group protesting when a school insists on instituting or continuing prayer practice, or perhaps in reaction to celebration of a religious holiday with denomination-specific displays. But there is an enormous gray area when it comes to distinguishing between what does and does not constitute religious practice that, upon closer inspection, brings into view possibilities for a consciousness-based, integral conception of religion, and approaches thereto, in public education. For one thing, establishing an environment whereby students could choose whatever practices or lineages they wish to engage may be entirely within existing legal constraints as they are now understood. Moreover, I believe this kind of environment could actually promote a level of critical inquiry into the nature of religion that counters the religious fundamentalism that the academic community generally abhors.[24] Imagine an educational environment in which celebration of denomination-specific religious/spiritual engagement coexisted, and coevolved, with transdenominational inquiry, meaning that a central criterion for religion in the schools was identification of common connecting principles across lineages, as well as lineage-specific features. Critical interrogation of the word *religion* would be paramount—where the principle of union of individual self with transcendent Self would catalyze transcendence of overlying dogma, and also ground belief in direct experience of pure consciousness and the wholeness in which all religion, and science and art, originate, and with which true religion, and science and art, reunite. Jazz-inspired transcultural musical navigation, where discrete lineages flow into a common musical ocean, combined with its PW/WP interplay, could powerfully set the stage for this exploration. Transposing the word *transcultural*, in other words, to *transdenominational* would reveal direct parallels that transform existing boundaries that fuel tensions and constrain religious understanding into gateways to new vistas of coevolutionary religious practice and wisdom.[25]

Needless to say, this is a highly charged and complicated discussion that could be the source of an entire volume in itself. I suggest this theme as yet another that distinguishes—much like transcultural versus multicultural diversity frameworks—between prevailing progressive and integral visioning, and that while church-state boundaries may have upheld an important function in response to the needs of one moment in time, they may, in fact, fuel the very fundamentalism that adherents of this legislation fear at the current moment in time and thus warrant reconsideration. I believe that just as an integral, transcultural conception of the word *jazz* is key to new frontiers in music studies, an integral conception of the term *religion*—inspired by the emergent conception of jazz—similarly provides a backdrop against which a critically robust paradigm of religious engagement could blossom in public education; I view this development as a key juncture in the overarching creativity-consciousness educational/societal revolution.

Closely related is a jazz-inspired integral view of transdisciplinarity.

Improvisation and Transdisciplinarity

Yet to be defined in a concise way, the term *transdisciplinarity*[26] generally refers to a level of experience that transcends typical discipline-specific inquiry and engagement. The jazz-based integral perspective gives considerable shape to this notion by situating it within the context of parts-to-whole and whole-to-parts epistemic trajectories. From a PW angle, one invokes transdisciplinary experience amid the turbulence of mental, physical, and/or sensory engagement, with one discipline or another serving as a point of departure. Heightened moment-to-moment improvisatory awareness yields openings to deeper strata of perception through some overlying disciplinary lens—whether it be mathematics, basketball, law enforcement, activism, philosophy, or strolling by the seashore. From a WP angle, one accesses transdisciplinary terrain from the vantage point of pure consciousness, where awareness is aware of nothing but awareness itself, exquisitely silent, entirely devoid of content, yet radiantly awake. Now, alternating between PW improvisatory activity and WP silence, one can then fathom the delicate intersection between undifferentiated wholeness and the subtlest strata of differentiation—which is the primordial junction point in which disciplines first begin to emerge. Integral transdisciplinarity is thus predicated on two means of access to an interior realm that, at once, lies beneath overarching knowledge areas, yet from which those knowledge areas emerge. As creativity and consciousness evolve, moreover, capacities blossom to fathom this realm in increasingly differentiated ways.

Several aspects of this model of transdisciplinarity are of particular value to the creativity-consciousness revolution in education and society. One is that it exemplifies understanding of not only educational disciplines but also the various overarching lines of inquiry—from environmental and social justice to peace—as richly intertwined differentiations from unified wholeness that, to varying degrees, have succumbed to dissociation. Environmental, social justice, economic, and epidemiological crises are forms of dissociation that have taken hold in the world at large, whereas conventional approaches to most every field in higher education are forms of dissociation, also to be viewed as crises, that have taken hold within the academy. Transdisciplinary grounding illuminates both the shared interiors—self-Self separation—of the crises, as well as domain-specific features. This reveals development of creativity and consciousness as the common foundation for addressing all areas, and domain-specific improvisatory engagement as a localized intervention.

In short, the deeper the penetration in the educational world into first-person interiors, particularly when individual and collective practice are involved, combined with improvisation-driven engagement with wide-ranging exteriors that span academic disciplines and real-world issues, the more the academy becomes a microcosm of the planetary improvising that needs to transpire on a heightened scale at this juncture in human history.

Clear parallels become evident between the transdisciplinary paradigm that is key to the broader educational shift and the transcultural musicianship paradigm, which is the localized manifestation of the overarching model. Direct experience of the inner workings of music, which is underpinned by the experience of pure consciousness, extends musical engagement far beyond conventional neo-Eurocentric (and multicultural) horizons in an interior, unifying direction. The crystallizing of basic musical elements in interaction with extramusical influences in the individual voice, which in turn gives rise to the wide scope of collective musical disciplines and genres that comprise the systematic improvisatory development continuum, extend the musicianship paradigm beyond the horizons currently in place or imagined in an outer direction. Jazz embodies the transcultural/transdisciplinary premise in both music studies and education, thus revealing the idiom as uniquely equipped to catalyze the overarching transformation, which would also encompass society at large—at which point the conversation comes full circle.

ADDRESSING THE CRISIS IN IMAGINATION: WHAT EXCITES US MOST?

For many years, my good friend and colleague Professor Frederick Amrine has taught a highly popular, far-reaching, and rigorous class called "Imagination" at the University of Michigan. When a few years ago he invited me to speak to his class, shortly following my publication of a prior book that viewed music through the lens of Integral Theory, I immediately panicked and did a "word find" that only confirmed the reasons for my panic: in the course of 475 pages, the word *imagination* appeared only a few times, and most of those were in quotations or titles from other authors. Although I made good use of this oversight through lighthearted self-deprecation to open my conversation with Fred's students, the experience had an important impact in my ongoing reform efforts in music studies and beyond. Whereas education should be about enlivening our imaginative capacities, the fact that it tends to have the opposite effect reflects fundamental shortcomings in educational and overarching worldviews that are in urgent need of rectification.

Following are thoughts about how this crisis might be resolved. The first involves the role of excitement in the ongoing cycles of worldview construction and dissolution that are uniquely possible with jazz-inspired PW/WP engagement, and essential to critically robust and meaningful visioning. I follow that with consideration of a framework called Deep Inquiry that connects educational visioning with the most far-reaching questions about the nature of the human being, creative and spiritual potential and purpose, and cosmic existence—hence, Ultimate Reality and Meaning. I think of this framework as a means by which the academy, which has become so dramatically disconnected from real-world issues, may transcend itself and establish this reconnection.

Igniting Excitement from the Transcendent Source

What if, in addition to asking ourselves about the logical coherence of an idea or worldview, the guiding question was "How does it feel?" I am not talking about feeling in mundane terms, as in the emotional mood swings or the boredom that pervade much of life, but in terms of a much wider range of feeling that includes subtle intuition at the faintest levels of perception and genuine excitement or passion for ideas that shake us at our core. Just as the jazz improviser, when he or she steps up to take a solo and, in the most profound jazz moments, digs deep into his reservoirs of imagination, passion, and purpose, the purpose of the educational institution could be seen as providing space for every participant—students, faculty, staff, administrative leadership—to do the same when it comes to any given idea, and most importantly the overarching worldview of the academy.

For me, the jazz-inspired integral worldview and its basic tenets—nondual relationship between individual consciousness and eternal universal wholeness, view of human beings as co-evolutionary participants in an improvisatory cosmic unfolding, compatibility between ancient and indigenous spiritual wisdom and cutting-edge science, central positioning of improvised musical art as global transformative catalyst, among other features—are infinitely more exciting, as well as philosophically coherent and resonant with my own experience, than the available alternatives. While the dualist notion of a universe comprised of ontologically separate realms of subjectivity and objectivity, or spirituality and science, has its merits, it pales on all fronts when compared to the subjective-objective unity of the integral. When it comes to the materialist platform (which when construed in its most fundamental form is based on the idea of the human being as an accidental outgrowth in a universe devoid of spirit, purpose, and meaning, and which categorically excludes contributions of most of the cultures across the globe, as well as foundational convictions—which lean strongly in an integral spiritual direction—of most of the world's artists), I find this worldview particularly devoid of excitement and imagination. Aside from its philosophical incoherence, inconsistency with most people's personal experience of, and intuitions about, the nature of our world, not to mention dramatic collapse in the face of cutting-edge empirical research into consciousness, materialism in my view is the result of an educational (learning and research) paradigm entirely devoid of improvisatory vitality. I am increasingly convinced that few individuals, if given the choice, would embrace this model. Just as few musicians, if given the choice, would opt for careers devoid of improvisation, let alone not predicated on improvisatory foundations.

Needless to say, individuals need to come to their own conclusions about worldview excitement level, and most important is that educational models enable them to make informed decisions of this kind. I propose a framework called Deep Inquiry that I believe may help address the problem. While there is no denying my nonmaterialist bias in formulating the framework, and my prediction that it will pose questions that prompt materialists to rethink their orientation, I believe that it will engage materialists and nonmaterialists alike with questions that are rarely posed in any educational setting, thereby helping individuals of both orientations define and refine their perspectives from a more informed and critically robust vantage point.

Deep Inquiry

Deep Inquiry is a process that helps practitioners across fields critically examine prevailing assumptions and practices and find coherence between day-to-day thinking and practice in a domain and their most heartfelt convictions about the biggest questions imaginable regarding the nature and purpose of the human being and cosmos. The model that follows is oriented toward education as the primary domain, although some version of the model could be applied to all fields. The point is not that individuals will articulate a personal worldview that is etched in stone from here till eternity, but rather to establish an ongoing basis for critical and self-critical interrogation that is the basis for new levels of meaning, fulfillment, and also the possibility of paradigmatic change. If the jazz/arts-driven revolution in creativity and consciousness is to take hold, change agents need to sustain the kind of "swinging" from localized considerations and overarching concerns on an individual scale. This will also enhance their capacities to engage in productive exchange with individuals of both similar and highly contrasting orientations. Much in the way of knee-jerk reaction to challenging ideas is rooted in worldview incoherence and confusion. Deep Inquiry is a tool that helps individuals move past these patterns.

Three overarching questions that correspond to third-person, second-person, and first-person integral perspectives guide the inquiry:

1. Tier I (third person): *What does it mean to be educated within a given field in the twenty-first century?*
2. Tier II (second person): *What does it mean to be an educated individual in twenty-first-century society?*
3. Tier III (first person): *What is the nature of the human being who is being educated?*

For each question, several subquestions further guide the inquiry and help illuminate ramifications across tiers. Additionally, Deep Inquiry involves jazz-inspired epistemologies—which might include improvisatory exercises, listening to recordings, and meditation—that complement reflection and dialogue. I recommend the formation of a Deep Inquiry Group (DIG) in order to sustain this kind of collective probing and exploration.

TIER I: What does it mean to be educated within a given field in the twenty-first century?

- What are the skills and knowledge that constitute competency in music, the sciences, broader arts and humanities disciplines, education, and so on?
- To what extent does one's personal response to this question align with conventional thinking and practice?
- To what extent does inquiry of this kind occur in one's day-to-day thinking and practice, and formal or informal conversations with colleagues?
- What does jazz, particularly when construed integrally (as a self-transcending gateway for creativity consciousness development) have to offer the above inquiry?

TIER II: What does it mean to be an educated individual in twenty-first-century society?

- What are the attributes of the ideal twenty-first-century citizen?
- To what extent do personal reflection or collective conversations transpire on these broader educational questions?
- How does response to the (primary tier II) question align with, or potentially challenge or expand, responses to tier I questions?
- What does jazz, particularly when construed integrally, have to offer the above inquiry?

TIER III: What is the nature of the human being who is being educated?

- Is the human being primarily a physical entity? Spiritual? A relational entity? All of these? Other? What happens after death? Is there a soul? What is its nature and purpose?
- Is there an inherent purpose in human existence? Cosmic existence?
- To what extent do personal reflection or collective conversations transpire on these questions in one's life and professional environment?
- What are the ramifications of one's response for the educational enterprise?
- How do responses to these questions align with responses to tier I and tier II questions?
- What does jazz, particularly when construed integrally, have to offer the above inquiry?
- What does meditation experience offer the above inquiry?

Note that each progressive tier has participants reflect on ramifications for responses to previous tiers in hopes for coherence across tiers. Elsewhere I examine common contradictions in worldview that are highlighted in this process—for example, where colleagues who might enter the process with tier III materialist leanings articulate expansive educational visions in response to tier II questions that prompt critical examination of their materialism from the newfound perspective of educational application. More precisely, if the purpose of education is considered more than vocational, but in fact to involve cultivation of moral and ethical qualities, are these facets of human consciousness mere by-products—let alone reducible to—a neurophysiological substrate? I do not believe most materialists would cling so firmly to that ideology in light of these kinds of questions.

Dualists might be challenged by the model in a different way, where they must confront inconsistency between their strong tier III convictions about spiritual dimensions of the human being and cosmos and tier II educational practices that, for most dualists, are excluded from the academy. Are these colleagues not engaging in the educational enterprise through a false identity, in which they leave important facets of their very being in the parking lot each morning they arrive at school?

I believe these kinds of questions and reflections may serve as compelling catalysts that help colleagues commit to breaking the current educational spell that represents such a crisis in the world, and render the academy a dynamic, self-transcending catalyst for individual and societal transformation.

CLOSING THOUGHTS

Who are we? What are we? Why are we? Where are we heading, and how will we get there?

If there is reason for optimism about the future, the seven-billion-plus-member improvising ensemble called humanity needs to place these kinds of questions front and center, not in place of rigorous engagement with the multitude of issues that define this moment in human history, but as a conceptual framework that, at once, sharpens this engagement while expanding our vision of possibilities for ourselves and the world. I think of this as a kind of "swinging"—between the most far-reaching ideas about human nature and potential and creative navigation of the rich tapestries of everyday life—for which jazz offers important guidance. Jazz inspires us to look beyond mere exterior survival, one type of improvisatory outcome, to another that is far more exemplary of human potential—an entirely new stride in creativity and consciousness evolution. Harmony among and between individuals, communities, and nations; fulfillment of the highest ideals of social and environmental justice; and unprecedented spiritual/religious vitality that is informed by cultural integrity and transcultural richness are all attainable in this new era for the world, providing we penetrate beyond the materialist inertia that has long overshadowed our educational and societal systems. While notions such as an improvisatory cosmos—with human beings as coevolutionary participants in its blossoming, the mechanics of which may be enlivened through collective creative and spiritual practice for global healing—may appear radical in terms of ordinary educational and societal discourse, the coherence of these ideas with cutting-edge consciousness research and age-old principles from wisdom traditions across the globe suggest that, in fact, the narrow horizons of prevailing discourse are what is radical. Most important is that this kind of arts-driven imagining becomes more the norm than the exception as humanity navigates the turbulent yet exciting waters that define the present moment in history.

Black music matters, and has never mattered more. I hope this book helps kindle excitement about these three words as a guiding axiom for future strides in music, education, and the re-envisioning of ourselves in relationship to the beautiful planet and vast and mysterious cosmos that we inhabit.

Epilogue

In April 1967, Martin Luther King Jr. delivered one of his most powerful sermons, titled "Beyond Vietnam: A Time to Break the Silence."[1] Interweaving the civil rights leadership for which he had already become legendary, his universal spiritual vision, and a poignant critique of the increasingly senseless U.S. military engagement in Southeast Asia, King framed his call to action in terms of the "fierce urgency of now."[2] It is difficult to imagine a more powerful and vivid example of key premises in this book: in response to a war that might be seen as among the worst series of improvisatory lapses in the history of our nation, where one decision after another shaped by untold conditioned responses and complete disconnection from the deepest realms of feeling and imagination resulted in unthinkable and unnecessary loss of life, King—a year before he was tragically and senselessly killed—exhorted the nation to penetrate deep into the moment at hand, break free from the inertia of prevailing patterns, and reorient itself in the love that "the great religions have seen as the supreme unifying principle of life."

Jazz—to articulate another key premise of the book—has much to teach us about the fierce urgency of the present moment in history, when humanity can either continue being swept along by the currents of habit, which almost inevitably spells doom, or alternatively invoke a revolution in creativity and consciousness that promotes entirely new levels of planetary flourishing.

Let us seize this moment by recognizing this musical treasure in our midst that has emerged from deep within our nation's soul, blossomed on its shores, flowed out to be cherished in distant lands, and that—exemplifying the second of the above pathways—offers unmatched hope for the near and distant future of our world.

To hone in on the central thrust of the book, let this newfound discovery of jazz take hold in our schools.

Think about the ramifications for our black children, newly awakened to the harsh realities of racism, that stem from the recognition that African American culture has produced not only the seminal American contribution to world culture, but also among the most extraordinary cultural expressions—one that may be unmatched in terms of unifying and transformative impact—in the history of the world.

Think about the ramifications of this vision for our white children, many of whom are also newly awakened to the harsh realities of racism even if not as direct victims of it, in enabling them to more fully apprehend the complicated racialized history of their own nation, including the manner in which foundational cultural contributions—from which they reap enrichment on a daily basis—by an oppressed constituency have been rendered invisible, both in attribution and in many ways reward. Think about how this might also help illuminate to these children the extent to which the holocaust of slavery remains deeply etched in the American psyche, impeding the self-esteem, sense of meaning and purpose, future visioning, let alone access to key educational and other essential resources for progressive development, in far too many of their black peers. Think about how this might alert these white children, particularly as they move into adolescence, to the ingrained tendencies that they continue to inherit from this holocaust, including a false sense of superiority, untold forms of privilege that breed entitlement and preclude opportunities for others, and susceptibility to superficial empathy for the oppressed that masks ongoing educational and societal policies of the oppressor.

Imagine, too, what this vision has to teach *all children* about the power of the arts—particularly the many forms of improvised musical art that are ubiquitous across the globe—to transcend overlying circumstance and connect human beings to the innermost recesses of the soul, and thus that jazz, the manifestation of this principle in America, did not come into being as a result of slavery, but rather came into being *despite* slavery—meaning that the divine improvisatory play—*lila*—of the cosmic creator that has flowed from time immemorial, continually seeking new outlets, would have availed itself of an infinitude of expressive channels whereby, in the inevitable and ever-blossoming cross-cultural navigation, Africa would encounter Europe and the rest of the world. When Dr. King so eloquently proclaimed in his opening remarks at the 1964 Berlin Jazz Festival that "God has wrought many things out of oppression,"[3] he did not declare that oppression was the source of jazz, but that the glory of the divine unfolding would shine forth regardless of the external conditions of life. "Long before the modern essayists and scholars wrote of racial identity as a problem for a multiracial world," he stated, "musicians were returning to their roots to affirm that which was stirring within their souls." When all is said and done, he reminded us, "this is triumphant music."[4]

In no way is this to negate the extent to which the unthinkably cruel circumstances of slavery catalyzed particularly deep penetration into the soul level and elicited musical expressions therefrom that reflect, as Cornell West states, "a greatness and magnanimity and integrity of self-respect," as well as "spiritual maturity."[5] It is simply to not lose sight of the primordial source of those qualities, and that what LeRoi Jones declared as core "Africanisms"[6] that could survive the atrocities of slavery originate from not only the innermost recesses of the African psyche but also the world psyche. While, of course, this kind of thinking runs counter to the postmodern entrenchment of much jazz scholarship, thus representing yet another instance of the multicultural veil, I believe that a transcultural era of jazz discourse that is at the heart of the emergent Integral Musicology paradigm is not far off.

From this affirmation of the primordial strata of spirit from which creativity flows extends important jazz-inspired guidance for the current geopolitical moment in our world. Just as the transcultural jazz artist identifies—within the realm of music—first as self-transcending global navigator, and secondarily as practitioner within a primary tradition, the time has come for all human beings to identify as planetary—if not cosmic—entities first, and members of nations and groups second. "I am a human being," states Herbie Hancock, "who happens to be a musician."[7] Neither ought the expanded musical identity be thought to compromise the integrity of jazz or whatever musical culture that one might identify as primary, nor an expanded human identity seen as compromising one's devotion to country. As I have argued at length, self-transcending engagement and identity enhance the integrity of engagement in the particular domain—musical, national, or otherwise—that serves as point of departure. "Every nation," to invoke Dr. King once more, "must now develop an overriding loyalty to mankind as a whole in order to preserve the best in their individual societies."[8] From this standpoint, notions such as America First, Russia First, China First, Brazil First, Israel First, Palestine First, India First, and so on through all nationalities across the globe, where superficial allegiance masquerades as genuine patriotism, must be recognized as relics of outmoded, spiritually impoverished, and unsustainable thinking and practice. Planetary leadership in the twenty-first century is predicated on a new paradigm of patriotism, based on the principle that what is good for one individual or nation is that which optimally serves the whole. Every individual and every nation has unique contributions to make to the good of the planet, and also obligations to listen intently, from the heart, and to celebrate the contributions of all individuals and nations as they step up to play their respective solos.

The destiny of America is to exemplify these principles for the world. Recalling my criteria for the characterization of knowledge systems that attain the status of wisdom systems through grounding their inquiry in the soul level, jazz is a shining example of this status in its creative, cultural, intellectual, and spiritual horizons. The time has come for America to establish this cultural treasure at the heart of its educational and societal identity, whereby this still-young country may emerge as a wisdom nation.

Notes

INTRODUCTION

1. Stuart Nicholson, November 3, 2004, Interview with Alice Coltrane, available online at http://bit.ly/2mV4M16.
2. HR 57, U.S. House of Representatives, sponsored by John Conyers, Detroit.
3. HR 57, U.S. House of Representatives.
4. I view Samuel Floyd's *The Power of Black Music: Interpreting Its History from Africa to the United States* (New York: Oxford University Press, 1995) among the best sources for a history of African American music and its impact. See also LeRoi Jones, *Blues People* (New York: HarperCollins/Perennial, 1963); William Banfield, *Cultural Codes: Makings of a Black Music Philosophy* (Lanham, MD: Scarecrow Press, 2010); Ingrid Monson, *Saying Something: Jazz Improvisation and Interaction* (Chicago: University of Chicago Press, 1996); and Guthrie Ramsey, *Race Music: Black Cultures from Bebop to Hip Hop* (Berkeley: University of California Press, 2003).
5. Jeff Pressing, 2002, "Black Atlantic Rhythm: Its Computational and Transcultural Foundations," *Music Perception* 19, no. 3: 285–310.
6. Jones, *Blues People*.
7. Here it is important to not conflate one or two courses in improvisation, or scattered electives, with even the moderate let alone substantive skill development needed. See Ed Sarath, David Myers, and Patricia S. Campbell, 2016, *Redefining Music Studies in an Age of Change* (New York: Routledge), for one of the most recent assessments of progress in rectifying this problem.
8. Michelle Obama, June 15, 2009, Remarks by the First Lady at the White House Music Series: The Jazz Studio (The White House, Washington, DC).
9. Christopher Small, 1994, *Music of the Common Tongue* (London: Calder Riverrun), 4.
10. In 2006, I founded the International Society for Improvised Music (www.isimprov.org), strongly inspired by the Association for Advancement of Creative Musicians (see George Lewis, 2008, *A Power Stronger Than Itself: The AACM and American Experimental Music* [Chicago: University of Chicago Press]) and Creative Music Studies (see Robert Sweet, 1996, *Music Universe, Music Mind* [Ann Arbor, MI: Arborville]), around this principle.
11. Ed Sarath, 2013, *Improvisation, Creativity and Consciousness: Jazz as Integral Template for Music, Education and Society* (Albany: State University of New York Press).
12. Lewis, *A Power Stronger Than Itself*, xii.
13. Sarath, *Improvisation, Creativity and Consciousness*.

14. For interesting inquiry into the rhythmic thrust of black music that extends beyond music per se into children's games, see Kyra Gaunt, 2006, *The Games Black Girls Play: From Double Dutch to Hip-Hop* (New York: New York University Press).

15. Sarath, *Improvisation, Creativity and Consciousness*.

16. See Ken Wilber, 2006, "Introduction to Integral Theory and Practice," *Journal of Integral Theory and Practice* 1, no. 1: 1–40, for more on the "transcend and include" integral axiom.

17. Lewis, *A Power Stronger Than Itself*, xi.

18. Lewis, *A Power Stronger Than Itself*, x.

19. For example, Karl Berger's Creative Music Studios, as Robert Sweet illuminates in his book, *Music Universe, Music Mind*.

20. For more on my distinctions between multicultural and transcultural paradigms, see Sarath, *Improvisation, Creativity and Consciousness,* and Sarath, Myers, and Campbell, *Redefining Music Studies*.

21. Christopher Small, 1996, *Music, Society, Education* (Hanover, NH: Wesleyan University Press), 48.

22. Braxton is quoted in Lewis, *A Power Stronger Than Itself*, 183.

23. Buckminster Fuller, 1969, *Utopia or Oblivion: The Prospects for Humanity* (New York: Bantam); Sarath, *Improvisation, Creativity and Consciousness.*

24. Wilber, "Introduction to Integral Theory and Practice," 1.

25. Wilber, "Introduction to Integral Theory and Practice."

26. As described by Maharishi Mahesh Yogi, in his *Apaurasheya Bhasha*, or commentary on Rig Veda, these are the *rishi, devata, chandas* qualities that unfold from cosmic creative intelligence. See *Constitution of India Fulfilled through Maharishi's Transcendental Meditation* New Delhi, India: Vishwa-Vidyalaya.

27. While my first-second-third-person/spirit-art-science correlations differ with those of Wilber, who correlates first-person with art, and second-person with religion, the idea that they represent the big three pillars of human endeavor that permeate the totality of creation is essentially shared.

28. Sarath, *Improvisation, Creativity and Consciousness.*

29. Mihaly Csikszentmihalyi, 1990, *Flow: The Psychology of Optimal Experience* (New York: Harper and Row); Abraham Maslow, 1971, *The Farther Reaches of Human Nature* (New York: Penguin).

30. Charles Alexander and Ellen Langer, eds., 1990, *Higher Stages of Human Development* (New York: Oxford University Press); Michael Murphy, 1988, *The Future of the Body* (Berkeley, CA: Conference Recording Service); Jenny Wade, 1996, *Changes of Mind* (Albany: State University of New York Press).

31. Alexander and Langer, *Higher Stages of Human Development*; Murphy, *The Future of the Body*; Wade, *Changes of Mind.*

32. Abrams is quoted in Lewis, *A Power Stronger Than Itself*, 154.

33. As Alice Coltrane recounts in an interview with Marion MacPartland (*Piano Jazz*, 1980) John introduced Alice to meditation, with Alice subsequently becoming strongly involved in lineage-specific, Vedantic practice.

34. Wilber, 2006, *Integral Spirituality: A Startling New Look at the Role for Religion in the Modern and Postmodern World* (Boston: Shambhala).

35. Scientific extremism is perhaps exemplified in the materialist/reductionist ideology, reducing consciousness to electrochemical activity in the brain; for religion, this is paralleled by the equally astonishing beliefs that the Earth is ten thousand years old, and that humans lived alongside dinosaurs.

36. Wilber, *Integral Spirituality*. Also see Ken Wilber, *The Marriage of Sense and Soul*, for insights on healing the science-spirituality divide.

37. Sarath, *Improvisation, Creativity and Consciousness.*

38. Wilber, "Introduction to Integral Theory and Practice."

1. CREATIVITY AS NEW ORGANIZING PRINCIPLE

1. "The way of preparing music educators in North America has changed very little over the past 150 years" (Clint Randle, ed., 2015, *Music Education: Navigating the Future* [New York: Routledge], 327). This is a guiding principle in the widely cited "Manifesto" of the College Music Society Task Force on the Undergraduate Music Major. The Manifesto is found in complete form in Ed Sarath, David Myers, and Patricia S. Campbell, 2016, *Redefining Music Studies in an Age of Change* (New York: Routledge). See also Henry Kingsbury, 1988, *Music, Talent and Performance: A Conservatory Cultural System* (Philadelphia: Temple University Press), and Bruno Nettl, 1995, *Heartland Excursions: Ethnomusicological Reflections on Schools of Music* (Urbana: University of Illinois Press), for important critiques of music studies. I view the present book as among the most recent contributions within this lineage.

2. The capacity for jazz to open up connections along the broader creativity and consciousness is the central theme in Ed Sarath, 2013, *Improvisation, Creativity and Consciousness: Jazz as Integral Template for Music, Education and Society* (Albany: State University of New York Press).

3. Music Educators National Conference, 1994, *National Standards for Arts Education: What Every Young American Should Know and Be Able to Do in the Arts*, Reston, VA: Author; improvising and composing were standards 3 and 4. See also "Contemporary Music Project," May 1973, *Music Educators Journal* 59, no. 9: 33–48; William J. Mitchell, May 1973, "Under the Comprehensive Musicianship Umbrella," *Music Educators Journal* 59, no. 9; and Laura Kautz Sindberg, 1998, "The Wisconsin CMP Project at Age 21," *Music Educators Journal* 85, no. 3: 37–42. "Traditional Western European Art Music," as Ward Steinman (1987) describes the Comprehensive Musicianship approach, "no longer dominates the curriculum, though it remains at the heart of it. We now include references to non-Western musics (principally from African, Indian, and Asian cultures), jazz, and a wide variety of twentieth century musics." Note that the conceptual and curricular core remain intact, with change happening at the edges. From the standpoint of higher order change visioning, "references" to broader musical regions are not remotely satisfactory.

4. See Juan Chattah et al., "Reflections on the Manifesto," 2016, http://www.academia.edu/28155924/Reflections_on_the_Manifesto, College Music Society website, cms.org, look under "Symposia," where Jenny Snodgrass argues that composition may be used more than is generally thought, but confirms that improvisation remains anomalous. Nonetheless, in my view these additive, pedagogical-enhancement applications fall far short of the creative identity shift I argue is needed.

5. Here is where my conception of musical identity as grounded in creative epistemology extends beyond much prevailing investigation on the topic. This is not at all incompatible with the prevailing notion, as Karen Salvador states, in "Identity and Transformation: (Re)claiming an Inner Musician" (in 2015, *Music Education: Navigating the Future*, edited by Clint Randle [New York: Routledge]), that identity is "socially constructed." From this standpoint, her commentary on all humans being musical, but "participation in school music convincing many students they were not musicians" (p. 230), is instructive.

6. Salvador, "Identity and Transformation."

7. Howard Gardner, 1993, *Multiple Intelligences: The Theory in Practice* (New York: Basic Books), 4.

8. I go into this in further detail in chapter 5. Also see Sarath, *Improvisation, Creativity and Consciousness* and Maharishi Yogi, *Bhagavad Gita: A New Translation and Commentary*.

9. Meki Nzewi, 1997, *African Music: Theoretical Content and Creative Continuum* (Oldershausen, Germany: Institut für Didaktik Populärer Musik), 13.

10. See Sarath, *Improvisation, Creativity and Consciousness*.

11. Sarath, *Improvisation, Creativity and Consciousness*.

12. I first present the systematic improvisatory development framework in Sarath, *Improvisation, Creativity and Consciousness*.

13. Steve Lacy, 1994, *Findings: My Experience with the Soprano Saxophone* (Paris: CMAP, Outre Mesure), 21.

14. Leonard Meyer, 1989, *Style and Music Theory, History, Ideology* (Philadelphia: University of Pennsylvania Press).

15. This addresses an interesting, though fundamentally erroneous, position advanced by Carol Gould and Kenneth Keaton in "The Essential Role of Improvisation in Musical Performance" (2000, *The Journal of Aesthetics and Art Criticism* 58, no. 2: 143–48), to the effect that improvisation in jazz and interpretive performance differs in degree, but not kind. The fact that interpretive performers can only manipulate a few nonsyntactic elements and none of the syntactic affirms that the forms of improvisation indeed differ in kind as well. See Sarath, *Improvisation, Creativity and Consciousness*, for further elaboration.

16. I present the exploratory-emulative interplay in Sarath, *Improvisation, Creativity and Consciousness*, 56, 68, and numerous places throughout the book. The exploratory component aligns with Randall Allsup's "open philosophy" of music education, presented in his *Remixing the Music Classroom: Toward an Open Philosophy of Music Education* (Indianapolis: Indiana University Press, 2016). However, I view his advocacy for that model, and positioning of it against a limiting master-apprentice, or closed pedagogical paradigm, as an example of unnecessary polarization of two necessary components that can work wonderfully together, and arguably must do so for either prong to optimally fulfill its function.

17. Gardner, *Multiple Intelligences*, 445.

18. Bowie is quoted in George Lewis, 2008, *A Power Stronger Than Itself: The AACM and American Experimental Music* (Chicago: University of Chicago Press), bookflap.

19. Here the integral vision guides us from egocentric to ethnocentric to worldcentric to cosmoscentric.

20. Sarath, *Improvisation, Creativity and Consciousness*, chapter 8. For Jung's account of individuation, see his *The Archetypes and the Collective Unconscious* (Princeton: Princeton University Press, 1990 [1959]).

21. Sarath, *Improvisation, Creativity and Consciousness*.

22. Paul Berliner, 1994, *Thinking in Jazz: The Infinite Art of Improvisation* (Chicago: University of Chicago Press), 151.

23. Robin D. G. Kelly, 2009, *Thelonious Monk: The Life and Times of an American Original* (New York: Free Press), 452.

24. Stuart Nicholson, November 3, 2004, Interview with Alice Coltrane, available online at http://bit.ly/2mV4M16.

25. Sarath, *Improvisation, Creativity and Consciousness*.

26. The astronaut Edgar Mitchell founded the Institute for Noetic Sciences based on an experience of transcendent awe glimpsed in space, which inspired him to commit to exploration to deeper dimensions of human experience, understanding, and development. See www.noetic.org.

27. Susanne Langer, 1948, *Philosophy in a New Key: A Study in the Symbolism of Reason, Rite, and Art* (New York: Mentor), 206.

28. Jung, *Archetypes and the Collective Unconscious*; useful commentary is also found in Jung's *The Spirit in Man, Art, and Literature* (Princeton: Princeton University Press, 1961), and Sarath, *Improvisation, Creativity and Consciousness*.

29. Sarath, *Improvisation, Creativity and Consciousness*.
30. Sarath, *Improvisation, Creativity and Consciousness*.
31. Sarath, *Improvisation, Creativity and Consciousness*.
32. Sarath, *Improvisation, Creativity and Consciousness*.

33. I am indebted to Christopher Small for this connection. See Small, 1994, *Music of the Common Tongue* (London: Calder Riverrun), 4.

34. See Sarath, Myers, and Campbell, *Redefining Music Studies in an Age of Change*.

2. MULTICULTURALISM, TRANSCULTURALISM, AND RACE

1. See Charles Fowler, 1996, *Strong Arts, Strong Schools: The Promising Potential and Shortsighted Disregard of the Arts in American Schooling* (New York: Oxford University

Press); Ed Sarath, David Myers, and Patricia S. Campbell, 2016, *Redefining Music Studies in an Age of Change* (New York: Routledge).

2. I therefore take important work done by Deborah Bradley, Juliet Hess, Lise Vaugeois, and others who have critiqued multiculturalism a significant step further in proposing jazz and black music, which eludes much of this work, as a pillar for a transcultural paradigm.

3. Bradley, Hess, Gustafson, Vaugeois are important exceptions.

4. For example, Huib Schippers, 2010, *Facing the Music: Shaping Music Education from a Global Perspective* (New York: Oxford University Press), 31, offers a highly informative continuum that extends from monocultural to multicultural, intercultural, and transcultural kinds of diversity strategies. However, I differentiate my notion of integral transculturalism from his correlate according to the parameter of creative identity shift about which he and the majority of thinkers on the topic remain ambivalent, as a vertical organizing principle that breaks free from prevailing horizontal orientation.

5. Schippers, *Facing the Music*.

6. In other words, musicking typically is devoid of key epistemic topographies, of which improvisation, as exemplified in the systematic improvisatory development continuum, is a primary example.

7. Meki Nzewi, 1997, *African Music: Theoretical Content and Creative Continuum* (Oldershausen, Germany: Insitut für Didaktik Populärer Musik), 13.

8. For example, in the College Music Society National Task Force on the Undergraduate Music Major, the statement was made that "no music should occupy the center of the curriculum." Although this never made its way into the report, the issue was never placed front and center.

9. Michelle Obama, June 15, 2009, Remarks by the First Lady at the White House Music Series: The Jazz Studio (The White House, Washington, DC).

10. Nzewi, *African Music*, 8.

11. In Robin Moore, 2017, *College Music Curricula in a New Century* (New York: Oxford), an excellent chapter on mariachi curriculum provides hints of openings for this direction in acknowledging experimental approaches to the genre, though stopping short of naming jazz as a transcultural gateway.

12. For example, throughout the first decades of the journal *Ethnomusicology*, the majority of titles correlate some particular theme with a geographical location. For a random sampling: Jose Maceda, May 1958, "Chants from Sagada Mountain Province, Phillipines," *Ethnomusicology* 2, no. 2: 45–55; Rose Brandel, September 1959, "The African Hemiola Style," *Ethnomusicology* 3, no. 3: 106–17; and George List, Fall 1997, "Hopi Kachina Dance Songs: Concept and Context," *Ethnomusicology* 41: 13–32.

Essays that explore connecting themes across boundaries are rarer in earlier years, and appear with greater frequency in more recent ones. Examples include Michael Tenzer, Winter 2015, "Meditations on Objective Aesthetics in World Music," *Ethnomusicology* 59, no. 1: 1–30; Izaly Zemtsoysky, 1997, "An Attempt at a Synthetic Paradigm," *Ethnomusicology* 41, no. 2: 185–205; Henry Kingsbury, Spring/Summer 1997, "Call and Response: Should Ethnomusicology Be Abolished?" *Ethnomusicology*: 243–62; and Sarah Weiss, Fall 2014, "Listening to the World but Hearing Ourselves: Hybridity and Perceptions of Authenticity in World Music," *Ethnomusicology* 58, no. 2: 506–24.

Still, even in many recent issues, the predominant thrust is tradition or culture-specific. Again, the point is not that there is no place for this kind of inquiry; it is essential. The problem is the extent to which it has overshadowed the diversity quest, at the expense of the transcultural gateway and overarching framework for understanding.

13. In Moore, *College Music Curricula in a New Century*, two notable exceptions to this aversion to a cultural center to American music might be noted. One involves bluegrass, the other mariachi communities. It is interesting, however, that in the same volume there is no correlate to grounding in African American music, which is arguably central to most Americans. This becomes particularly conspicuous given the significant status of Christopher Small in musical diversity conversations. Although Small's status in ethnomusicology is not quite as iconic as it has been in music education, it has not been inconsequential. However, of three seminal aspects of Small's work, only two have seemed to take hold. One is musicking,

which I have already examined as a kind of multicultural flatlining of the process scope. Second is his particular critique of the systemic impact of the European classical paradigm. Overlooked is his acknowledgment of the central status of African American music—as the dominant music of the West—which would surely represent a powerful argument for self-cultural grounding in America.

14. Argumentation along these lines appears in "Reflections on the Manifesto," Chattah et al.

15. I therefore address from a different angle shared concerns with Schippers (*Facing the Music*) and Bradley (2015, *Hidden in Plain Sight: Race and Racism in Music Education*, Oxford Handbooks Online [Oxford: Oxford University Press]) about notions of authenticity being an obstacle to culturally diverse engagement.

16. Jazz literature provides ample accounts of such transcultural innovators. See George Lewis, 2008, *A Power Stronger Than Itself: The AACM and American Experiemental Music* (Chicago: University of Chicago Press); Robert Sweet, 1996, *Music Universe, Music Mind* (Ann Arbor, MI: Arborville); Joachim-Ernst Berendt, 1991, *The World Is Sound: Nada Brahma* (Rochester, VT: Destiny).

17. I am thinking of the guitarist John MacLaughlin, or the percussionists Jamey Haddad and Dan Weiss, all of whom had intensive immersion with Indian music as examples of transcultural artists with tradition-specific grounding who have yielded powerful expressions.

18. In Mantle Hood, 1960, "The Challenge of Bi-Musicality," *Ethnomusicology* 4, no. 1: 55–59, Hood suggests that aspiring scholars define their aims from what I would call culture-specific/multicultural vantage point, but not transcultural. In other words, he asks whether or not they seek a baseline proficiency in the culture to conduct research from a reasonably informed perspective, or the kind of competency that might make them competitive with professionals in the culture. The question of whether or not they wish to gain skills that inform their particular creative voice does not arise.

19. Weiss, "Listening to the World but Hearing Ourselves," 521.

20. Among the most recent resources that confirms this assessment, not by what it addresses but by what it omits, is Svanibor Pettan and Jeff Todd Titon, 2016, *The Oxford Handbook of Applied Ethnomusicology* (New York: Oxford University Press), an otherwise extraordinary collection of essays that deal with numerous issues in the field.

21. "Global Musical Citizenship" was a common slogan at the 2015 Summit for 21st Century Music School Design convened by the College Music Society.

22. Drawing from my own experience, I recently have collaborated with musicians from North India, South India, Korea, and Brazil. I have regularly found that my jazz grounding enables me to go further into common terrain with these musicians than any other background in Western music.

23. Again, I believe my analysis takes further important concerns articulated by Juliet Hess, 2015, "Upping the 'Anti-': The Value of an Anti-Racist Theoretical Framework in Music Education," *Action, Criticism, and Theory for Music Education* 14, no. 1: 66–92; Juliet Hess, 2017, "Equity in Music Education: Euphemisms, Terminal Naivety, and Whiteness," *Action, Criticism, and Theory for Music Education* 16, no. 3: 15–47; Deborah Bradley, *Hidden in Plain Sight*; Ruth Gustafson, 2009, *Race and Curriculum: Music in Childhood Education* (New York: Palgrave MacMillan); and Julia Eklund Koza about the multicultural paradigm.

24. John Covach, January 2015, "Rock Me Maestro," *Chronicle of Higher Education*.

25. Randall Allsup in *Remixing the Music Classroom: Toward an Open Philosophy of Music Education* (Indianapolis: Indiana University Press, 2016) notes that European classical music comprises over 90 percent of music curricula.

26. For example, Moore, *College Music Curricula for a New Century*, makes significant mention of popular music with little recognition of the black roots of the music. The same holds for Carlos Rodriquez, ed., 2017, *Coming of Age: Teaching and Learning Popular Music in Academia* (Ann Arbor, MI: Maize Books); and John Covach, "Rock Me Maestro." Covach's chapter, "High Brow, Low Brow, Knot Now, Now How: Music Curriculum in a Flat World," in Rodriquez's volume is yet another example. Even Trevor de Clercq's excellent exploration of rhythm, "Swing, Shuffle, Half-Time, Double: Beyond Traditional Time Signatures in the

Classification of Meter in Pop/Rock Music," in that same volume, falls short in acknowledging the black roots of popular music.

27. Moore, *College Music Curricula for a New Century*.

28. Samy Alim, 2015, *Raciolinguistics: How Language Shapes Our Ideas about Race*, ed. John R. Rickford and Arnetha F. Ball (Oxford: Oxford University Press).

29. The practice pervades Moore's *College Music Curricula for a New Century*, even as the book lays claim to social justice as among its primary tenets.

30. Robert Freeman, 2014, *The Crisis of Classical Music in America* (Lanham, MD: Rowman and Littlefield).

31. See Lewis, *A Power Stronger Than Itself*, where I first encountered this term. See Sarath, *Improvisation, Creativity and Consciousness*.

32. John Cage, 1961, *Silence* (Middletown, CT: Wesleyan University Press), 72.

33. Ed Sarath, 2013, *Improvisation, Creativity and Consciousness: Jazz as Integral Template for Music, Education and Society* (Albany: State University of New York Press).

34. Jay Gorden and Bryan Van Norden, May 11, 2016, "If Philosophy Won't Diversify, Let's Call It What It Really Is," *New York Times* Opinion Pages, originally appeared in the *Stone*.

35. As Schippers (*Facing the Music*), Weiss ("Listening to the World but Hearing Ourselves"), and others point out, there are a range of connotations to be found in the heading "world music." However, my generalizations about jazz, popular, and European classical are not unreasonable. At the very least, European classical music is almost never considered a world music, which reifies its centrality.

36. See Cathy Benedict and Patrick Schmidt, 2014, "Educating Teachers for 21st Century Challenges: The Music Educator as Cultural Citizen," in *Promising Practices in 21st Century Music Teacher Education*, ed. Michelle Kaschub and Janice Smith, 79–104 (Oxford: Oxford University Press), for an example of renaming conventional musical disciplines.

37. Kristin Anderson, *Benign Bigotry: The Psychology of Subtle Prejudice* (Cambridge: Cambridge University Press, 2009).

38. For more on Critical Race Theory, see the work of Derrick Bell.

39. A February 2015 symposium at the University of Michigan on racism research focused on this more nuanced account of this lingering pathology.

40. Juliet Hess, Deborah Bradley, and Ruth Gustafson are notable exceptions.

41. Among the concerns that fuel this aversion is that of "essentialism"—meaning that broaching transcendent interiors risks extremist convictions by which a given racial/ethnic constituency might be deemed intrinsically inferior or superior according to essential traits, thus opening up possibilities for the worst kind of racist transgressions that one need not look far to see outside of the academy. The integral paradigm resolves this decidedly postmodern concern by grounding discourse in transcendent unity, where all ethnicities, races, and genders unite, and then identifying a primordial junction point at which these streams begin to differentiate, and emphasizing that all streams exist in our consciousness. This provides a basis for a newfound, vastly deepened consciousness-based commitment to diversity that replaces deficit-driven postmodern concerns about essentialism with the highest forms of celebratory embrace.

42. Alim, *Raciolinguistics*.

43. See Robin Diangelo, 2011, "White Fragility: Overcoming Racism," *International Journal of Critical Pedagogy* 3, no. 3: 54–70. Also on this topic, see Robin Diangelo, 2007, "I'm Leaving: White Fragility in Racial Dialogue," in *Inclusion in Urban Educational Environments: Addressing Issues of Diversity, Equity, and Social Justice*, ed. B. McMahon and D. Armstrong, 213–40 (Charlotte, NC: Information Age Publishing).

44. Deborah Bradley makes observations consistent with this point in *Hidden in Plain Sight*, as she recounts tendencies among music studies colleagues to interpret appeals for diversification as inherently rooted in denigrating views of European classical music.

45. W. E. B. Du Bois, 2007 (1903), *The Souls of Black Folk* (New York: Oxford University Press).

46. John Covach's ("Rock Me Maestro") statement suggesting *classical* and *music* are typically on a par can be seen as a form of musical double-consciousness skewing a coherent assessment of prevailing practice.

47. George Lewis alerts us to a further example of important black contributions eluding recognition, this—perhaps occupying the opposite end of the commercial continuum than pop music—in the case of musical experimentalism: "Historians of experimentalism have stood at a crossroads, facing a stark choice: to grow up and recognize a multicultural, multiethnic, base for experimentalism in music . . . or to remain the chroniclers of an ethnically bound, and ultimately limited tradition that appropriates freely, yet furtively from other traditions, yet cannot recognize any histories as its own other than those based in whiteness" (Lewis, *A Power Stronger Than Itself*, xii).

48. Musicians and pedagogues who go to great lengths to sustain this aversion can be described as having well-developed "LAMB chops."

49. While one cannot judge a book by its index, important patterns can be inferred that are corroborated by the overall narrative. The word *jazz* does not appear in the index for *College Music Curricula in a New Century*, even if the book makes highly sporadic mention of the term. *African American* has three listings in the index.

50. See Bradley, *Hidden in Plain Sight*, and Hess, "Upping the 'Anti-'" and "Equity in Music Education," for discussion of musical whiteness. Both stop short, however, of engaging or even mentioning musical blackness in any significant way.

3. MUSIC SCHOOL FOR A TRANSCULTURAL AGE

1. "Contemporary Music Project," May 1973, *Music Educators Journal* 59, no. 9: 33–48; William J. Mitchell, May 1973, "Under the Comprehensive Musicianship Umbrella," *Music Educators Journal* 59, no. 9; Laura Kautz Sindberg, 1998, "The Wisconsin CMP Project at Age 21," *Music Educators Journal* 85, no. 3: 37–42.

2. Randall Allsup provides a particularly strong and thoughtful critique of the master-apprentice foundations of the prevailing model in *Remixing the Music Classroom: Toward an Open Philosophy of Music Education* (Indianapolis: Indiana University Press, 2016). Although I believe he succumbs to the opposite extreme when he suggests the overthrow of that model, he weaves a powerful and compelling account.

3. Ed Sarath, 2013, *Improvisation, Creativity and Consciousness: Jazz as Integral Template for Music, Education and Society* (Albany: State University of New York Press).

4. Allsup, *Remixing the Music Classroom*.

5. Sarath, ibid.

6. This perspective, of course, takes issue with that of the College Band Directors National Organization, as made clear in their "Position Paper," written in response to the CMS Manifesto cited above. See www.cbdna.org and search under "Publications."

7. I first proposed the Integral Learning Environment in Ed Sarath, 2013, *Improvisation, Creativity and Consciousness: Jazz as Integral Template for Music, Education and Society* (Albany: State University of New York Press), chapter 10, "Music School of the Future." The overarching scheme for ILE is predicated on the three-part rhythm of learning cycle—romance, precision, and generalization—put forth in a general educational context in Alfred North Whitehead, 1929, *The Aims of Education* (New York: Free Press).

8. See Ed Sarath, David Myers, and Patricia S. Campbell, 2016, *Redefining Music Studies in an Age of Change* (New York: Routledge), for an earlier articulation of this idea.

9. Sarath, *Improvisation, Creativity and Consciousness*, chapter 10.

10. Lucy Green, 2014, "Popular Music Education in and for Itself," in *Music Education as Critical Theory and Practice: Selected Essays*, 248 (Surrey, UK: Ashgate).

11. Green, "Popular Music Education in and for Itself," 248 fn 6, and Ed Sarath, 2010, *Music Theory through Improvisation: A New Approach to Musicianship Training* (New York: Routledge).

12. Sarath, *Music Theory through Improvisation*. Also see Michael Tenzer, 2016, "In Honor of What We Can't Groove to Yet," in *College Music Curricula for a New Century*, ed. Robin Moore, 119–35 (New York: Oxford University Press), where he makes a compelling case for transcription.

13. Sarath, *Music Theory through Improvisation.*

14. See, for example, David Kulma and Meghan Naxer, 2014, "Beyond Part-Writing: Modernizing the Curriclum," in *Engaging Students: Essays in Music Pedagogy*, vol. 2 (Mountain View, CA: Creative Commons). The authors state: "Research in music theory has diversified in its stylistic reach and historical application, yet the breadth of tools and repertoire introduced to undergraduates has not changed alongside it" (p. 2). The content distribution in the typical core curriculum as outlined in many popular textbooks heavily emphasizes part writing, voice leading, and harmonic syntax in the eighteenth- and nineteenth-century styles that has appeared in textbooks since Walter Piston's *Harmony*. It is the most-covered topic in these textbooks, and occupies the largest portion of our core sequence. Part writing becomes a set of memorized rules rather than a flexible tool; it limits the engagement and agency of our students.

15. Kulma and Naxer, "Beyond Part-Writing: Modernizing the Curriculum."

16. Jeff Pressing, 2002, "Black Atlantic Rhythm: Its Computational and Transcultural Foundations," *Music Perception* 19, no. 3: 285–310.

17. "For the African," states Meki Nzewi, "'rhythm' does not ride on one plane of affect or perception, is not created or practiced in isolation, embodies extramusical intentions, is multidimensional in conception and manifestation. It is doubtful that any African culture has a music-specific term or expression for rhythm. This does not imply that African has no concept of what this European term applies to. The African philosophy of musical motion in time, and how it is rationalized in performance, has more profound, multi-dimensional perception" (Meki Nzewi, 1997, *African Music: Theoretical Content and Creative Continuum* [Oldershausen, Germany: Institut für Didaktik Populärer Musik], 13).

18. Patricia Sheehan Campbell has offered important commentary on musical embodiment, including from the perspective of *ngoma*—which not only is a kind of drum, but also refers to the integration of movement, sound, and ritual. See Sarath, Myers, and Campbell, *Redefining Music Studies in an Age of Change*. See also Sonia T. Seeman, 2016, "Embodied Pedagogy," in *College Music Curricula for a New Century*, ed. Robin Moore, 190–203 (New York: Oxford University Press), for insightful analysis of this important aspect of musicianship.

19. I elaborate on this point in my book *Music Theory through Improvisation*.

20. See David J. Chalmers, 2010, "The Singularity: A Philosophical Analysis," *Journal of Consciousness Studies* 17: 7–65.

21. Evan Tobias, 2015, "Inter/Trans/Multi/Cross/New Media(ting): Navigating an Emerging Landscape of Digital Media for Music Education," in *Music Education: Navigating the Future*, ed. Clint Randle, 91–121 (New York: Routledge), delineates a range of technological approaches involving various media—from multimedia to intermedia to transmedia—that underscores the virtual explosion in the field. See also Frank Heuser, 2015, "Understanding the Tools: Technology as a Springboard for Reflective Musicking," in *Music Education: Navigating the Future*, ed. Clint Randle, 155–66 (New York: Routledge). "The pursuit of strategies that would continue to enable the modern scientifically-technologically obsessed man remain human in thoughts and behavior," states Meki Nzewi, is essential "for world peace, stability, survival and inter-personal understanding within and between cultures and races and colours and sexes" (*African Music*, 8).

22. The idea of a hidden curriculum has a long history, traceable back to at least John Dewey, and visited by a range of thinkers, including Phillip Jackson (*Life in Classrooms*), Henri Giroux, Paulo Freire, and bell hooks. For a particularly informative account, see Jane Martin, 1983, "What Should We Do with a Hidden Curriculum When We Find One?" in *The Hidden Curriculum and Moral Education*, ed. Henry Giroux and David Purpel, 122–39 (Berkeley, CA: McCutchan).

23. Time Theory, see Ravi Shankar, 1968, *My Music, My Life* (New York: Simon and Schuster); Charles Diserens and Harry Fine, 1939, *A Psychology of Music* (Cincinnati: Cincinnati College of Music); and Alain Danielou, 1995 (1943), *Music and the Power of Sound: The Influence of Tuning and Interval on Consciousness* (Rochester, VT: Destiny).

24. See Edith Boxhill, 1989, *Music Therapy for Living: Principles of Normalization Embodied in Music Therapy* (St. Louis: MMB Music Inc.); Peter Westbrook, 2007, "Unstruck Sound and Forgotten Truth," *Ultimate Reality and Meaning* 30, no. 1: 93–120.

25. Pressing, "Black Atlantic Rhythm."

26. Robert Freeman, 2014, *The Crisis of Classical Music in America* (Lanham, MD: Rowman and Littlefield).
27. George Lewis, 2008, *A Power Stronger Than Itself: The AACM and American Experimental Music* (Chicago: University of Chicago Press), ix.
28. For example, see Robert O'Meally, Brent Hayes Edwards, and Farah Jasmine Griffin, eds., 2004, *Uptown Conversation: The New Jazz Studies* (New York: Columbia University Press).
29. Sarath, *Improvisation, Creativity and Consciousness*.
30. Nzewi, *African Music*, 11.
31. I say "intriguing" because the primary thrust of his visioning is to emphasize what I call self-culturing grounding in music studies in Africa. This is not to deny his powerful spiritual commentary from which one might infer broader cultural application; but he elaborates far less on that.
32. Sarath, *Improvisation, Creativity and Consciousness*, chapter 10.
33. I thus veer from Deborah Bradley's argument that a music education–ethnomusicology nexus is key to a new model of music studies that embodies the diversity of today's musical world. See Deborah Bradley, 2017, "In the Shadows of Mozart," in *College Music Curricula for a New Century*, ed. Robin Moore, 217 (New York: Oxford University Press). My concern is that the multicultural orientation of both fields would reinforce each other, further shrouding the rebuilding on the necessary transcultural CICP foundations.
34. As noted in the previous chapter; Juliet Hess, Deborah Bradley, Lisa Vaugeois, and Ruth Gustafson are among the leaders in this multicultural critique.
35. I go into this at length in *Improvisation, Creativity and Consciousness*, chapter 5, "Jazz and the Academy," citing critiques from a number of thinkers.
36. Lewis, *A Power Stronger Than Itself*, xi. Or a jazz education model that, as AACM trumpeter Leo Smith puts it, is based in the embrace and integration of "all forms of music . . . anything and everything is valuable" (Lewis, ibid.). Joseph Jarman described the AACM aesthetic, "we create sounds, period" (Lewis, ibid.).
37. Jazz studies programs at California Institute for the Arts, New England Conservatory, University of Iowa, University of Michigan, and University of Nevada–Reno are notable exceptions to the conventional model.

4. NEW CONVERSATIONS WITH CONSERVATIVES

1. For example, in addresses in 2013 and 2014 to several hundred leaders of music schools at the National Association of Schools of Music. NASM is the accrediting body in the field.
2. Therefore, Brian Pertl's playful characterization of my visioning, appreciated in reform circles, is not likely to go over so well in conversations with conservatives: "I'd like to suggest a thought experiment inspired by Ed Sarath and his visionary works on institutional change. The rules are simple: Blow up your curriculum" (2017, "Reshaping Undergraduate Music Education in Turbulent Times," in *College Curricula for a New Century*, ed. Robin Moore, 38 [New York: Oxford University Press]).
3. Thomas Kuhn, 1962, *The Structure of Scientific Revolutions* (Chicago: University of Chicago Press).
4. The CMS Manifesto appears in Ed Sarath, David Myers, and Patricia S. Campbell, 2016, *Redefining Music Studies in an Age of Change* (New York: Routledge).
5. Ed Sarath, 2013, *Improvisation, Creativity and Consciousness: Jazz as Integral Template for Music, Education and Society* (Albany: State University of New York Press).
6. This model first appears in my book, *Improvisation, Creativity and Consciousness*.
7. I would include discourse on critical thinking in Robin Moore's 2017 edited volume, *College Music Curricula in a New Century* (New York: Oxford), in this assessment. While compelling commentary is offered in support of the importance of critical thinking, little if any definition of the term, nor analysis of the means for critical thinking development, is provided. Therefore, one can reasonably infer that, consistent with multicultural ambivalence to episte-

mology, critical thinking is construed as externally mediated—where an instructor instigates discussion on various topics. This is important, but only part of the broader epistemic framework called for.

8. May Kokkidou, 2013, "Critical Thinking and School Music Education: Literature Review, Research Findings, and Perspectives," *Journal for Learning through the Arts* 9, no. 1. Also see Betty Anne Younker, 2002, "Critical Thinking," in *The New Handbook of Research on Music Teaching and Learning*, ed. Richard Colwell and Carol Richardson, 162–70 (New York: Oxford University Press).

9. Kokkidou, "Critical Thinking and School Music Education."

10. Cornell West, 2001, *Race Matters* (New York: Vintage Books).

11. Sarath, *Improvisation, Creativity and Consciousness*.

12. Sarath, *Improvisation, Creativity and Consciousness*.

13. Here music studies reform discourse might take its cue from philosophy-of-mind discourse, where thinkers imagine what it might be like to have the consciousness of a bat, or a zombie.

14. I encountered this response early on in CMS Task Force deliberations.

15. A common theme in reform literature is that the core curriculum has remained largely unchanged since at least the mid-1950s. See Robin Moore, "Introduction," in his volume, *College Music Curricula in a New Century*; see also, Sarath, Myers, and Campbell, *Redefining Music Studies in an Age of Change*.

16. See, for example, David Kulma and Meghan Naxer, 2014, "Beyond Part-Writing: Modernizing the Curriclum," in *Engaging Students: Essays in Music Pedagogy*, vol. 2 (Mountain View, CA: Creative Commons): "Part writing becomes a set of memorized rules rather than a flexible tool, it limits the engagement and agency of our students." See also Nicholas Bannan, Spring 2016, "Embodied Music Theory: New Pedagogy for Creative and Aural Development," *Journal of Music Theory Pedagogy*, vol. 24: 201, where he advances a model that seeks to address "the disconnection between music theory and actual musical practice"; and Sam Richards, 2015, "Rethinking the Theory Classroom: Towards a New Model for Undergraduate Instruction," in *Engaging Students: Essays in Music Pedagogy*, vol. 3 (Mountain View, CA: Creative Commons).

17. The 2016 Position Paper of the College Band Directors National Association (see CBDNA.org, under "Publications") in response to the College Music Society "Manifesto" (see Sarath, Myers, and Campbell, *Redefining Music Studies in an Age of Change*, chapter 3) advances this concern that diversification may inhere tendencies to dilute resultant skills and understanding.

18. Bruno Nettl underscores this point in his 1995 *Heartland Excursions: Ethnomusicological Reflections on Schools of Music*, 138 (Urbana: University of Illinois Press).

19. Deborah Bradley acknowledges this pattern in Bradley, 2015, *Hidden in Plain Sight: Race and Racism in Music Education*, Oxford Handbooks Online (Oxford: Oxford University Press).

20. In addition to my many years of curriculum experience noted above, I am also professionally active in the emergent field of consciousness studies; I gave the first keynote address at the newly formed Society for Consciousness Studies conference.

21. See, for example, Juan Chattah, Melissa Hoag, Steven Laitz, Elizabeth Sayrs, and Jennifer Sterling Snodgrass, "Reflections on the Manifesto," http://http://www.academia.edu/28155924/Reflections_on_the_Manifesto, and Carol Gould and Kenneth Keaton, 2000, "The Essential Role of Improvisation in Musical Performance," *The Journal of Aesthetics and Art Criticism* 58, no. 2: 143–48.

22. The College Music Society "Manifesto" is among the first documents in the music studies reform literature, even if on a very preliminary scale, to fulfill this criterion. This occurs when the document sets itself apart from prevailing change commentary. I take this further in Sarath, Myers, and Campbell, *Redefining Music Studies in an Age of Change*.

23. Much of the commentary in Moore's *College Music Curricula for a New Century*, if not outright supporting my assessment, at the very least supports the case for placing these kinds of questions (about the effectiveness of theory and history paradigms) front and center.

24. See, for example, James Zull, 2006, "Key Aspects of How the Brain Learns," in *The Neuroscience of Adult Learning: New Directions for Adult and Continuing Education*, ed. Sandra Johnson and Kathleen Thompson, 3–10 (San Francisco, CA: Jossey-Bass).

25. Zull, "Key Aspects of How the Brain Learns."

26. Martin Luther King Jr., 1967, "Beyond Vietnam: The Time to Break the Silence," www.beliefnet.com/columnists/christianityfortherestofus/2011/01/martin-luther-king-jr-fierce-urgency-of-now.html.

27. Ruth Gustafson, 2009, *Race and Curriculum: Music in Childhood Education*, 3 (New York: Palgrave MacMillan). I would add that Kate Fitzpatrick, 2015, *Urban Music Education: A Practical Guide for Teachers* (New York: Oxford University Press), offers important representation of fine work being done in a number of inner-city music programs. She also dispels prevailing stereotypes that surround this area.

JAZZ AND THE CONSCIOUSNESS TURN

1. See, for example, Alphonso Montouri and Robert Purser, 1994, "Miles Davis in the Classroom: Using the Jazz Ensemble Metaphor for Enhancing Team Learning," *Journal of Management Education* 18, no. 1: 21–31, and Robert O'Meally, Brent Hayes Edwards, and Farah Jasmine Griffin, eds., 2004, *Uptown Conversation: The New Jazz Studies* (New York: Columbia University Press).

5. A JAZZ-BASED INTEGRAL PERSPECTIVE ON CONSCIOUSNESS

1. Ed Sarath, 2013, *Improvisation, Creativity and Consciousness: Jazz as Integral Template for Music, Education and Society* (Albany: State University of New York Press), see chapter 11.

2. Sarath, *Improvisation, Creativity and Consciousness*.

3. Sarath, *Improvisation, Creativity and Consciousness*. Also see Robert Forman, ed., 1990, *The Problem of Pure Consciousness* (New York: Oxford University Press).

4. For a similar argument, see Phillip Goldberg, 2010, *American Veda: How Indian Spirituality Changed the West* (New York: Harmony/Random House), for an account of the influence of Vedanta on Western culture.

5. Hua Hsu, April 25, 2017, "Alice Coltrane's Devotional Music," *New Yorker*, p. 1.

6. Interesting commentary on emergent, contemporary spiritual pathways is found in Elizabeth Lesser, 1999, *The New American Spirituality: A Seeker's Guide* (New York: Random House), and Robert Forman, 2004, *Grassroots Spirituality* (Charlottesville, VA: Imprint Academic), and particularly toward tendencies whereby Westerners disengage from Judeo-Christian roots, engage with Eastern practices, and then gravitate back toward their original roots—often retaining newfound practices. See also Goldberg, *American Veda*.

7. Amit Goswami, 1993, *The Self-Aware Universe: How Consciousness Creates the Material World* (New York: Tarcher), offers a comprehensive synopsis of philosophies of mind. See also Candace Pert, 1997, *Molecules of Emotion: The Science behind Mind-Body Medicine* (New York: Touchstone), and Imants Barruss and Julia Mossbridge, 2017, *Transcendent Mind: Rethinking the Science of Consciousness* (Washington, DC: American Psychological Association).

8. Stephen Jay Gould, 1999, *Rock of Ages: Science and Religion in the Fullness of Life* (New York: Ballantine).

9. A. S. Dalal, 2001, *A Greater Psychology: The Psychological Thought of Sri Aurobindo* (New York: Tarcher/Putnam), 336.

10. Planck is quoted in the *Observer*, January 1931. Also see his remarks in Das Wesen der Materie [The Nature of Matter], speech at Florence, Italy (1944) (from Archiv zur Geschichte der Max-Planck-Gesellschaft, Abt. Va, Rep. 11 Planck, Nr. 1797):

> As a man who has devoted his whole life to the most clear headed science, to the study of matter, I can tell you as a result of my research about atoms this much: There is no matter as such. All matter originates and exists only by virtue of a force which brings the particle of an atom to vibration and holds this most minute solar system of the atom together. We must assume behind this force the existence of a conscious and intelligent mind. This mind is the matrix of all matter.
>
> It cannot be emphasized strongly enough that the view of consciousness as primary involves an eternal realm of spirit as the source of creation, not the notion that some aspect of objective reality does not exist unless some human being is conscious of it.

11. See David Skrbina, 2005, *Panpsychism in the West* (Cambridge, MA: MIT).

12. Skrbina, *Panpsychism in the West*. Also see Quartz Media LLC, https://qz.com/1184574/the-idea-that-everything-from-spoons-to-stones-are-conscious-is-gaining-academic-credibility/2018, for indications of recent interest in panpsychism among thinkers who previously subscribed to materialist viewpoints.

13. For leading materialist accounts, see Daniel Dennett, 1991, *Consciousness Explained* (Boston: Back Bay); Patricia Churchland, 1998, "Can Neurobiology Teach Us Anything about Consciousness?" in *The Nature of Consciousness: Philosophical Debates*, ed. N. Block, O. Flanagan, and G. Guzelder, 127–39 (Cambridge, MA: MIT). See also Francis Crick and Christof Koch, 1998, "Towards a Neurobiological Theory of Consciousness," in *The Nature of Consciousness: Philosophical Debates*, ed. N. Block, O. Flanagan, and G. Guzelder, 277–92 (Cambridge, MA: MIT). For one of the most compelling recent critiques of materialism, its limitations, and the ideological underpinnings that keep it in place, see Barruss and Mossbridge, *Transcendent Mind*.

14. John R. Searle, 1997, *The Mystery of Consciousness* (New York: New York Review of Books).

15. Steven Weinberg, 1977, *The First Three Minutes* (New York: Basic Books).

16. The Society for Study of Human Ideas on Ultimate Reality and Meaning. See https://utorontopress.com/us/ultimate-reality-and-meaning for a description of the organization and its journal.

17. Webster's dictionary.

18. Teilhard de Chardin, 1965, *The Hymn of the Universe* (New York: Harper and Row), 93.

19. This range of practices is called "Integral Methodological Pluralism" in Ken Wilber, Terry Patten, Adam Leonard, and Marco Morelli, 2008, *Integral Life Practice: A 21st-Century Blueprint for Physical Health, Emotional Balance, Mental Clarity, and Spiritual Awakening* (Boston: Integral Books).

20. See Charles Alexander and Ellen Langer, eds., 1990, *Higher Stages of Human Development* (New York: Oxford University Press). See also Forman, *The Problem of Pure Consciousness*.

21. Abraham Maslow's notion of "peak experience," discussed in his landmark 1971 book, *The Farther Reaches of Human Nature* (New York: Penguin), is a precursor to Csikszentmihalyi's "flow"; see Mihalyi Csikszentmihalyi, 1990, *Flow: The Psychology of Optimal Experience* (New York: Harper and Row).

22. Ken Wilber, 2000, *Collected Works*, vol. 4 (Boston: Shambhala), provides a cross-cultural cartology of spiritual experiences across traditions that illuminates parallels in the stage model. While the experience may be mediated by cultural influences, the essential core is remarkably similar across traditions.

23. Craig Pearson, 2011, *Supreme Awakening: Experiences of Higher States of Consciousness* (Fairfield, IA: Maharishi University of Management Press).

24. Pearson, *Supreme Awakening*. See also F. Travis, A. Arenander, and D. DuBois, 2004, "Psychological and Physiological Characteristics of a Proposed Object-Referral/Self-Referral

Continuum of Self-Awareness," *Consciousness and Cognition* 13: 401–20, for among the very first set of neurophysiological data in support of higher enduring stages.

25. Ken Wilber elaborates on these general principles in much of his writing; see, for example, Ken Wilber, 2000, "Integral Psychology," in *Collected Works*, vol. 4 (Boston: Shambhala).

26. Wilber, "Integral Psychology."

27. Richard Tarnas, 2006, *Cosmos and Psyche: Intimations of a New World View* (New York Viking), provides among the most powerful accounts of the wide-ranging correlates to archetypal principles in Western thought. This includes mythic gods and goddesses, Aristotelian immanent universals, Platonic forms, Schopenarian universal essences of life, Husserlian essences of life, Wittgensteinian linguistic family resemblances, and Whiteheadian eternal objects (p. 84). One can easily see correlates to Hindu devatas and Buddhist boddhisatvas.

28. C. G. Jung, 1960, *On the Nature of the Psyche* (Princeton: Princeton University Press).

29. Jung, *On the Nature of the Psyche*.

30. Sarath, *Improvisation, Creativity and Consciousness*.

31. Sarath, *Improvisation, Creativity and Consciousness*.

32. Alexander and Langer, *Higher Stages of Human Development*.

33. Pearson, *Supreme Awakening*, 322.

34. Pearson, *Supreme Awakening*, 235.

35. Maharishi Mahesh Yogi, 1999, *Constitution of India Fulfilled through Maharishi's Transcendental Meditation* (New Delhi, India: Vedic Vishwa-Vidyalaya).

36. Pearson, *Supreme Awakening*, 347.

37. Pearson, *Supreme Awakening*, 354.

38. Here potentially fruitful intersections between Western and Eastern perspectives on the strata at which matter and consciousness intersect come into view. Whereas penetration to the underpinnings of matter through the discoveries (and conundrums) of contemporary physics reveals a world not comprised of the particulate phenomena observed at classical scales but rather of energy waves, probability, and indeterminacy, with some physicists taking the next step of viewing this as fluctuations in consciousness, the ancient Vedantic approach can be seen as arriving at the same stratum from the angle of consciousness. The first, scientific approach can be thought of as parts-to-whole, the second, consciousness-based approach as whole-to-parts.

39. Maharishi Mahesh Yogi explains the self-referential principles of creation as the interplay of three aspects of consciousness that interact at cosmic and individual scales. These are knower (*rishi*); process of knowing, or self-referential curving back (*devata*); and object of knowing (*chandas*). In his *Apaurusheya Bhāshya*, commentary on Rig (Rk) Veda, he locates this self-referential interaction, and ensuing dynamics of creation, within a single syllable of the Vedic literature: "AK (the first syllable of Rk Veda) describes the collapse of fullness of consciousness—A collapses within itself to its own point value, K. This collapse, which represents the eternal dynamics of consciousness knowing itself, occurs in eight successive stages." In other words, the syllable A represents *rishi*, the collapse of A represents the *devata* value, and K represents the *chandas* value. The resultant syllable AK is the first sound emerging from this interaction, and as these interactions continue, they result in the "eight syllables of the first Pada, which emerge from and provide a further commentary on the first syllable of Rk Veda, AK. These eight syllables pertain to the eight Prakrti or eight fundamental qualities of intelligence, which constitute the divided nature of pure consciousness" (in Kai Druhl, 1997, "Consciousness as the Subject and Object of Physics: Toward a New Paradigm for the Physical Sciences," *Modern Science and Vedic Science* 7, no. 1: 156).

40. Abhinavagupta is cited in Paul Eduardo Muller-Ortega, 1989, *The Triadic Heart of Siva: Kaula Tantricism of Abhinavagupta in the Non-Dual Shaivism of Kashmir* (Albany: State University of New York Press).

41. Maharishi Mahesh Yogi, *Constitution of India*. See also Theresa Olson-Sorflaten, 1995, *Increased Personal Harmony and Integration as Effects of Maharishi Gandharva Veda Music on Affect, Physiology, and Behavior: The Psychophysiology* (PhD dissertation, Maharishi International University).

42. In Hazrat Inayat Kahn, 1988, *The Music of Life* (New Lebanon, NY: Omega), Kahn offers powerful commentary on this music-cosmos connection.

43. Joachim-Ernst Berendt, 1991, *The World Is Sound: Nada Brahma* (Rochester, VT: Destiny), 63.

44. Berendt, *The World Is Sound*, 63.

45. Fred Alan Wolff and John Hagelin, are among contemporary physicists who ascribe to this correlation. From a Vedantic standpoint, Maharishi Mahesh Yogi has elaborated on this at length in *Constitution of India*.

46. Ananda K. Coomaraswamy, 1941, "Lila," *Journal of the American Oriental Society* 61: 98–101.

47. Edward C. Dimock, 1989, "Lila," *History of Religions* 29, no. 2: 159.

48. William S. Sax, 1990, November. "The Ramnagar Ramlila: Text, Performance, Pilgramage," *History of Religions* 30: 129.

49. For example, Susan Blackmore is among the more prominent deniers of free will from a materialist perspective.

50. See Llewellyn Vaughn-Lee, 2009, *The Return of the Feminine and the World Soul* (Inverness, CA: The Golden Sufi Center), 1, 3, 4. I am more inclined toward the participatory spirituality inferred in Richard Tarnas's work (e.g., *Cosmos and Psyche*) than the participatory hermeneutics inferred in that of Jorge Ferrer (2002, *Revisioning Transpersonal Theory: A Participatory Vision of Human Spirituality* [Albany: State University of New York Press]), however impressive his arguments are.

51. See Christopher Bache, 2008, *The Living Classroom: Teaching and Collective Consciousness* (Albany: State University of New York Press), for compelling support for educational application of the intersubjective consciousness principle. For transformative impact on society, see John Hagelin, Maxwell V. Rainforth, David W. Orme-Johnson, Kenneth L. Cavanaugh, Charles N. Alexander, Susan F. Shatkin, John L. Davies, Anne O. Hughes, and Emanuel Ross, June 1999, "Effects of Group Practice of the Transcendental Meditation Program on Preventing Violent Crime in Washington, D.C.; Results of the National Demonstration Project to Reduce Crime and Improve Governmental Effectiveness in Washington, D.C., June-July, 1993," *Social Indicators Research* 47, no. 2: 153–201; and D. Orme-Johnson, C. Alexander, J. Davies, H. Chander, and W. Larimore, 1988, "International Peace Project: The Effects of the Maharishi Technology of the Unified Field," *Journal of Conflict Resolution* 32, no. 4: 776–812. Also see Hari Sharma and Christopher Clark, 1998, *Contemporary Ayurveda: Medicine and Research in Maharishi Ayurveda* (Philadelphia: Churchill Livingstone). For general argumentation for collective consciousness, see Lynne M. McTaggart, 2002, *The Field: The Quest for the Secret Force of the Universe* (New York HarperCollins).

52. Ibid.

53. See Lynne Mason, Robert P. Patterson, and Dean I. Radin, 2007, "Exploratory Study: The Random Number Generator and Group Meditation," *Journal of Scientific Exploration* 21: 295–317, for findings that are suggestive of both mind-matter interaction and collective consciousness. See also McTaggart, *The Field*, for compelling commentary in this direction.

54. Among the strongest recent sources of this support is Barruss and Mossbridge, *Transcendent Mind*.

55. Barruss and Mossbridge, *Transcendent Mind*, 15–17.

56. See, for example, Charles Tart, 2009, *The End of Materialism: How Evidence of the Paranormal Is Bringing Science and Spirit Together* (Oakland, CA: New Harbinger), and Barruss and Mossbridge, *Transcendent Mind*.

57. Tart, *The End of Materialism*, chapter 1, p. 18.

58. Dean Radin, 1997, *The Conscious Universe* (San Francisco: Harper).

59. In addition to the above sources (Radin, Tart, and Barruss and Mossbridge), Larry Dossey, 2013, *One Mind: How Our Individual Mind Is Part of a Greater Consciousness and Why It Matters* (Carlsbad, CA: Hay House), and Rupert Sheldrake, 2012, *Science Set Free: 10 Paths to New Discovery* (New York: Deepak Chopra Books), offer powerful commentary on the critical integrity lapse that underpins much scientific materialist ideology and literature.

60. David Chalmers originally articulated the "hard problem." See David J. Chalmers, 1996, *The Conscious Mind: In Search of a Fundamental Theory* (New York: Oxford University Press).

61. Fred Alan Wolff, 1999, *The Spiritual Universe: One Physicist's Vision of Spirit, Soul, Matter, and Self* (Needham, MA: One Moment Press).

62. Quartz Media LLC, https://qz.com/1184574/the-idea-that-everything-from-spoons-to-stones-are-conscious-is-gaining-academic-credibility/2018.

63. It is interesting to note that among former materialists, such as Chalmers, who have begun to make an exodus from that ideology, psi research—which could powerfully support their new trajectory—minimally informs their reasoning. I view this as a result of the lingering inertia of the conventional paradigm, even as it topples from another direction.

64. Sarath, *Improvisation, Creativity and Consciousness*.

65. See my paper, "On Earth as It Is in Heaven," found in Gunnlaugson, O., Bai, Heesoon, Scott, C. and Sarath, E., 2017, *The Intersubjective Turn: Theoretical Approaches to Contemplative Learning and Inquiry across Disciplines* (State University of New York), and *Improvisation, Creativity and Consciousness* for preliminary accounts of the second-tier hard problem.

66. Sarath, *Improvisation, Creativity and Consciousness*.

67. See Owen Flanagan, 2002, *The Problem of the Soul* (New York: Basic Books), and similar misunderstandings in Sam Harris, 2004, *The End of Faith: Religion, Terror, and the Future of Reason* (New York: W.W. Norton), and Stephen Batchelor, 2010, *Confessions of a Buddhist Atheist* (New York: Spiegel and Grau/Random House).

68. Nan Huaijin, 1997, *Basic Buddhism: Exploring Buddhism and Zen* (York Beach, NY: Weiser Books).

69. This underscores a question I pose to materialists, which parallels that which I pose to practitioners in the neo-Eurocentric musical paradigm: To what extent is your orientation the result of careful consideration of a wide spectrum of possible pathways/worldviews?

70. Sarath, *Improvisation Creativity and Consciousness*.

71. Sarath, *Improvisation Creativity and Consciousness*.

72. See Mary Murphy and Sabrina Zirkel, 2015, "Race and Belonging in School: How Anticipated and Experienced Belonging Affect Choice, Persistence, and Performance," *Teachers College Record* 117, no. 12: 1–40. For research on hope, see Song Wang, Xin Xu, Ming Zhou, Taolin Chen, Xun Yang, Guangxlang Chen, and Quyong Gong, August 2017, "Hope and the Brain: Trait Hope Mediates the Protective Role of Medial Orbitofrontal Cortex Spontaneous Activity against Anxiety," *NeuroImage* 157: 439–47.

73. Dennett, *Consciousness Explained*

74. Allan Combs, 2009, *Consciousness Explained Better: Toward an Integral Understanding of the Multi-Faceted Nature of Consciousness* (St. Paul, MN: Paragon House).

6. A CONSCIOUSNESS-BASED INTEGRAL PERSPECTIVE ON IMPROVISATION

1. Ed Sarath, 2013, *Improvisation, Creativity and Consciousness: Jazz as Integral Template for Music, Education and Society* (Albany: State University of New York Press).

2. Paul Berliner, 1994, *Thinking in Jazz: The Infinite Art of Improvisation* (Chicago: University of Chicago Press), 36; chapter 2 is titled "Composing in the Moment." Similarly, Phillip Alperson (1984, "Thoughts on Improvisation," *Journal of Aesthetics and Art Criticism* 43: 17–29) defines improvisation as "the creation of a musical work while it is performed." In, moreover, assessing a given improvisation according to "what has proven to be possible within the demands of improvisatory musical activity," one senses default recourse to a norm that improvisation is inherently incapable of achieving, at which point our only recourse is to appreciate the noble attempt. Similar implications might be inferred in the title and thrust of Ted Goia's book on improvisation, *The Imperfect Art: Reflections on Jazz and Modern Culture* (New York: Oxford, 1988). Even more overtly limiting is the idea that "improvisation," as

composer Luciano Berio puts it, "may be of therapeutic value to uptight performers," but lacks the capacity inherent in composition for "coherent discourse that develops along multiple levels" (1985, *Two Interviews* [New York: Marion Boyars]).

3. Ed Sarath, 1996, "A New Look at Improvisation," *Journal of Music Theory* 40, no. 1: 1–39.

4. Steve Lacy, 1994, *Findings: My Experience with the Soprano Saxophone* (Paris: CMAP, Outre Mesure), 21.

5. Jonathan Kramer, 1988, *The Time of Music* (New York: Schirmer), deploys the concept of nonlinearity largely from the standpoint of composed music, as in compositions that elicit more of a moment-to-moment sensibility as opposed to linear, formal architecture. In this sense, there is compatibility with my model, the only difference being that I argue compositional nonlinearity will never achieve that which is possible in improvisation (nor can improvisation, even amid the most robust attempts at such, achieve the linearity of composition).

6. Kramer, *The Time of Music*.
7. Sarath, *Improvisation, Creativity and Consciousness*.
8. Ibid.
9. This first appears in my essay, "A New Look at Improvisation."
10. Sarath, *Improvisation, Creativity and Consciousness*.
11. Ibid.
12. Ibid.
13. Ibid.
14. Ibid.
15. Ibid.
16. Ibid.
17. Ibid.
18. Ibid.
19. Ibid.
20. Ibid.
21. Ibid.
22. Sarath, *Improvisation, Creativity and Consciousness*, chapter 6.
23. James Gleick, 1987, *Chaos* (New York: Viking).
24. Paul Hindemith, 1952, *A Composer's World: Horizons and Limitations* (Cambridge, MA: Harvard University Press), 71. Quotations from Mozart, Brahms, and Beethoven are found in Willis Harmon and Howard Rheingold, 1984, *Higher Creativity: Liberating the Unconscious for Breakthrough Insights* (New York: Tarcher), 41.

25. Quoted in Berliner, *Thinking in Jazz*, 356. Stephen Nachmanovitch has written eloquently on this facet of the improvisatory experience in his book *Free Play: Improvisation in Art and Life*.

26. What I call "either/or and creativity as novelty" fallacies are implicit in Csikszentmihalyi's "systems view" of creativity, as articulated in his 1996 book, *Creativity: Flow and the Psychology of Discovery and Invention* (New York: Harper Perennial); and Jason Townbee's "radius of creativity," in his "Music, Culture and Creativity," in *The Cultural Study of Music: A Critical Introduction*, ed. Richard Middleton, 102–12 (New York: Routlege, 2003). In addition to the above, the "creativity as object," see David Elliott, 1995, *Music Matters* (New York: Oxford University Press).

27. See Margaret Barrett, 2005, "A Systems View of Creativity," in *Praxial Music Education*, edited by David Elliott, 177–95 (New York: Oxford University Press), for an argument along these lines.

28. For example, Keith Sawyer made this argument in his keynote address at the College Music Society annual meeting in 2014 in St. Louis. It is also implicit in Carol Gould and Kenneth Keaton's interesting, yet fundamentally flawed, 2000 argument, in "The Essential Role of Improvisation in Musical Performance" (*The Journal of Aesthetics and Art Criticism* 58, no. 2) that improvisation in interpretive performance differs in degree, but not kind, when compared to jazz improvisation. (From an integral standpoint, the two kinds of improvisation differ in both degree *and* kind.) For a critique of the motive explanation, see George Lewis,

Spring 1996, "Improvised Music since 1950: Afrological and Eurological Perspectives," *Black Music Research* 16: 91–119; I believe my account elaborates on his important analysis.

29. Jeff Pressing, 1987, "Improvisation: Methods and Models," in *Generative Processes in Music*, ed. John Sloboda, 129–76 (London: Oxford University Press).

30. Sarath, *Improvisation, Creativity and Consciousness*.

31. I first drew these distinctions in Sarath, "A New Look at Improvisation."

32. Dorothy Lee, 1974, "Codifications of Reality: Lineal and Nonlineal," in *The Nature of Human Consciousness*, ed. Robert Ornstein, 128–42 (New York: Viking), 132.

33. Judith Becker, 1981, "Hindu-Buddhist Time in Javanese Gamelan Music," in *Explorations in the Study of Time*, ed. J. T. Fraser, Nathaniel Lawrence, and David Park, 161–72 (New York: Springer Verlag), 165. John Broomfield, 1997, *Other Ways of Knowing: Recharting Our Future with Ageless Wisdom* (Rochester, VT: Inner Traditions International).

34. Heide Göttner-Abendroth, *The Dancing Goddess: Principles of a Matriarchal Aesthetic* (Boston: Beacon Press), 47–48.

35. See Martin Luther King Jr., 1964, "On the Importance of Jazz: Introductory Remarks at the 1964 Berlin Jazz Festival," http://wclk.com/dr-martin-luther-king-jr-importance-jazz.

36. LeRoi Jones, 1963, *Blues People* (New York: HarperCollins/Perennial).

37. For example, music and artificial intelligence, computer-generated composition and improvisation, and various listener reception theories would come under systematic musicology. While, unlike historical and ethnomusicological branches, systematic musicology might lay claim to a culturally neutral orientation, a hidden resort to neo-Eurocentric patterns may be noted. Music cognition, for instance, tends to focus far more heavily on listener reception to composed-notated music than artist creation, which reifies the centrality of the composed-work paradigm.

38. Generally speaking, jazz interpretations of standard repertory that derives from Tin Pan Alley or Broadway shows, as well as original compositions particularly from the 1960s on, are more conducive to what I am talking about than bebop. With bebop, the improvising tends to remain within the density/textural level of the main theme. With standards and originals, the improvising can venture to distant realms.

7. JAZZ AND THE INTEGRAL REVOLUTION

1. Cornell West, 2001, *Race Matters* (New York: Vintage Books).

2. See Ed Sarath, 2003, "Meditation in Higher Education: The Next Wave?" *Innovative Higher Education* 27: 215–34, for in-depth analysis of the structure of the curriculum. See Ed Sarath, 2007, "Improvisation, Consciousness, and the Play of Creation: Music as a Lens into Ultimate Reality and Meaning," *Ultimate Reality and Meaning* 30, no. 1: 54–77, for commentary on a previous innovation. See Ed Sarath, 2006, "Meditation, Creativity, and Consciousness: Charting Future Terrain within Higher Education," *Teachers College Record* 108, no. 9: 1816–41, and Ed Sarath, 2010, "Jazz, Creativity, and Consciousness: Blueprint for Integral Education," in *Integral Education: New Directions for Higher Learning*, ed. Sean Esbjörn-Hargens, Jonathan Reams, and Olen Gunnlaugson (Albany: State University of New York Press), for reflections on improvisation-meditation advocacy intersections.

3. See Ed Sarath, 2013, *Improvisation, Creativity and Consciousness: Jazz as Integral Template for Music, Education and Society* (Albany: State University of New York Press), chapter 10, for a critical analysis of the contemplative studies movement that situates the present orientation within a multistage evolutionary sequence.

4. Sarath, *Improvisation, Creativity and Consciousness*.

5. This statement is typically attributed to Woodrow Wilson.

6. Perhaps ironically, this reactionary imagining may have worked in the proposal's favor. Several colleagues who were initially ambivalent if not averse to the proposal confided to me that the vociferous and what they perceived to be extremist nature of the resistance to the proposal compelled them to vote in its favor.

7. In light of Brian Pertl's argument (see chapter 4, note 2) for cultural change as also important if not more important than curricular change, this is not to deny that important dimensions of learning take place outside the classroom. However, the curriculum is the bloodstream of the academy; it is where vital nutrients—in terms of not only information and skills but also more fundamentally transformative experiences, ideas, critical inquiry capacities, and expansive visioning—may be transmitted to students and by extension to society: I see the two—curricula and culture—as closely intertwined.

8. Yogi, *Apaurasheya Bhashya*, in his *Constitution of India*, is the most compelling account of this relationship. See *Constitution of India Fulfilled through Maharishi's Transcendental Meditation* New Delhi, India: Vishwa-Vidyalaya.

9. See Robert Oates, 2002, *Permanent Peace: How to Stop Terrorism and War—Now and Forever* (Fairfield, IA: Institute for Science, Technology, and Public Policy).

10. Dean Radin, 2007, "A Brief History of the Potential Future," in *Mind Before Matter: Visions of a New Science of Consciousness*, ed. Trish Pfeiffer and John E. Mack (Winchester, UK: O Books/John Hunt).

11. Here is where an advanced form of Transcendental Meditation (TM) called the TM-Sidhis program, as conceived by Maharishi Mahesh Yogi, may be ideal on both accounts. The practice provides powerful episodes of pure consciousness and also involves the navigation of primordial interstices from that basis. Studies on healing results of collective meditation have involved large groups of TM-Sidhis practitioners. See Yogi, *Constitution of India*, and John Hagelin, Maxwell V. Rainforth, David W. Orme-Johnson, Kenneth L. Cavanaugh, Charles N. Alexander, Susan F. Shatkin, John L. Davies, Anne O. Hughes, and Emanuel Ross, June 1999, "Effects of Group Practice of the Transcendental Meditation Program on Preventing Violent Crime in Washington, D.C.; Results of the National Demonstration Project to Reduce Crime and Improve Governmental Effectiveness in Washington, D.C., June-July, 1993," *Social Indicators Research* 47, no. 2: 153–201.

12. Ibid., Hagelin et al.

13. As I argue in chapter 4, readers are encouraged to consider epistemological diversity as a key criterion for critical and self-critical vitality of any knowledge system.

14. This is not to deny materialist implications that might be inferred in the worldview of someone like Democritus, but simply to put this in broader perspective of Western thought.

15. David Chalmers in his 2012 "The Singularity: A Philosophical Analysis" (*Journal of Consciousness Studies* 17: 7–65) acknowledges possibilities no less chilling than the "end of the human race, an arms race of warring machines, and the destruction of the planet."

16. For commentary on educare and educere, see Randall V. Bass and J. W. Good, 2004, Winter, "Educare and Educere: Is a Balance Possible in the Educational World?" *The Educational Forum* 68, no. 2: 161–68. Alfred North Whitehead, 1929, *The Aims of Education* (New York: Free Press).

17. Abraham Maslow, 1971, *The Farther Reaches of Human Nature* (New York: Penguin).

18. bell hooks, 1994, *Teaching to Transgress: Education as the Practice of Freedom* (New York: Routledge), 206.

19. See Sarath, *Improvisiation, Creativity and Consciousness*, chapter 11, for a historically based critique of contemplative studies.

20. Owen Flanagan, 2002, *The Problem of the Soul* (New York: Basic Books).

21. Erwin Schroedinger, Niels Bohr, and Werner Heisenberg were significantly influenced by Vedic texts. More recently, John Hagelin, Fred Alan Wolff, Menas Kafatos, and Amit Goswami are physicists to be added to this list.

22. Pierre Hadot, 2002, *What Is Ancient Philosophy?* (Cambridge, MA: Harvard University Press), 2, 6.

23. Sarath, *Improvisation, Creativity and Consciousness*, chapter 11.

24. Ibid.

25. Ibid.

26. Basarab Nicolescu, 2002, *Manifesto of Transdisciplinarity* (Albany: State University of New York Press).

EPILOGUE

1. Martin Luther King Jr., 1967, "Beyond Vietnam: The Time to Break the Silence," www.beliefnet.com/columnists/christianityfortherestofus/2011/01/martin-luther-king-jr-fierceurgency-of-now.html. Diana Bass, 2011, "Martin Luther King, Jr. The Fierce Urgency of Now," www.beliefnet.com/columnists/christianityfortherestofus/2011/01/martin-luther-king-jr-fierce-urgency-of-now.html. Also inspired by King's words is a fine collection of essays titled *The Fierce Urgency of Now: Improvisation, Rights and Cocreation* (Chapel Hill: Duke University Press, 2013) compiled and coauthored by Ajay Heble, Daniel Fischlin, and George Lipsitz.

2. Bass, "Martin Luther King, Jr."

3. Martin Luther King Jr., 1964, "On the Importance of Jazz: Introductory Remarks at the 1964 Berlin Jazz Festival," http://wclk.com/dr-martin-luther-king-jr-importance-jazz.

4. King, "On the Importance of Jazz." Here I might add that this does not in any way negate the extent to which the circumstances of slavery catalyzed particularly deep penetration into the soul level.

5. West's comments are from William C. Banfield, 2015, *Ethnomusicologizing* (Lanham, MD: Rowman and Littlefield), 84.

6. LeRoi Jones, *Blues People* (New York: HarperCollins/Perennial, 1963), 13.

7. Herbie Hancock with Lisa Dickey, 2014, *Possibilities* (New York: Viking), 384.

8. King, "Beyond Vietnam."

References

Alexander, Charles, and Ellen Langer, eds. 1990. *Higher Stages of Human Development*. New York: Oxford University Press.
Alim, Samy. 2015. *Raciolinguistics: How Language Shapes Our Ideas about Race*. Edited by John R. Rickford and Arnetha F. Ball. Oxford: Oxford University Press.
Allsup, Randall. 2016. *Remixing the Music Classroom: Toward an Open Philosophy of Music Education*. Indianapolis: Indiana University Press.
Alperson, Phillip. 1984. "Thoughts on Improvisation." *Journal of Aesthetics and Art Criticism* 43: 17–29.
Anderson, Kristin. 2009. *Benign Bigotry: The Psychology of Subtle Prejudice*. Cambridge: Cambridge University Press.
Bache, Christopher. 2008. *The Living Classroom: Teaching and Collective Consciousness*. Albany: State University of New York Press.
Banfield, William C. 2010. *Cultural Codes: Makings of a Black Music Philosophy*. Lanham, MD: Scarecrow Press.
———. 2015. *Ethnomusicologizing*. Lanham, MD: Rowman and Littlefield.
Bannan, Nicholas. 2016, Spring. "Embodied Music Theory: New Pedagogy for Creative and Aural Development." *Journal of Music Theory Pedagogy* vol. 24: 197–215.
Barrett, Margaret. 2005. "A Systems View of Creativity." In *Praxial Music Education*, edited by David Elliott, 177–95. New York: Oxford University Press.
Barruss, Imants, and Julia Mossbridge. 2017. *Transcendent Mind: Rethinking the Science of Consciousness*. Washington, DC: American Psychological Association.
Bass, Diana. 2011. "Martin Luther King, Jr. The Fierce Urgency of Now." www.beliefnet.com/columnists/christianityfortherestofus/2011/01/martin-luther-king-jr-fierce-urgency-of-now.html.
Bass, Randall V., and J. W. Good. 2004, Winter. "Educare and Educere: Is a Balance Possible in the Educational World?" *The Educational Forum* 68, no. 2: 161–68.
Batchelor, Stephen. 2010. *Confessions of a Buddhist Atheist*. New York: Spiegel and Grau/Random House.
Becker, Judith. 1981. "Hindu-Buddhist Time in Javanese Gamelan Music." In *Explorations in the Study of Time*, edited by J. T. Fraser, Nathaniel Lawrence, and David Park, 161–72. New York: Springer Verlag.
Benedict, Cathy, and Patrick Schmidt. 2014. "Educating Teachers for 21st Century Challenges: The Music Educator as Cultural Citizen." In *Promising Practices in 21st Century Music Teacher Education*, edited by Michelle Kaschub and Janice Smith, 79–104. Oxford: Oxford University Press.
Berendt, Joachim-Ernst. 1991. *The World Is Sound: Nada Brahma*. Rochester, VT: Destiny.

Berio, Luciano. 1985. *Two Interviews*. New York: Marion Boyars.
Berliner, Paul. 1994. *Thinking in Jazz: The Infinite Art of Improvisation*. Chicago: University of Chicago Press.
Boxhill, Edith, 1989. *Music Therapy for Living: Principles of Normalization Embodied in Music Therapy*. St. Louis: MMB Music Inc.
Bradley, Deborah. 2015. *Hidden in Plain Sight: Race and Racism in Music Education*. Oxford Handbooks Online. Oxford: Oxford University Press.
———. 2017. "In the Shadows of Mozart." In *College Music Curricula for a New Century*, edited by Robin Moore. New York: Oxford University Press.
Brandel, Rose. 1959, September. "The African Hemiola Style." *Ethnomusicology* 3, no. 3: 106–17.
Broomfield, John. 1997. *Other Ways of Knowing: Recharting Our Future with Ageless Wisdom*. Rochester, VT: Inner Traditions International.
Cage, John. 1961. *Silence*. Middletown, CT: Wesleyan University Press.
Chalmers, David J. 1996. *The Conscious Mind: In Search of a Fundamental Theory*. New York: Oxford University Press.
———. 2010. "The Singularity: A Philosophical Analysis." *Journal of Consciousness Studies* 17: 7–65.
Chattah, Juan, Hoag, Melissa, Laitz, Steven, Sayres, Elizabeth, and Snodgrass, Jennifer Sterling. 2016, August. *Reflections on the Manifesto*. http://www.academia.edu/28155924/Reflections_on_the_Manifesto.
Churchland, Patricia. 1998. "Can Neurobiology Teach Us Anything about Consciousness?" In *The Nature of Consciousness: Philosophical Debates*, edited by N. Block, O. Flanagan, and G. Guzelder, 127–39. Cambridge, MA: MIT.
Combs, Allan. 2009. *Consciousness Explained Better: Toward an Integral Understanding of the Multi-Faceted Nature of Consciousness*. St. Paul, MN: Paragon House.
"Contemporary Music Project." 1973, May. *Music Educators Journal* 59, no. 9: 33–48.
Coomaraswamy, Ananda K. 1941. "Lila." *Journal of the American Oriental Society* 61: 98–101.
Covach, John. 2015, January. "Rock Me Maestro." *Chronicle of Higher Education*.
———. 2017. "High Brow, Low Brow, Knot Now, Now How: Music Curriculum in a Flat World." In Carlos Xavier Rodriguez, *Coming of Age: Teaching and Learning Popular Music in Academia*. Ann Arbor, MI: Maize Books.
Crick, Francis, and Christof Koch. 1998. "Towards a Neurobiological Theory of Consciousness." In *The Nature of Consciousness: Philosophical Debates*, edited by N. Block, O. Flanagan, and G. Guzelder, 277–92. Cambridge, MA: MIT.
Csikszentmihalyi, Mihaly. 1990. *Flow: The Psychology of Optimal Experience*. New York: Harper and Row.
———. 1996. *Creativity: Flow and the Psychology of Discovery and Invention*. New York: Harper Perennial.
Dalal, A. S. 2001. *A Greater Psychology: The Psychological Thought of Sri Aurobindo*. New York: Tarcher/Putnam.
Danielou, Alain. 1995 (1943). *Music and the Power of Sound: The Influence of Tuning and Interval on Consciousness*. Rochester, VT: Destiny.
de Chardin, Teilhard. 1965. *The Hymn of the Universe*. New York: Harper and Row.
de Clercq, Trevor. 2017. "Swing, Shuffle, Half-Time, Double: Beyond Traditional Time Signatures in the Classification of Meter in Pop/Rock Music." In Carlos Xavier Rodriguez, *Coming of Age: Teaching and Learning Popular Music in Academia*, 139–168. Ann Arbor, MI: Maize Books.
Dennett, Daniel. 1991. *Consciousness Explained*. Boston: Back Bay.
Diangelo, Robin. 2007. "I'm Leaving: White Fragility in Racial Dialogue." In *Inclusion in Urban Educational Environments: Addressing Issues of Diversity, Equity, and Social Justice*, edited by B. McMahon and D. Armstrong, 213–40. Charlotte, NC: Information Age Publishing.
———. 2011. "White Fragility: Overcoming Racism." *International Journal of Critical Pedagogy* 3, no. 3: 54–70.

Dimock, Edward C. 1989. "Lila." *History of Religions* 29, no. 2: 159–73.
Diserens, Charles, and Harry Fine. 1939. *A Psychology of Music*. Cincinnati: Cincinnati College of Music.
Dossey, Larry. 2013. *One Mind: How Our Individual Mind Is Part of a Greater Consciousness and Why It Matters*. Carlsbad, CA: Hay House.
Druhl, Kai. 1997. "Consciousness as the Subject and Object of Physics: Toward a New Paradigm for the Physical Sciences." *Modern Science and Vedic Science* 7, no. 1: 143–64.
Du Bois, W. E. B. 2007 (1903). *The Souls of Black Folk*. New York: Oxford University Press.
Elliott, David. 1995. *Music Matters*. New York: Oxford University Press.
Ferrer, Jorge. 2002. *Revisioning Transpersonal Theory: A Participatory Vision of Human Spirituality*. Albany: State University of New York Press.
Fitzpatrick, Kate. 2015. *Urban Music Education: A Practical Guide for Teachers*. New York: Oxford University Press.
Flanagan, Owen. 2002. *The Problem of the Soul*. New York: Basic Books.
Floyd, Samuel A. 1995. *The Power of Black Music: Interpreting Its History from Africa to the United States*. New York: Oxford University Press.
Forman, Robert, ed. 1990. *The Problem of Pure Consciousness*. New York: Oxford University Press.
———. 2004. *Grassroots Spirituality*. Charlottesville, VA: Imprint Academic.
Fowler, Charles. 1996. *Strong Arts, Strong Schools: The Promising Potential and Shortsighted Disregard of the Arts in American Schooling*. New York: Oxford University Press.
Freeman, Robert. 2014. *The Crisis of Classical Music in America*. Lanham, MD: Rowman and Littlefield.
Fuller, R. Buckminster. 1969. *Utopia or Oblivion: The Prospects for Humanity*. New York: Bantam.
Gardner, Howard. 1993. *Multiple Intelligences: The Theory in Practice*. New York: Basic Books.
Gaunt, Kyra. 2006. *The Games Black Girls Play: From Double Dutch to Hip-Hop*. New York: New York University Press.
Gleick, James. 1987. *Chaos*. New York: Viking.
Goia, Ted. 1988. *The Imperfect Art: Reflections on Jazz and Modern Culture*. New York: Oxford.
Goldberg, Phillip. 2010. *American Veda: How Indian Spirituality Changed the West*. New York: Harmony/Random House.
Gorden, Jay, and Bryan Van Norden. 2016, May 11. "If Philosophy Won't Diversify, Let's Call It What It Really Is." *New York Times* Opinion Pages. Originally appeared in the *Stone*.
Goswami, Amit. 1993. *The Self-Aware Universe: How Consciousness Creates the Material World*. New York: Tarcher.
Göttner-Abendroth, Heide. *The Dancing Goddess: Principles of a Matriarchal Aesthetic*. Boston: Beacon Press.
Gould, Carol, and Kenneth Keaton. 2000. "The Essential Role of Improvisation in Musical Performance." *The Journal of Aesthetics and Art Criticism* 58, no. 2: 143–48.
Gould, Stephen Jay. 1999. *Rock of Ages: Science and Religion in the Fullness of Life*. New York: Ballantine.
Green, Lucy. 2014. "Popular Music Education in and for Itself." In *Music Education as Critical Theory and Practice: Selected Essays*, 101–118. Surrey, UK: Ashgate.
Gunnlaugson, O., Bai, Heesoon, Scott, C., and Sareth, E. 2017. *The Intersubjective Turn: Theoretical Approaches to Contemplative Learning and Inquiry across Disciplines*. State University of New York.
Gustafson, Ruth. 2009. *Race and Curriculum: Music in Childhood Education*. New York: Palgrave MacMillan.
Hadot, Pierre. 2002. *What Is Ancient Philosophy?* Cambridge, MA: Harvard University Press.
Hagelin, John, Maxwell V. Rainforth, David W. Orme-Johnson, Kenneth L. Cavanaugh, Charles N. Alexander, Susan F. Shatkin, John L. Davies, Anne O. Hughes, and Emanuel Ross. 1999, June. "Effects of Group Practice of the Transcendental Meditation Program on Preventing Violent Crime in Washington, D.C.; Results of the National Demonstration

Project to Reduce Crime and Improve Governmental Effectiveness in Washington, D.C., June–July, 1993." *Social Indicators Research* 47, no. 2: 153–201.

Hancock, Herbie, with Lisa Dickey. 2014. *Possibilities.* New York: Viking.

Harmon, Willis, and Howard Rheingold. 1984. *Higher Creativity: Liberating the Unconscious for Breakthrough Insights.* New York: Tarcher.

Harris, Sam. 2004. *The End of Faith: Religion, Terror, and the Future of Reason.* New York: W.W. Norton.

Heble, Ajay, Fischlin, Daniel, and Lipsitz, George, eds. 2013. *The Fierce Urgency of Now: Improvisation, Rights and the Ethics of Cocreation.* Chapel Hill: Duke University Press.

Hess, Juliet. 2015. "Upping the 'Anti-': The Value of an Anti-Racist Theoretical Framework in Music Education." *Action, Criticism, and Theory for Music Education* 14, no. 1: 66–92

———. 2017. "Equity in Music Education: Euphemisms, Terminal Naivety, and Whiteness." *Action, Criticism, and Theory for Music Education* 16, no. 3: 15–47.

Heuser, Frank. 2015. "Understanding the Tools: Technology as a Springboard for Reflective Musicking." In *Music Education: Navigating the Future*, edited by Clint Randle, 155–66. New York: Routledge.

Hindemith, Paul. 1952. *A Composer's World: Horizons and Limitations.* Cambridge, MA: Harvard University Press.

Hood, Mantle. 1960. "The Challenge of Bi-Musicality." *Ethnomusicology* 4, no. 1: 55–59.

hooks, bell. 1994. *Teaching to Transgress: Education as the Practice of Freedom.* New York: Routledge.

Huaijin, Nan. 1997. *Basic Buddhism: Exploring Buddhism and Zen.* York Beach, NY: Weiser Books.

Hsu, Hua. 2017, April 25. "Alice Coltrane's Devotional Music." *New Yorker*, p. 1.

Jones, LeRoi. 1963. *Blues People: Negro Music in White America.* New York: HarperCollins/Perennial.

Jung, C. G. 1960. *On the Nature of the Psyche.* Princeton: Princeton University Press.

———. 1961. *The Spirit in Man, Art, and Literature.* Princeton: Princeton University Press.

———. 1990 (1959). *The Archetypes and the Collective Unconscious.* Princeton: Princeton University Press.

Kahn, Hazrat Inayat. 1988. *The Music of Life.* New Lebanon, NY: Omega.

Kaschub, Michele, and Janice Smith, eds. 2014. *Promising Practices in 21st Century Music Teacher Education.* Oxford: Oxford University Press.

Kelly, Robin D. G. 2009. *Thelonious Monk: The Life and Times of an American Original.* New York: Free Press.

King, Martin Luther, Jr. 1964. "On the Importance of Jazz: Introductory Remarks at the 1964 Berlin Jazz Festival." http://wclk.com/dr-martin-luther-king-jr-importance-jazz.

———. 1967. "Beyond Vietnam: The Time to Break the Silence." www.beliefnet.com/columnists/christianityfortherestofus/2011/01/martin-luther-king-jr-fierce-urgency-of-now.html.

Kingsbury, Henry. 1988. *Music, Talent and Performance: A Conservatory Cultural System.* Philadelphia: Temple University Press.

———. 1997, Spring/Summer. "Call and Response: Should Ethnomusicology Be Abolished?" *Ethnomusicology*: 243–62.

Kokkidou, May. 2013. "Critical Thinking and School Music Education: Literature Review, Research Findings, and Perspectives." *Journal for Learning through the Arts* 9, no. 1.

Kramer, Jonathan. 1988. *The Time of Music.* New York: Schirmer.

Kuhn, Thomas. 1962. *The Structure of Scientific Revolutions.* Chicago: University of Chicago Press.

Kulma, David, and Meghan Naxer. 2014. "Beyond Part-Writing: Modernizing the Curriculum." In *Engaging Students: Essays in Music Pedagogy*, vol. 2. Mountain View, CA: Creative Commons.

Lacy, Steve. 1994. *Findings: My Experience with the Soprano Saxophone.* Paris: CMAP, Outre Mesure.

Langer, Susanne. 1948. *Philosophy in a New Key: A Study in the Symbolism of Reason, Rite, and Art.* New York: Mentor.

Lee, Dorothy. 1974. "Codifications of Reality: Lineal and Nonlineal." In *The Nature of Human Consciousness*, edited by Robert Ornstein, 128–42. New York: Viking.
Lesser, Elizabeth. 1999. *The New American Spirituality: A Seeker's Guide*. New York: Random House.
Lewis, George. 1996, Spring. "Improvised Music since 1950: Afrological and Eurological Perspectives." *Black Music Research* 16: 91–119.
———. 2008. *A Power Stronger Than Itself: The AACM and American Experimental Music*. Chicago: University of Chicago Press.
List, George. 1997, Fall. "Hopi Kachina Dance Songs: Concept and Context." *Ethnomusicology* 41: 13–32.
Maceda, Jose. 1958, May. "Chants from Sagada Mountain Province, Phillipines." *Ethnomusicology* 2, no. 2: 45–55.
Maharishi Mahesh Yogi. 1969. *Bhagavad Gita: A New Translation and Commentary*. New York: Penguin.
———. 1999. *Constitution of India Fulfilled through Maharishi's Transcendental Meditation*. New Delhi, India: Vedic Vishwa-Vidyalaya.
Martin, Jane. 1983. "What Should We Do with a Hidden Curriculum When We Find One?" In *The Hidden Curriculum and Moral Education*, edited by Henry Giroux and David Purpel, 122–39. Berkeley, CA: McCutchan.
Maslow, Abraham. 1971. *The Farther Reaches of Human Nature*. New York: Penguin.
Mason, Lynne, Robert P. Patterson, and Dean I. Radin. 2007. "Exploratory Study: The Random Number Generator and Group Meditation." *Journal of Scientific Exploration* 21: 295–317.
McMahon, B., and D. Armstrong, eds. 2006. *Inclusion in Urban Educational Environments: Addressing Issues of Diversity, Equity, and Social Justice*. Charlotte, NC: Information Age Publishing.
McTaggart, Lynne M. 2002. *The Field: The Quest for the Secret Force of the Universe*. New York: HarperCollins.
Meyer, Leonard. 1989. *Style and Music Theory, History, Ideology*. Philadelphia: University of Pennsylvania Press.
Mitchell, William J. 1973, May. "Under the Comprehensive Musicianship Umbrella." *Music Educators Journal* 59, no. 9: 71–78.
Monson, Ingrid. 1996. *Saying Something: Jazz Improvisation and Interaction*. Chicago: University of Chicago Press.
Montouri, Alphonso, and Robert Purser. 1994. "Miles Davis in the Classroom: Using the Jazz Ensemble Metaphor for Enhancing Team Learning." *Journal of Management Education* 18, no. 1: 21–31.
Moore, Robin, ed. 2017. *College Music Curricula in a New Century*. New York: Oxford.
Muller-Ortega, Paul Eduardo. 1989. *The Triadic Heart of Siva: Kaula Tantricism of Abhinavagupta in the Non-Dual Shaivism of Kashmir*. Albany: State University of New York Press.
Murphy, Mary, and Sabrina Zirkel. 2015. "Race and Belonging in School: How Anticipated and Experienced Belonging Affect Choice, Persistence, and Performance." *Teachers College Record* 117, no. 12: 1–40.
Murphy, Michael. 1988. *The Future of the Body*. Berkeley, CA: Conference Recording Service.
Music Educators National Conference. 1994. *National Standards for Arts Education: What Every Young American Should Know and Be Able to Do in the Arts*. Reston, VA: Author.
Nachmanovitch, Stephen. 1990. *Freeplay: Improvisation in Art and Life*. New York: Tarcher/Putnam.
Nettl, Bruno. 1995. *Heartland Excursions: Ethnomusicological Reflections on Schools of Music*. Urbana: University of Illinois Press.
Nicholson, Stuart. 2004, November 3. Interview with Alice Coltrane. Available online at http://bit.ly/2mV4M16.
Nicolescu, Basarab. 2002. *Manifesto of Transdisciplinarity*. Albany: State University of New York Press.
Nzewi, Meki. 1997. *African Music: Theoretical Content and Creative Continuum*. Oldershausen, Germany: Institut für Didaktik Populärer Musik.

Oates, Robert. 2002. *Permanent Peace: How to Stop Terrorism and War—Now and Forever.* Fairfield, IA: Institute for Science, Technology, and Public Policy.
Obama, Michelle. 2009, June 15. Remarks by the First Lady at the White House Music Series: The Jazz Studio. The White House, Washington, DC.
Olson-Sorflaten, Theresa. 1995. *Increased Personal Harmony and Integration as Effects of Maharishi Gandharva Veda Music on Affect, Physiology, and Behavior: The Psychophysiology.* PhD dissertation, Maharishi International University.
O'Meally, Robert, Brent Hayes Edwards, and Farah Jasmine Griffin, eds. 2004. *Uptown Conversation: The New Jazz Studies.* New York: Columbia University Press.
Orme-Johnson, D., C. Alexander, J. Davies, H. Chander, and W. Larimore. 1988. "International Peace Project: The Effects of the Maharishi Technology of the Unified Field." *Journal of Conflict Resolution* 32, no. 4: 776–812.
Pearson, Craig. 2011. *Supreme Awakening: Experiences of Higher States of Consciousness.* Fairfield, IA: Maharishi University of Management Press.
Pert, Candace. 1997. *Molecules of Emotion: The Science behind Mind-Body Medicine.* New York: Touchstone.
Pertl, Brian. 2017. "Reshaping Undergraduate Music Education in Turbulent Times." In *College Curricula for a New Century*, 33–46, edited by Robin Moore. New York: Oxford University Press.
Pettan, Svanibor, and Jeff Todd Titon. 2016. *The Oxford Handbook of Applied Ethnomusicology.* New York: Oxford University Press.
Pressing, Jeff. 1987. "Improvisation: Methods and Models." In *Generative Processes in Music*, edited by John Sloboda, 129–76. London: Oxford University Press.
———. 2002. "Black Atlantic Rhythm: Its Computational and Transcultural Foundations." *Music Perception* 19, no. 3: 285–310.
Radin, Dean. 1997. *The Conscious Universe.* San Francisco: Harper.
———. 2007. "A Brief History of the Potential Future." In *Mind before Matter: Visions of a New Science of Consciousness*, 170–178, edited by Trish Pfeiffer and John E. Mack. Winchester, UK: O Books/John Hunt.
Ramsey, Guthrie. 2003. *Race Music: Black Cultures from Bebop to Hip Hop.* Berkeley: University of California Press.
Randle, Clint, ed. 2015. *Music Education: Navigating the Future.* New York: Routledge.
Richards, Sam. 2015. "Rethinking the Theory Classroom: Towards a New Model for Undergraduate Instruction." In *Engaging Students: Essays in Music Pedagogy*, vol. 3. Mountain View, CA: Creative Commons.
Rodriquez, Carlos, ed. 2017. *Coming of Age: Teaching and Learning Popular Music in Academia.* Ann Arbor, MI: Maize Books.
Salvador, Karen. 2015. "Identity and Transformation: (Re)claiming an Inner Musician." In *Music Education: Navigating the Future*, 215–232, edited by Clint Randle. New York: Routledge.
Sarath, Ed. 1996. "A New Look at Improvisation." *Journal of Music Theory* 40, no. 1: 1–39.
———. 2002. "Improvisation and Curriculum Reform." In *The New Handbook of Research on Music Teaching and Learning*, edited by Richard Colwell and Carol Richardson, 188–98. New York: Oxford University Press.
———. 2003. "Meditation in Higher Education: The Next Wave?" *Innovative Higher Education* 27: 215–34.
———. 2006. "Meditation, Creativity, and Consciousness: Charting Future Terrain within Higher Education." *Teachers College Record* 108, no. 9: 1816–41.
———. 2007. "Improvisation, Consciousness, and the Play of Creation: Music as a Lens into Ultimate Reality and Meaning." *Ultimate Reality and Meaning* 30, no. 1: 54–77.
———. 2010. "Jazz, Creativity, and Consciousness: Blueprint for Integral Education." In *Integral Education: New Directions for Higher Learning*, 169–184, edited by Sean Esbjörn-Hargens, Jonathan Reams, and Olen Gunnlaugson. Albany: State University of New York Press.
———. 2010. *Music Theory through Improvisation: A New Approach to Musicianship Training.* New York: Routledge.

———. 2013. *Improvisation, Creativity and Consciousness: Jazz as Integral Template for Music, Education and Society*. Albany: State University of New York Press.
———. 2017. "On Earth as it is in Heaven: Toward a Nondual Integral Understanding of Intersubjectivity as Primordial in Cosmos," in Gunnlaugson, O, Bai, Heesoon, Scott, C. and Sarath, E. The Intersubjective Turn: Theoretical Approaches to Contemplative Learning and Inquiry across Disciplines. State University of New York.
Sarath, Ed, David Myers, and Patricia S. Campbell. 2016. *Redefining Music Studies in an Age of Change*. New York: Routledge.
Sax, William S. 1990, November. "The Ramnagar Ramlila: Text, Performance, Pilgramage." *History of Religions* 30: 129–53.
Schippers, Huib. 2010. *Facing the Music: Shaping Music Education from a Global Perspective*. New York: Oxford University Press.
Searle, John R. 1997. *The Mystery of Consciousness*. New York: New York Review of Books.
Seeman, Sonia T. 2016. "Embodied Pedagogy." In *College Music Curricula for a New Century*, edited by Robin Moore, 190–203. New York: Oxford University Press.
Shankar, Ravi. 1968. *My Music, My Life*. New York: Simon and Schuster.
Sharma, Hari, and Christopher Clark. 1998. *Contemporary Ayurveda: Medicine and Research in Maharishi Ayurveda*. Philadelphia: Churchill Livingstone.
Sheldrake, Rupert. 2012. *Science Set Free; 10 Paths to New Discovery*. New York: Deepak Chopra Books.
Sindberg, Laura. 1998. "The Wisconsin CMP Project at Age 21." *Music Educators Journal* 85, no. 3: 37–42.
Skowlimowski, Henryk. 2010. *Let There Be Light: The Mysterious Voyage of Cosmic Creativity*. New Delhi: Wisdom Tree.
Skrbina, David. 2005. *Panpsychism in the West*. Cambridge, MA: MIT.
Small, Christopher. 1994. *Music of the Common Tongue*. London: Calder Riverrun.
———. 1996. *Music, Society, Education*. Hanover, NH: Wesleyan University Press.
Steinman, David Ward. 1987. "Comprehensive Musicianship at San Diego State University." *Journal of Music Theory Pedagogy* vol. 1: 127–140.
Sweet, Robert. 1996. *Music Universe, Music Mind*. Ann Arbor, MI: Arborville.
Tarnas, Richard. 2006. *Cosmos and Psyche: Intimations of a New World View*. New York: Viking.
Tart, Charles. 2009. *The End of Materialism: How Evidence of the Paranormal Is Bringing Science and Spirit Together*. Oakland, CA: New Harbinger.
Tenzer, Michael. 2015, Winter. "Meditations on Objective Aesthetics in World Music." *Ethnomusicology* 59, no. 1: 1–30.
———. 2016. "In Honor of What We Can't Groove to Yet." In *College Music Curricula for a New Century*, edited by Robin Moore, 119–35. New York: Oxford University Press.
Tobias, Evan. 2015. "Inter/Trans/Multi/Cross/New Media(ting): Navigating an Emerging Landscape of Digital Media for Music Education." In *Music Education: Navigating the Future*, edited by Clint Randle, 91–121. New York: Routledge.
Townbee, Jason. 2003. "Music, Culture and Creativity." In *The Cultural Study of Music: A Critical Introduction*, edited by Richard Middleton, 102–12. New York: Routledge.
Travis, F., A. Arenander, and D. DuBois. 2004. "Psychological and Physiological Characteristics of a Proposed Object-Referral/Self-Referral Continuum of Self-Awareness." *Consciousness and Cognition* 13: 401–20.
Vaughn-Lee, Llewellyn. 2009. *The Return of the Feminine and the World Soul*. Inverness, CA: The Golden Sufi Center.
Vaugeois, L. 2007. "Social Justice and Music Education: Claiming the Space of Music Education as a Site of Postcolonial Contestation." *Action, Criticism, and Theory for Music Education* 6, no. 4: 163–200. Available online at http://act.maydaygroup.org/articles/Vaugeois6_.
Wade, Jenny. 1996. *Changes of Mind*. Albany: State University of New York Press.
Wang, Song, Xin Xu, Ming Zhou, Taolin Chen, Xun Yang, Guangxlang Chen, and Quyong Gong. 2017, August. "Hope and the Brain: Trait Hope Mediates the Protective Role of Medial Orbitofrontal Cortex Spontaneous Activity against Anxiety." *NeuroImage* 157: 439–47.

Weinberg, Steven. 1977. *The First Three Minutes*. New York: Basic Books.
Weiss, Sarah. 2014, Fall. "Listening to the World but Hearing Ourselves: Hybridity and Perceptions of Authenticity in World Music." *Ethnomusicology* 58, no. 2: 506–24.
West, Cornell. 2001. *Race Matters*. New York: Vintage Books.
Westbrook, Peter. 2007. "Unstruck Sound and Forgotten Truth." *Ultimate Reality and Meaning* 30, no. 1: 93–120.
Whitehead, Alfred North. 1929. *The Aims of Education*. New York: Free Press.
Wilber, Ken. 1998. *The Marriage of Sense and Soul: Integrating Science and Religion*. New York: Broadway Books.
———. 1999. "Foreword to *The Mission of Art*, by Alex Grey." In *Collected Works*, vol. 4: 394–395. Boston: Shambhala.
———. 2000. "Integral Psychology." In *Collected Works*, vol. 4: 423–719. Boston: Shambhala.
———. 2000. *Sex, Ecology, Spirituality*. Boston: Shambhala.
———. 2006. *Integral Spirituality: A Startling New Look at the Role for Religion in the Modern and Postmodern World*. Boston: Shambhala.
———. 2006. "Introduction to Integral Theory and Practice." *Journal of Integral Theory and Practice* 1, no. 1: 1–40.
Wilber, Ken, Terry Patten, Adam Leonard, and Marco Morelli. 2008. *Integral Life Practice: A 21st-Century Blueprint for Physical Health, Emotional Balance, Mental Clarity, and Spiritual Awakening*. Boston: Integral Books.
Wolff, Fred Alan. 1999. *The Spiritual Universe: One Physicist's Vision of Spirit, Soul, Matter, and Self*. Needham, MA: One Moment Press.
Younker, Betty Anne. 2002. "Critical Thinking." In *The New Handbook of Research on Music Teaching and Learning*, edited by Richard Colwell and Carol Richardson, 162–70. New York: Oxford University Press.
Zemtsoysky, Izaly. 1997. "An Attempt at a Synthetic Paradigm." *Ethnomusicology* 41, no. 2: 185–205.
Zull, James. 2006. "Key Aspects of How the Brain Learns." In *The Neuroscience of Adult Learning: New Directions for Adult and Continuing Education*, edited by Sandra Johnson and Kathleen Thompson, 3–10. San Francisco, CA: Jossey-Bass.

Index

Abhinavagupta, 115
Abrams, Muhal Richard, xxi
Advaita, 105, 148
Africanisms, x, 150, 189
African music, 77
Afro-Euro nexus, 10, 79; Afro-Euro-global, 10
Afrological, 118, 150, 170, 207n28
Alexander, Charles, 114
Alim, Samy, 197n28, 197n42
Allsup, Randall, 194n16
Amrine, Frederick, 180
Anatta, 123, 175
Anderson, Kristin, 47, 197n37
anomaly centering, 120
Apaurusheya Bhashya, 7, 115, 209n8
Archetype, xxviii, 15, 113, 147, 194n20
art music: critique of heading, xvii, xxv, 26, 43, 47, 67, 97, 193n3
Association for the Advancement of Creative Musicians (AACM), xv, 11, 49, 73–74, 78, 200n36
Atma, 8, 13, 14, 29, 96, 115, 117, 118, 119, 152, 153, 157
Aurobindo, Sri, 105
Ayer, Vijay, 34

Bache, Christopher, 205n51
Banfield, William, 210n5
Barrett, Margaret, 207n27
Barruss, Imants, 121

Bass, Diana, 210n1, 210n2
Becker, Judith, 147, 208n33
Benedict, Cathy, 197n36
Berendt, Joachim, 149, 196n16
Berliner, Paul, 194n22
bhagavat chetena, 111–119, 166
Black Atlantic Rhythm, x, xiii, 42, 63, 69, 113, 118, 191n5
Black Music: defined, x
Bloom, Jane Ira, 37
Blues, x, xi, xii, 10, 63, 145–151; as archetypally rich, 149; and emotion, 149; as modal, 149; problems in defining of, 149; as triumphant, 149
Bowie, Lester, 11, 194n18
Bradley, Deborah, 50, 98, 195n2
brahman, 7–8, 115, 116, 148
brahmi chetena, 114, 118
Braxton, Anthony, xviii, 37
Broomfield, John, 147
Brown, James, 72
Buddhism, 123–124, 175, 206n68; critique of Western conception of, 123

Cage, John, 44
Campbell, Patricia, 193n1, 199n18
Carter, Regina, 37
Central Impasse, xxv, 4, 5, 9, 87
Chalmers, David, 122
de Chardin, Teillhard, 107, 123
Cherry, Don, xxi

Combs, Alan Leslie, 206n74
cognitive event cycle, 138, 143; frequency, 138; inflated points, 138; weak spans, 142
Coleman, Steve, 37
College Music Society, 80; Manifesto, 80
Coltrane, Alice, ix, xxi, 13, 104, 112
Coltrane, John, xxi, 36, 37, 43, 104, 112, 166
Combs, Alan, 127
composition: contrasted with improvisation, 131; extemporaneous (contrasted with solo improvisation), 145
consciousness, xxvii; hard problem of, xxvii; higher developmental stages, 110; intersubjective, 119; relationship with music, 68. *See also bhagavat*; *brahmi*; *turiyitata*
contemplative studies: contrast with consciousness studies, 175; movement in higher education, 124, 161, 175, 208n3
Contemporary Improviser Composer Performer (CICP), xvii, 4, 13, 14, 16, 17, 21–22, 29–30, 31, 33, 35, 37, 40, 51, 53, 54, 58, 61, 64, 68, 74, 79, 80, 83, 84, 86, 87, 89, 92, 94, 95, 96, 131–132, 137, 148, 153, 156, 171, 200n33; CICP-plus, xxiv, 12, 13
Coomaraswamy, Ananda, 116
Covach, John, 41
creativity: cosmic source of, 7, 17; research, 143. *See also* musical creativity
critical race theory, 48
critical thinking, 4, 5, 20, 24, 54, 81, 82–83, 97, 111, 200n7, 201n8
Csikszentmihalyi, Mihaly, 144

Dalal, A.S., 202n9
Deep Inquiry, 74, 107, 180, 181–182
Dennett, Daniel, 127
Descartes, Rene, 105
Diangelo, Robin, 197n43
differentiation (as evolutionary stride), xxii, xxiv, 4, 9–10, 19, 23, 81, 95, 111, 143, 148, 153, 157, 165, 178–179

Dissociation, xxii, xxiv, 4, 19–20, 49, 125, 135, 179
division of labor, 4, 19, 20–21, 22, 60, 156
double consciousness, 48; double musical consciousness, 48
Du Bois, W.E.B., 48, 197n45
Dualism, xii, xxvii, 69, 103, 105, 107, 110, 112, 122, 131

education: church-state boundaries, 124, 177; contemplative roots of (academic amnesia), 176; *educere* and *educare*, 174; leadership of, 162; music education, 21–22, 27, 30, 31, 41, 65, 67–68, 70, 77–78, 98; place of black music in, xi; racism in, 48; reform, xviii, xxiii, 4, 5, 8, 34, 39, 47, 74, 81, 87, 96, 103–104, 107, 124, 125, 126, 159, 161, 162–163, 164, 169, 174, 175, 176–177, 177, 179, 181, 184, 188, 189; role of imagination in, 162
Ellington, Duke, 112, 144
Elliott, David, 207n27
embodied musicianship, xxv, 6, 61, 63
embodied musical racism, 63
entrepreneurship (musical), xxv, 6, 9, 70, 73
environment: creative, 16, 139, 143; ecological, 6, 74, 88, 93, 101, 108, 117, 118, 126, 134, 141, 163, 164–167, 169, 179; learning, 5, 17, 39, 40, 58, 60, 73, 173, 177. *See also* Integral Learning Environment
Epiphenomalism, 106, 131
epistemology: diverse forms, xiv, xx, 48, 68, 81, 105, 119, 132, 158, 176, 182
ethnology/epistemology relationship, 158, 176
ethnomusicology, xvi, 21, 22, 30, 38, 41, 45, 64, 68, 97, 153, 158, 159, 170; paradox of, 34, 35
exnomination, xxv, 44, 45, 46, 97

Farmer, Art, 13
first-person reality. *See* Integral Theory
Fitzpatrick, Kate, 202n27
Flannagan, Owen, 123, 175
Forman, Robert, 202n4
Freeman, Robert, 43, 197n30

Fuller, Buckminster, xviii
fundamentalism: musical, 11, 171; religious, 171; scientific, 171

Gardner, Howard, 5
Gleick, James, 207n23
Goia, Ted, 206n2
Goldberg, Phillip, 202n4
Göttner-Abendroth, Heide, 147
Gould, Stephen Jay, 105
Green, Lucy, 198n10
Gustafson, Ruth, 98

Hadot, Pierre, 176, 209n22
Hagelin, John, 205n51, 209n11, 209n21
Hancock, Herbie, xxi, 189
Hess, Juliet, 98
Heuser, Frank, 199n21
higher order change discourse, xvi, xvii, 3
Hindemith, Paulm, 143, 207n24
Hood, Mantle, 196n18
hooks, bell, 174
horizontal change, xxiv
Hsu, Hua, 202n5
Huaijin, Nan, 124

Imagination, 180
Improvisation, xxvii; across fields, 74; defined, 131–133; distinguished from composition, 10; in jazz, 145; large ensemble stylistically open, 151; and meditation, 151; and peace, 167; systematic approach to development, 8–9; unaccompanied, 145. *See also* parts to whole/whole to parts interplay
individuation, 4, 13
Integral Learning Environment, 60, 64, 72
Integral Musicology, 146, 153, 158–159, 189; bridging musical and spiritual realms, 156; profile of integral musicologist, 149
Integral Theory, x, xviii; AQAL, xix; first-person, second-person, third-person, xix, 7, 8, 74, 82, 83, 107, 115, 150, 165, 171–172, 182; integral jazz studies, 74
Interpretive Performance Specialist, xvii, xx, 12, 13, 14, 16, 29, 58, 60, 63, 92, 111, 113

Jarman, Joseph, 200n36
Jazz: and contemplative studies, BFA degree, 161; freedom fighter, 161; jazz education, xv, xvi, 22, 78, 200n36; as national treasure, ix; and Vedanta, 104, 175; writ large, xiv
Jones, LeRoi, x, 150, 189, 208n35
Jung, C. G., xii, xxi, 4, 13, 15, 111, 120, 149, 194n20, 208n35, 210n1

Kayser, Hans, 115
Kelly, Robin D. G., 194n23
King, Martin Luther Jr., 98, 149, 187, 188, 202n26, 210n2, 210n3, 210n4, 210n7, 210n8
Kingsbury, Henry, 193n1
Kokkidou, Mayn, 201n8, 201n9
Kramer, Jonathan, 207n5
Kuhn, Thomas, 53, 79, 121, 200n3
Kulma, David, 199n14

Lacy, Steve, 10
Langer, Suzanne, 15, 82
Lee, Dorothy, 147
Leonard, Adam, 203n19
Lewis, George, xiii, xv, 37, 73, 78, 197n31, 198n47, 200n27, 200n36, 207n28
Liebman, David, 61
lila, 114, 115, 116, 148, 188, 205n46, 205n47
Lingering Aversion to Musical Blackness, 50
Liston, Melba, 143
Lloyd, Charles, xxi
lower order change discourse, xvi, 3

Maharishi Mahesh Yogi, 7, 114, 115, 116, 167, 192n26, 204n35, 204n39, 204n41, 205n45, 207n23, 209n11
Maslow, Abraham, 174
Materialism, xxvii, 69, 89, 103, 105, 106–107, 128, 171, 181, 184; Buddhism and, 123; collapse of, 120–123, 127, 203n13; matrix of, xxii, xxiii, 123
McFerrin, Bobby, 37, 43
McLaughlin, John, xxi, 196n17
Meditation, xx, 18, 54, 56, 66, 68, 83, 84, 108; features/benefits associated with,

107, 108, 109, 110; large group, effects on society, xxvii; types of, 108
Meyer, Leonard, 10
Meyers, Edgar, 37
Mitchell, Edgar, 120
Mitchell, Nicole, 37
Monk, Thelonious, 13, 144
Montouri, Alphonso, 202
Moore, Robin, 195n11, 195n13, 196n26
Morelli, Marco, 203n19
Mossbridge, Julia, 121
Muller-Ortega, Paul, 204n40
Multicultural, xv, xvii, xxiii, 4, 11, 13, 21, 26; Aims, 39; conception of popular music, 41–43; correlated with lower order change discourse, 4; distinguished from transcultural, 26, 27–30; exemplars, 36–39; place of self-cultural grounding, 31–34; types (conceptual, idealized), 30; view of jazz, xvi, xxii
multiple paradigms principle, 81, 91
musical creativity, 6; creativity turn, xxv, 3; direct creative experience (part of individuation), 13, 15; emulative-exploratory interaction, 11, 13, 27, 31, 35, 40, 78, 156, 174, 194n16; identity shift, 30; primary and secondary, 156
musicking, xviii, 23; transcultural critique of, 30, 50, 195n6, 195n13
music of the spheres, 7
Myers, David, 193n1

Naxer, Meghan, 199n14
Nettl, Bruno, 201n18
neo-Eurocentric, xvii, 4, 20
neo-Eurocentric-plus orientation, xxiv, 3, 4, 11, 13, 20, 22, 30, 51, 57, 59, 60, 65, 66, 67, 70, 71–72, 73, 75, 86, 92, 96, 97, 101, 107, 121, 148, 156, 159
nested synergies, 153; Improvisation anchored, 153; Meditation anchored, 154
New Jazz Studies, 74
Nicholson, Stuart, 194n24
Nicolescu, Basarab, 209n26
Noetic, xxii, 15, 18, 20, 22, 53, 120
nonlinear time dynamics, xxvii, 132, 135, 140, 144, 145, 146, 153, 158, 159

Nzewi, Meki, 7, 32, 77, 193n9, 199n17, 200n30

Oates, Robert, 209n9
Obama, Michelle, xi, 77
Olson-Sorflaten, Theresa, 204n41
Orme-Johnson, David, 205n51

Panpsychism, 69, 106, 112, 131, 203n11
parts-to-whole engagement, xx, xxi, xxv, xxvii, 56, 68, 83, 101, 108, 119, 151, 154, 163, 164, 165, 167, 174, 178, 204n38
Patten, Terry, 203n19
peak experience, xx, 110, 134, 143, 172, 203n21
Pearson, Craig, 203n23, 203n24, 204n33, 204n36, 204n37, 205n44
pedagogy: as one of five pillars, 54, 67; integrative, 22; jazz pedagogy without jazz foundations, 67; performance and private instruction, 57; relationship with research, 39; student-driven vs. institution-driven, xii, xxv, 4, 17; transcultural vs multicultural, 27, 38, 40, 41
Pertl, Brian, 200n2
Pettan, Svanibor, 196n20
Planck, Max, 105
popular music, 41; multicultural and transcultural conceptions, 41; separation from black roots, 159; separation from jazz, 159
Pressing, Jeff, 72, 113
Psi, xxvii, 120–122
Ptanjali: Yoga sutras, 120
pure consciousness, 83, 104, 107, 108, 109, 118, 129, 135, 148, 154, 155, 163, 165, 178, 179, 203n20, 204n39; as contemplative anchor, 109; defined, 83, 109; role in transdisciplinary experience, 178

race, 125, 191n4; racism, xxi, xxiv, xxv, xxviii, 26, 48, 94, 126, 188, 197n39, 197n43; racism research, 26, 48, 197n39; racist bias, xxv, 20, 26, 41, 43, 46, 48, 51, 52, 67, 71, 73, 81, 93, 97,

Index

98, 126, 127, 144, 158, 188, 196n23, 197n41
Radin, Dean, 121, 166
Randle, Clint, 193n1, 193n5, 199n21
Reductionism, 106
reflection: As part of individuation process, 14, 16, 18, 84
religion: integral view of, xix, xxii, 17, 108, 124, 170, 172, 173, 177, 178, 187, 192n27; relationship with science, xxii, 101, 103, 173
Richards, Sam, 201n16

Sawyer, Keith, 207n28
Sax, William, 116
Schippers, Huib, 195n4
Schmidt, Patrick, 197n36
science: integral view of, xix, xx, xxii, 8, 11, 79, 82, 101, 103, 105, 119, 121, 124, 148, 169, 170, 172, 173, 177, 181, 183, 192n27, 194n26, 202n7; scientism, xxii, xxiii, 121. *See also* fundamentalism; materialism
Searle, John, 106
self-cultural, 29, 31, 32, 34, 35, 69, 76, 80, 94, 118
self-driven, 5, 17, 18, 29, 40, 53, 73. *See also* self-organizing
self-motivational, 16, 17, 27, 53. *See also* self-organizing
self-navigational, 16, 17, 18, 27, 53, 73. *See also* self-organizing
self-organizing, xii, xxiv, xxv, 4, 5, 13, 14, 15, 16, 20, 23, 25, 27, 39, 52, 53, 54, 69, 73, 81, 97, 118, 154, 167. *See also* self-driven
self-referral, 7, 38, 69, 81, 107, 108, 112, 115, 116, 117, 118, 134, 135, 140, 152, 154, 155, 156, 157, 163, 165, 203n24, 217
self-transcending, xi, xiv, xv, xvi, xix, xx, xxi, xxii, xxiv, 11, 12, 13, 25, 26, 33, 51, 73, 75, 83, 86, 98, 101, 119, 124, 171, 173, 184, 189
Shorter, Wayne, xxi
Shyu, Jen, 37
Skirbina, David, 203n11
Slavery, x, 48, 148, 150, 188–189
Small, Christopher, xii, xvii, 79

Smith, Wadada Leo, 200n36
Sorey, Tyshawn, 37
Soul, ix, x, xi, xxiv, xxviii, 8, 9, 10, 11, 13, 14, 29, 32, 33, 34, 48, 52, 56, 68, 75, 96, 104, 106, 114, 115, 116, 117, 118, 123, 124, 128, 152, 153, 156, 157, 166, 175, 183, 187, 188, 189, 197n45, 205n50, 206n61, 206n67, 206n69, 210n4
Spaulding, Esperanza, 37
Spirituality, x, xi, xiii, xix, xx, xxi, xxvi, xxviii, 3, 7, 8, 9, 11, 38, 40, 48, 54, 56, 69, 75, 82, 101, 103, 104, 106, 125, 128, 147, 148, 171, 173, 177, 181, 192n34, 202n4, 205n50
spiritual-but-not-religious, critique of, xxii, xxiv
Sweet, Robert, 196n16
syntactic parameters, 10, 15, 20, 144, 145, 194n15; nonsyntactic parameters, 10, 15, 194n15

Tagore, Rabindranath, 116
Tarnas, Richard, 204n27, 205n50
Technology, 6, 65
Tenzer, Michael, 198n12
terrorism: and consciousness, 168, 173; meditation as antidote for, 118, 165, 168, 209n9
time theorym, 7, 69, 115, 117, 199n23
Titon, Jeff Todd, 196n20
Tobias, Evan, 199n21
Transcultural, xv, xvii, xxi, xxv, xxvi, 4, 11, 21, 26–43, 53, 63, 66, 67, 69, 77, 78, 83, 84, 94, 95, 96, 97, 98, 101, 113, 118, 134, 146, 151, 156, 157, 158, 166, 170, 173, 175, 177, 178, 179, 189, 191n5, 192n20, 195n3, 195n4, 195n11, 195n12, 196n16, 196n18, 200n34, 216
Transdenominational, 177
Transdisciplinary, 6, 164, 178, 179
turiyatita chetena, 110, 111, 112, 113, 149

Vaugeois, Lise, 98
Vaughn-Lee, Lllewellyn, 205n50
Vedanta, xxi, 104, 105, 148, 175, 176

Weinberg, Stephen, 106
Weiss, Sara, 38, 196n19

West, Cornell, 82, 161, 189
white fragility, 48; white musical fragility, 48
Whitehead, Alfred North, 174
white privilege, 48; white epistemic privilege, 126; white musical privilege, 48
whole-to-parts, xx, xxi, xxv, xxvii, 56, 68, 83, 101, 108, 119, 151, 152, 154, 163, 165, 167, 174, 178
Wilber, Ken, xviii, xxii, 192n16, 192n24, 192n25, 192n27, 192n34, 203n19, 203n22, 204n25, 204n26
Williams, Mary Lou, xxi, 112
Wolff, Fred Alan, 122
world music, xvii, 26, 27, 46, 64, 68, 89, 97, 195n12, 197n35, 217, 218
worldview/workplace paradox, 81, 93, 127

yoga: integral view of, xix, xxii, 15, 17, 108, 120; related to creative process, 15
Younker, Betty Anne, 201n8

About the Author

Ed Sarath is a professor of music at the University of Michigan, director of the UM Program in Creativity and Consciousness Studies, and active worldwide as a performer, composer, recording artist, and scholar. He is founder and president of the International Society for Improvised Music. His prior book, *Improvisation, Creativity, and Consciousness* (2013), is the first to apply principles of Integral Theory to music. An earlier book, *Music Theory through Improvisation: A New Approach to Musicianship Training* (2010), is based on his innovative approach to core curriculum musicianship. He is lead author of the widely read CMS Manifesto, which appears in a co-authored book, *Redefining Music Studies in an Age of Change* (2016). His recording *New Beginnings* features the London Jazz Orchestra performing his large ensemble compositions.

www.ingramcontent.com/pod-product-compliance
Lightning Source LLC
Chambersburg PA
CBHW021848300426
44115CB00005B/60